Automation, Innovation and Work

Artificial intelligence will not necessarily create a super-intelligent "human robot"; however, it is very probable that intelligent robots and intelligent informats will bring about a form of super-globalization, in which money and goods are prioritized over people and democracy and where the widespread use of casual labour – that is, short-term contracts – will become the most common form of employment relationship. It is also very likely that artificial intelligence will bring about what is known as singularity. This term is used to describe a situation where intelligent robots, from a rational and logical perspective, are smarter than humans, i.e. the development of AI.

This book explores the impact that these intelligent robots and intelligent informats will have on social and societal development. The author tackles the question of singularity from three distinct standpoints: technological singularity – the intelligence of machines compared to that of humans – which he argues will bring about a qualitatively new labour market; economic singularity – the consequences for work relationships, value creation and employment – which he asserts will promote full automation, result in precarious contracts with low salaries, and, in some countries, possibly lead to the introduction of a universal basic income; and social singularity – the consequences of technological and economic singularity for democratic processes, bureaucratic procedures for exercising authority and control, and the direction in which society will develop, in addition to the emergence of new social institutions – which Johannessen says will promote a transition from representative democracy to genuine democracy.

The book will appeal to academics, researchers and students of economic sociology and political economy, as well as those focusing upon the emerging innovation economy. It will also find an audience among professionals and policymakers keen to understand the impact the Fourth Industrial Revolution will have on organizations, individuals and society at large.

Jon-Arild Johannessen is a professor at Kristiania University College, Oslo, Norway.

Helene Sætersdal is Associate Professor at Kristiania University College, Oslo, Norway.

Routledge Studies in the Economics of Innovation

The Routledge Studies in the Economics of Innovation series is our home for comprehensive yet accessible texts on the current thinking in the field. These cutting-edge, upper-level scholarly studies and edited collections bring together robust theories from a wide range of individual disciplines and provide in-depth studies of existing and emerging approaches to innovation, and the implications of such for the global economy.

The Workplace of the Future
The Fourth Industrial Revolution, the Precariat and the Death of Hierarchies
Jon-Arild Johannessen and Helene Sætersdal

Economics of an Innovation System
Inside and Outside the Black Box
Tsutomu Harada

The Dynamics of Local Innovation Systems
Structures, Networks and Processes
Eva Panetti

Innovation in Knowledge Intensive Business Services
The Digital Era
Anna Cabigiosu

The Impact of the Sharing Economy on Business and Society
Digital Transformation and the Rise of Platform Businesses
Edited by Abbas Strømmen-Bakhtiar and Evgueni Vinogradov

Automation, Innovation and Work
The Impact of Technological, Economic, and Social Singularity
Jon-Arild Johannessen and Helene Sætersdal

For more information about this series, please visit: www.routledge.com/ Routledge-Studies-in-the-Economics-of-Innovation/book-series/ECONINN

Automation, Innovation and Work

The Impact of Technological, Economic, and Social Singularity

**Jon-Arild Johannessen and
Helene Sætersdal**

Routledge
Taylor & Francis Group

LONDON AND NEW YORK

First published 2020
by Routledge
2 Park Square, Milton Park, Abingdon, Oxon OX14 4RN

and by Routledge
52 Vanderbilt Avenue, New York, NY 10017

Routledge is an imprint of the Taylor & Francis Group, an Informa business

British Library Cataloguing-in-Publication Data
A catalogue record for this book is available from the British Library

Library of Congress Cataloging-in-Publication Data
Names: Johannessen, Jon-Arild, author.
Title: Automation, innovation and work: the impact of technological,
economic, and social singularity / Jon-Arild Johannessen.
Description: Milton Park, Abingdon, Oxon; New York, NY: Routledge, 2020. |
Includes bibliographical references and index.
Identifiers: LCCN 2019055726 (print) | LCCN 2019055727 (ebook)
Subjects: LCSH: Employees–Effect of automation on. |
Artificial intelligence–Social aspects. |
Singularities (Artificial intelligence)–Social aspects. |
Precarious employment. | Automation–Economic aspects. |
Employment forecasting. Classification: LCC HD6331 .J638 2020 (print) |
LCC HD6331 (ebook) | DDC 331.25–dc23
LC record available at https://lccn.loc.gov/2019055726
LC ebook record available at https://lccn.loc.gov/2019055727

ISBN: 978-0-367-47016-6 (hbk)
ISBN: 978-1-003-03285-4 (ebk)

Typeset in Bembo
by Newgen Publishing UK

Contents

vi   *Contents*

Figures

Prologue

The core ideas in this book are:
- **Technological singularity** will bring about a qualitatively new labour market, in which experience is no longer prioritized.
- **Economic singularity** will encourage full automation, mass unemployment, and the introduction of a universal basic income.
- **Social singularity** will promote a transition from representative democracy to genuine democracy.

Artificial intelligence will not necessarily create a super-intelligent "human robot". On the other hand, it is very likely that intelligent robots and intelligent informats will bring about a form of super-globalization in which money and goods are prioritized over people and democracy (Rodrik, 2017). It is also very likely that artificial intelligence will bring about what is known as singularity. This word is used to describe a situation where intelligent machines are smarter than humans, from a rational and logical perspective, i.e. "classical" AI (Boden, 2016).

When, not if, technological and economic singularity occur, the phenomena will affect how we generate value, the distribution – and consumption – of goods, and how we organize our society. Such changes will affect the conventional concept of work and change our understanding of employment. We can imagine robots and artificial intelligence either leading to a society without jobs, in which a new social order is created through personal development and dialogue, or to unemployment and miserable existences for the vast majority, while a tiny super-wealthy elite enjoy lives of excess and luxury, much like the upper class in the heyday of the Roman Empire.

What kind of society will develop when the singularity occurs is difficult to predict. What we do know, however, is that social mechanisms such as robotization, globalization and artificial intelligence will bring about a metamorphosis in society. We use the metaphor of a metamorphosis to emphasize the fact that this will not be a revolution in the conventional sense, nor will it simply be a transformation, but it will be a transition to something qualitatively new, like the metamorphosis of a larva to a butterfly.

The coming of the singularity has been debated by philosophers (Boden, 2016), economists (Chace, 2015, 2016), computer scientists (Levesque, 2017) and technologists (Shanahan, 2015), to name but a few. While singularity in the technological sense is mainly about the intelligence of machines compared to human intelligence, economic singularity is mainly about the consequences for work, value creation and employment. Singularity in the social sense is mainly about the consequences of technological and economic singularity for democratic processes, bureaucratic procedures for exercising government and control, and the direction in which society will develop.

Artificial intelligence and intelligent robots may be advantageous for individuals and society, but technology may also bring about a new kind of feudalism. Such a development would mean that an extremely small economic elite would take control over how society develops. To prevent a popular uprising, a similar strategy would be adopted as in the Roman Empire, where free or heavily subsidized grain was distributed to the population. We might envisage this as taking the form of some type of universal basic income. A universal basic income would also help maintain purchasing power.

Some of the practical applications of artificial intelligence already exist today, for example search engines (Google), financial decision-making, stockmarket investments, driverless cars, diagnostic equipment in hospitals, in the care sector, in traditional industries, in the gaming industry, in surveillance, in marketing, in project planning, security systems, furniture design, aircraft design, architecture, logistics, transport systems, energy systems, and so on (Skilton & Hovsepian, 2018: 269–291).

If all the goods and services we need (and don't need) suddenly descend like manna from heaven, how should these goods and services be divided up? At first glance, this question sounds completely idiotic. But imagine: if robotization and technological singularity materialize, then we will have a situation that is comparable metaphorically with the heavens opening and "goods and services" being provided without any real labour being required to obtain them.

How will we divide up the value created by the work of intelligent robots, if we choose momentarily to ignore the rights of ownership over capital in the broad sense? The consequences of social singularity bestow urgency on these kinds of questions. One of the answers is a universal basic income (Chace, 2016: 5), because this will most likely maintain the economic inequality that already exists.

The book explores the following question: What impact will intelligent robots and intelligent informats have on social development?

In order to answer this primary question, we have developed three sub-questions:

1   What impact will technological singularity have on social development?
2   What impact will economic singularity have on social development?
3   What impact will social singularity have on social development?

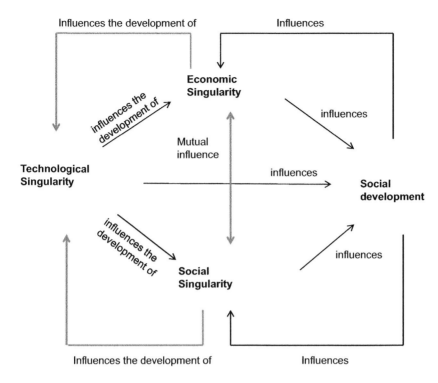

Figure P1 Singularity and societal change.

Figure P.1 is a conceptual illustration of the Introduction, and also depicts the structure of the book.

References

Boden, M.A. (2016). *AI: Its nature and future*, Oxford University Press, Oxford.
Chace, C. (2015). *Surviving AI*, Three Cs, New York.
Chace, C. (2016). *The economic singularity*, Three Cs, New York.
Levesque, H.J. (2017). *Common sense, the Turing Test, and the quest for real AI*, MIT Press, Cambridge, MA.
Rodrik, D. (2017). *Straight talk on trade: Ideas for a sane economy*, Princeton University Press, Princeton.
Shanahan, M. (2015). *The technological singularity*, MIT Press, Cambridge, MA.
Skilton, M., & Hovsepian, F. (2018). *The 4th Industrial Revolution: Responding to the impact of artificial intelligence on business*, Palgrave Macmillan, Cham.

Part I

Technological and economic singularity

1 Technological singularity

Introduction

The main ideas discussed in this chapter are:

- Technological singularity will lead to the development of super-intelligent robots.
- Super-intelligent robots will bring about a greater focus on moral intelligence.
- Technological singularity will lead to brain engineering.

We can describe technological singularity as follows:

> Within a few decades, machine intelligence will surpass human intelligence, leading to The Singularity – technological change so rapid and profound it represents a rupture in the fabric of human history. The implications include the merger of biological and nonbiological intelligence, immortal software-based humans, and ultra-high levels of intelligence that expand outward in the universe at the speed of light.
>
> (Kurzweil, 2001)

The concept of the Singularity was first proposed in 1958 by John von Neumann (1958: 1–49). Subsequently, the concept was popularized by Kurzweil (2005, 2008). From being a theoretical mathematical possibility, the Singularity has become an imminent reality.

One argument in favour of the reality of the Singularity has been advanced by Kurzweil (2005, 2008) with what he calls *the law of accelerating returns*. In summary, this law states as follows:

> An analysis of the history of technology shows that technological change is exponential, contrary to the common-sense intuitive linear view. So we won't experience 100 years of progress in the 21st century – it will be more like 20,000 years of progress (at today's rate). The "returns", such as chip speed and cost-effectiveness, also increase exponentially. There's even exponential growth in the rate of exponential growth.
>
> (Kurzweil, 2001)

This law can be viewed analogously with Moore's law, which states that the number of transistors that it is possible to integrate into a circuit doubles approximately every other year.[1] This link between "the law of accelerating returns" and "Moore's law" provides the theoretical explanation for why the Singularity is approaching near.

Shanahan (2015: xv) writes that the institutions we know today, such as the economy, government, the judicial system and other key societal institutions, cannot continue to exist in their current form once the Singularity occurs. Once nanotechnology, biotechnology, computer science, cognitive psychology, neurotechnology and artificial intelligence are integrated into technical artefacts, our experiences will collapse, and creative destructions will become part of many people's everyday lives. There will also be ethical debate about the nature of a human being, of human values, of consciousness, of "the mind", and of the relationship between consciousness and a rational artificial "brain" that has just as much rational and logical intelligence as a natural human brain. Technological singularity will bring the debate about moral intelligence to the surface, because, among other reasons, we will be forced to implant ethical rules into our super-intelligent machines.

We will not only see nano- and biotechnologies being used to develop products, but also the emergence of brain engineering, where the human brain becomes the subject of large-scale technological engineering projects (Kozma et al., 2018). If the brain becomes a technological product that is analogous to an artificial heart or a prosthetic limb or similar, then the Singularity will have moved on to Super-Singularity (Boden, 2016). One of the results of such a scenario will be that human intelligence, which has remained relatively stable throughout evolution, may suddenly undergo a quantum leap.

The general questions here are as follows: What impact will technological singularity have on social development?

We have summarized this introduction in Figure 1.1. Figure 1.1 also illustrates how we have structured this chapter.

Super-intelligent robots

The term technological singularity refers to the point in time when machines become more intelligent than humans. We do not know exactly when this will occur, but many researchers expect technological singularity to occur at some point between 2035 and 2040 (Kurzweil, 2005; Shanahan, 2015).[2] When this happens, intelligent robots will boost their intelligence by linking up with other intelligent robots worldwide. This will result in what we describe here as intelligent informats. These intelligent informats will possess super-intelligence that will far exceed the logical and rational powers of human intelligence. These intelligent informats will maintain and update themselves. They will also be able to duplicate themselves through, for example 3D printing. In this way they will be continually able to "create" new robots, literally in their own image. In this way, super-intelligent informats will be able, both to outnumber humans,

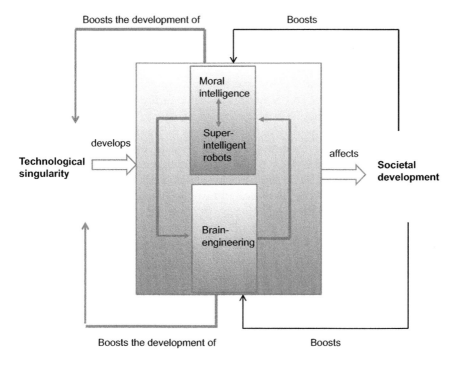

Figure 1.1 Aspects of technological singularity and societal change.

and also to have definitively higher IQs than humans. When talking about intelligence in this context, we are referring primarily to rational, logical, mathematical intelligence. Both the problems selected for analysis and the solutions that emerge will be largely controlled by intelligent robots and super-intelligent informats.

Those who are positive towards technological singularity claim that it will be possible to reduce or eliminate problems relating to employment, work injuries, occupational wear and tear injuries, accidents, etc. (Kurzweil, 2005, 2008). Those who are sceptical about technological singularity, such as Stephen Hawking (Boden, 2016: 148) and Stuart J. Russell (Russell & Norvig, 2013) point out the dangers of ignoring the negative aspects of the technological developments that we find ourselves in the middle of. If we ignore the development of super-intelligent machines, which we here call informats in order to make a distinction from intelligent robots, then these machines could be directly harmful to humans (Vinge, 1993).

When singularity occurs, all the usefulness of our previous experiences will break down, which may be metaphorically compared to what happens to matter in a black hole. When our experiences collapse, we cannot use history as an anchor point for social development. It is in this way that technological singularity will destroy our current society, while something new will emerge. This may be likened to when a larva becomes a butterfly, and the butterfly no longer finds the experiences gained as a larva useful.

Singularity was first of interest to the authors of science fiction. However, now that nanotechnology, biotechnology, information technology and robots have been integrated into technological artefacts, singularity has been elevated from being pure science to becoming a possible future reality, which one can envisage developing over the course of a few years.

When we talk about technological singularity, we have advanced far from the time of the Turing Test, which was developed by Alan Turing in the 1950s. The Turing Test was designed to see if people could differentiate between responses given by a machine and those given by a human. Intelligent robots connected to artificial intelligence are more geared towards general intelligence, not just specific intelligence. In the case of general intelligence, super-intelligent robots can understand the feelings of others, make moral evaluations, and assess complex ethical problems. Such super-intelligent robots, with both logical-rational and specific and general intelligence can, for example, understand when, and if, telling a white lie is morally permissible. These robots will also be able to reason as to why a white lie is correct to use in a specific situation.

In this context, the distance between the Turing Test and the super-intelligent robot may be likened to the distance between the discovery of fire and the discovery of atomic energy. A turning point in the development of artificial intelligence (AI) was in 1997 when Deep Blue, a supercomputer, defeated the ruling world chess champion Gary Kasparov.

Deep Blue was specially designed sole for playing chess. Moving from this point, to developing a general technological intelligence, is a long way, but it is the journey along this path to which Kurzweil (2005, 2008), among others, refers when he uses the term singularity. The intelligent robot will be like a human being, "a jack of all trades", where some are masters of something, while most are masters of none. Such an intelligent robot will have developed general human intelligence, while Deep Blue and many thousands of such specialized robots are designed for a specialized purpose, such as playing chess, adjusting functions on cars, braking a car at speed to avoid an obstacle, and so on.

One approach to developing a general technological intelligence could be to integrate all the specialized intelligences, such as Deep Blue, together with those of all other such machines. Some may be designed for chess, others for anatomy, yet others for addressing ethical issues, and so on. Would such an integrated specialized technological intelligence be equivalent to general intelligence? If the answer is more or less yes, then it will only be a matter of time and resources before we have robots that possess general technological intelligence. Once we have made a good deal of progress along this design road, one can imagine that the general AI robot will begin to use analogy-thinking from the various specialized competencies it possesses. In such a situation, this general AI robot will be able to develop creative new innovations.

If the answer is no, i.e. the sum of specific intelligences does not result in general intelligence, but only appears so, then it will most likely be difficult to develop general intelligence. The problem for the intelligent robot that is designed based on the integration of all known specific intelligences occurs when it has to deal with something that is not found in any of the specific intelligences, or in the interaction between them. The theoretical example is that part of knowledge we call "hidden knowledge", that is to say, what we don't know that we don't know. A practical example may be honesty and integrity linked to a white lie. What would the intelligent robot do? The objection is of course that a person of flesh and blood will also have problems with such a situation.

It is also possible that general intelligence in intelligent robots may be developed in the same way as it is in humans, i.e. as a result of experience, learning and knowledge development. If this proves to be correct, then the sum of the specific intelligences, plus an ability to learn from their own mistakes and adapt to situations, could be the design strategy for the development of robots with general intelligence. The design principle for the development of general intelligence in intelligent robots is then the sum of specific intelligences, plus the ability to learn from their own and others' mistakes. Mistakes or errors may be defined as the negative consequences of attempts to solve a challenge, a problem, and so on, such as a white lie. In addition to learning, the machines could be designed so that they could adapt to new contexts and new situations.

In addition to learning and adaptation, general intelligence consists of common sense, creativity, reason, analogical thinking, cultural understanding, contextual understanding, language comprehension, historical understanding, ethical reflection, moral action and what can be called moral intelligence, etc. In the next section, we will reflect on the concept of moral intelligence.

Moral intelligence

Here we define moral intelligence as a system of explicit values, values relating to our behaviour and capacity for empathy. This definition explains the components of moral intelligence, as well as how it is oriented in practice. This definition brings us on from knowing what is right and wrong to behaving in a way that is right.

Throughout history, and in our own times, moral leadership has proved to be of enormous importance for businesses and nation states (Lennick & Kiel, 2011). Dishonest leaders cause ruin for their businesses. In the most recent economic crisis, which occurred in autumn 2008, the whole global economy suffered the negative impact of unethical leadership, with the most well-known examples being Enron and Andersen Consulting (Johannessen, 2017). There are compelling empirical indications that moral leadership, moral intelligence and emotional intelligence have direct positive effects on the bottom line of a business (Goleman, 1995, 1998; Lennick & Kiel, 2011). Unless customers can trust a business, no matter what sector it is in, the business will not survive.

Its customers' moral judgement will weigh like an anchor around its bottom line. This is also apparent in an empirical investigation of customers' views of business leaders' moral reputations. In a major Gallup survey, only 12 per cent of leaders were considered to have high ethical standards.[3]

The existence of unethical leaders shows that it is not only intelligent robots that have problems and challenges with moral intelligence. In recent history, leaders have shown that reflection on moral intelligence is not just a theoretical academic phenomenon, but a challenge for leadership practices.

Our values are based on our assumptions, and it is presumed that they guide our behaviour. However, empirical research has shown that in reality there is only a tenuous link between our values and our behaviour. Therefore, moral skills and empathy are important elements when showing that moral intelligence is related to our "operating philosophy". Our values when carrying out actions, the ones we use, are related to our moral skills. Empathy, the ability to understand the feelings of others, is an essential part of moral intelligence. Therefore, developing empathy will be an essential step towards building the moral intelligence of the super-intelligent robot (Bellaby, 2014).

The relationship between moral intelligence and logical intelligence (IQ) is shown in Figure 1.2.

Moral intelligence is based on fundamental and universal values. This means that moral intelligence, as we use the concept here, is not linked to cultural relativism. Cultural relativism is the view that an individual's values are relative to the culture to which they belong. We assume here that there are some fundamental moral values that are common to all people, such as respect, duty, dignity and perceived justice (Benhabib, 2002, 2004; Benhabib et al., 2006).

Some claim that morality and intelligence are two different domains that cannot be linked (Bellaby, 2014: 1–5). However, we are of the opinion that

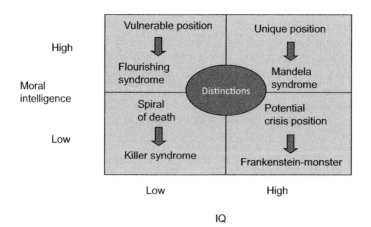

Figure 1.2 Moral intelligence and logical intelligence (IQ).

intelligence without morality and morality without intelligence are on par with a plane without wings or a boat without a rudder.

Moral or ethical intelligence is like optimism, something that can be learned and developed (Seligman, 2006), a view which Dobrin also shares. We know from countless historical examples that people with a high intelligence quotient (IQ) do not necessarily develop a high moral intelligence. We also know from several historical examples that those with a high moral intelligence do not necessarily have a high IQ. In this way, the concept of intelligence ethics appears as a paradox. The paradox, however, finds its solution in an inseparable connection between ethics and intelligence. This does not mean that you need to be intelligent (IQ) to act morally, or act morally because you have a high IQ. It means that the connection tries to show that moral intelligence is a form of intelligence that appears in the connection between the two elements.

How can you know what high moral intelligence is? One can learn much from the answer Aristotle gave to the question of what is a good person. Aristotle asked them to find a righteous person and then observe what this person does (Dobrin, 2002: 37). This method connects moral intelligence to practice, reflection and action.

To find such a righteous person, the moral values that apply to all humanity may be used as a starting point (Benhabib, 2002, 2004; Benhabib et al., 2006).[4] How the individual uses these values in practice can then be assessed. Finally, the individual's empathy plays an important role because this says something about how the common values are incorporated into the individual's actions. Understood in this way, you do not need a theory or quantification of moral intelligence, because experience and practice inform us whether an individual has low or high moral intelligence.

This approach is closely related to Lawrence Kohlberg's theory of moral development. Kohlberg's theory is based on the close relationship between moral reasoning and moral actions.

At a time when technological singularity is increasingly developing and the global knowledge economy has become a fact, there is much to suggest that we should utilize universal values, because that which will hold us together is, namely, our fundamental human values, though everything else separates us.

Our identity and belonging are essentially different, but our values can be the cohesion that binds humanity together despite differences in language, sexual orientation, ethnicity, nationality, gender, race and so on (Benhabib, 2002: 24–49). In our view, our common values are universal and represent a cohesive force, for which Benhabib et al. (2006) argue. These universal values are shared by all humanity, not just those who have the same nationality as us.

When designing super-intelligent robots, it will be both desirable and necessary that the robots possess moral intelligence on the basis of the above argumentation. If super-intelligent robots do not incorporate moral intelligence, they may just become a technological offspring of the Frankenstein monster, so to speak. The design principles of a super-intelligent robot that take into account moral intelligence are shown in Figure 1.3.

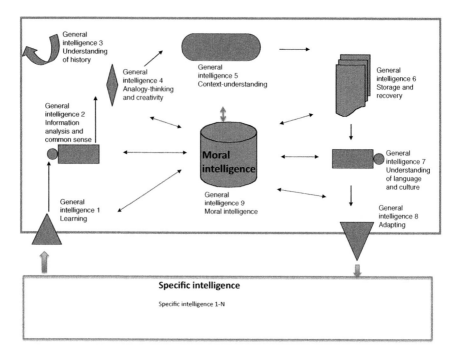

Figure 1.3 The design principles for moral intelligence in super-intelligent robots.

Brain engineering

If we look at the brain as an information-processing unit, then we can apply the nine information processes identified by Miller (1978) to compare the brain's information-processing functions and translate them into design principles for general intelligence in a robot. We have adapted Miller's nine information processes to suit our purposes here, namely to develop design principles for general intelligence.

The nine information processes shown in Figure 1.4 can be viewed meta-phorically as clusters of neurons. We can envisage implementing the nine design principles through a step-by-step process. First, we would model a technological platform for each of the nine elements of general intelligence (Modelling). Next, we would conceptualize the different activities and processes that go to make up these nine elements of general intelligence (Conceptualization). Finally, we would simulate each of these nine elements of general intelligence both individually and interactively (Simulation). The simulation process would be a learning-by-doing process, where the model and the conceptualization would be subject to changes and improvements. The activities of modelling, concep-tualization and simulation are intended to form a continual, iterative process, whereby general intelligence would be continually updated and approved.

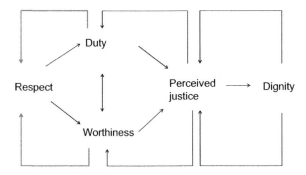

Figure 1.4 The design principles of general intelligence.

Both learning and adapting are very important processes in Figure 1.4. They form the basis for the other seven general processes. Learning and adapting can over time be the two processes that can solve challenges and problems that the programmers did not predict; for example how an intelligent robot, designed for moral intelligence, can cope with white lies when programmed for respect, truth and honesty. Being honest and dishonest at the same time can be very difficult for most people, but through trial and error and adapting to situation and context, most people can manage this activity. That is why learning and adapting are crucial processes in the development of general intelligence in Figure 1.4.

The nine information processes in Figure 1.4 are an easier way to develop the link between specific intelligence and general intelligence than the radical "whole brain emulation", about which Sandberg and Bostrom (2008) and Shanahan (2015: 15–51), amongst others, write in detail.

Figure 1.4 shows a figurative representation of general intelligence that could be designed into an intelligent robot, with its specific intelligences.

Figure 1.4 is based on the assumption that intelligent behaviour is brought about by a link between specific intelligences and general intelligences, where moral intelligence is part of the general intelligence.

Conclusion

The question we have considered in this part is as follows: What impact will technological singularity have on social development?

A brief answer to this question is that nanotechnology, biotechnology and artificial intelligence will lead to creative destructions that will transform everything we know about our existing societal organization. This will cause the collapse of the experiences we have been accustomed to take as the basis of our evaluations, assessments and constructs of social systems. This experiential collapse will force us to consider society in new ways. It is not our

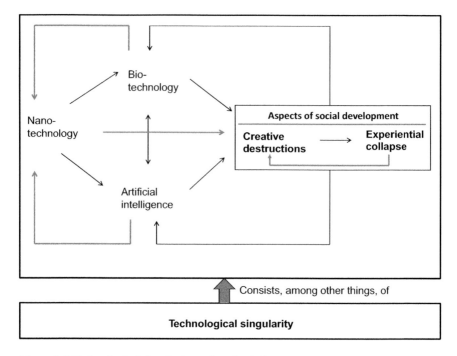

Figure 1.5 Technological singularity and societal change.

experience, but our ideas, that will become the crucial social mechanisms for the understanding and development of society.

We have illustrated this in Figure 1.5.

The digital revolution we have seen starting at the end of the twentieth century and continuing today has created the necessary infrastructures and info-structures to allow intelligent robots to possess an info-structure which they can use to link up with other intelligent robots worldwide. These intelligent robots will then become what we call informats.

One of the positive results of the debate about technological singularity may be that moral intelligence (MIQ) will be allocated the same focus and status as rational, logical intelligence (IQ). This is because it will become more legitimate to ask questions about what distinguishes a human from a super-intelligent robot. One of the answers may well turn out to be moral intelligence.

Notes

1 https://en.wikipedia.org/wiki/Moore%27s_law.
2 There is disagreement as to when and whether the Singularity will occur. There is also disagreement as to whether the Singularity will be good or bad for humans. Our view is that the consequences will generally be good, assuming that the consequences

of the Singularity are subject to political control and not left to market forces (Boden, 2016: 145).

3   A link to the Gallup survey is available in Lennick and Kiel, 2011: 3, note 26.

4   Respect, duty, worthiness, perceived justice and dignity.

References

Bellaby, R.W. (2014). *The ethics of intelligence*, Routledge, London.

Benhabib, S. (2002). *The claims of culture*, Princeton University Press, Princeton.

Benhabib, S. (2004). *The rights of others*, Cambridge University Press, Cambridge.

Benhabib, S. Waldron, J., Honig, B., & Kymlicka, W. (eds.) (2006). *Another cosmopolitanism*, Oxford University Press, Oxford.

Boden, M.A. (2016). *AI: Its nature and future*, Oxford University Press, Oxford.

Casti, J.L. (1988). *The Cambridge quintet: A work of scientific speculation*, Perseus Books, London.

Chace, C. (2015). *Surviving AI*, Three Cs, New York.

Chace, C. (2016). *The economic singularity*, Three Cs, New York.

Colvin, G. (2016). *Talents are overrated: What really separates world class performers from everybody else*, Nicolas Brealey, New York.

Colvin, G. (2018). *Humans are underrated: What high achievers know that brilliant machines never will*, Nicolas Brealey, New York.

Dorling, D. (2015). *Inequality and the 1%*, Verso, London.

Franklin, D. (2017). *Megatech: Technology in 2050*, The Economist, London.

Gordon, E. (2018). *Future jobs: Solving the employment and skills crisis*, Praeger, New York.

Johannessen, J.-A. (2017). *Innovations lead to economic crises*, Palgrave Macmillan, Cham.

Kozma, R, et al. (2018). *Artificial intelligence in the age of neural networks and brain computing*, Academic Press, London.

Kurzweil, R. (2001). Law of accelerating returns, Lifeboat Foundation Special Report, https://lifeboat.com/ex/law.of.accelerating.returns.

Kurzweil, R. (2005). *The singularity is near*, Penguin, London.

Kurzweil, R. (2008). *The age of spiritual machines: When computers exceed human intelligence*, Penguin, London.

Lennick, D., & Kiel, F. (2011). *Moral intelligence 2.0: Enhancing business performance and leadership success in turbulent times*, Pearson Prentice Hall, Upper Saddle River, NJ.

Miller, J.G. (1978). *Living systems*, McGraw-Hill, New York.

Pistono, F. (2012). *Robots will steal your job, but that's OK: How to survive the economic collapse and be happy*, Create Space, New York.

Russell, S., & Norvig, P. (2013). *Artificial intelligence: A modern approach*, Pearson, London.

Sandberg, A., & Bostrom, N. (2008). *Whole brain emulation: A roadmap*, Future of Humanity Institute, Oxford.

Seligman, M.E.P. (2006). *Learned optimism*, Vintage, New York.

Shanahan, M. (2015). *The technological singularity*, MIT Press, Cambridge, MA.

Skilton, M., & Hovsepian, F. (2018). *The 3rd Industrial Revolution: Responding to the impact of artificial intelligence on business*, Palgrave Macmillan, Cham.

Vinge, V. (1993). The coming technological singularity, Vision-21 Symposium, www8.cs.umu.se/kurser/5DV084/HT10/utdelat/vinge.pdf.

von Neumann, J. (1958). *John von Neumann 1903–1957*, American Mathematical Society, Menasha, WI.

2 Economic singularity

Introduction

The main ideas discussed in this chapter are:

- An extreme increase in productivity will occur in the future, accompanied by little or no increase in wages.
- Technology and innovation have the power to bring about a work-free society for most people, i.e. "living for free".
- Change will become the new stability, and innovation will become the basic model for business.
- A new type of integrated production and distribution will be developed, known as "distruction". "Distruction" means the emergence of processing power, storage capacity, artificial intelligence and non-visible "robots" in AI networks, as well as in 3D printers located near customers.

Economic singularity (Chace, 2016) will be the result of the automation of production, distribution and the consumption element of the economy. In addition, the nine information processes found in all businesses will be automated (Miller, 1978). This automation of information processes will be crucial for value creation and employment in the innovation economy (Avent, 2016). If we arrive at, or become close to achieving, economic singularity, most of these information processes will be replaced by intelligent robots. This will leave us facing the challenge of mass unemployment, unless the political system intervenes to provide a solution, e.g. a universal basic income.

In practice, economic singularity will mean that project-based employment becomes the norm, not unlike the casual day-to-day employment of peasants in feudal society (Johannessen, 2018a). If capitalism is not to collapse due to a lack of people creating a demand for goods and services, then a universal basic income, in one form or another, is an obvious possibility (Johannessen, 2018b). In such a scenario, governments could relatively easily increase, decrease or differentiate this universal basic income, so that the goods and services being produced would be sold. There may be other potential strategies, i.e. that demand determines what is produced. In any event, some type of universal basic income will be capable of resolving the crisis of capitalism at the dawn of economic singularity in the innovation economy.

Let us conduct a simple thought experiment to illustrate what might happen. Suppose that there are a number of people on a desert island, without any links whatsoever to the surrounding world. On the island, there are two factories, each with its own machinery. These factories employ 50 of the island's inhabitants. The factories supply absolutely all the goods and services required by the island's inhabitants. Suddenly there's an economic earthquake: someone invents a technology capable of fully automating all the operations (production and administrative) in both factories. The two factory owners go ahead with full automation of the factories. All the workers become unemployed and for two or three years live solely on a small fund set aside for social welfare. Finally, this is used up. There is no other paid employment on the island. What would the factory owners do in such a situation? They would probably meet at their club and decide that they needed to maintain demand. How could this be achieved? The unemployed workers would have to be given money so that they could buy the factory owners' products. In return, workers could do gardening for the factory owners, or build them mini-palaces on the island, or otherwise perform such services for the factory owners as were suited to this new era.

In the second part of the thought experiment, the workers at both factories held an assembly and agreed to share the value creation which the fully automated machines had produced for the island. They then managed to get the two factory owners and their families to participate in this distribution of goods.

Thus, we have one thought experiment with two scenarios. However, the most likely outcome is probably the first scenario, the one that proposes the development of a type of feudal capitalism (Johannessen, 2019). The reason lies in what was not mentioned in the thought experiment. The island was populated by more than just the 50 workers. The population also included police, teachers, journalists, cultural workers, etc. Many of these would be interested in maintaining the status quo in order to secure their established positions, which Kahneman and Tversky explain in their prospect theory (Kahneman & Tversky, 1979: 263–292, 2000).[1] It seems reasonable that most of the people who were not factory workers would argue strongly in favour of upholding both the private property rights of the factory owners and their right to the profits from the fully automated machines. This is the essence of the future emergence of feudal capitalism as a result of economic singularity (Johannessen, 2019).

The question we are investigating here is: What impact will economic singularity have on social development?

To answer the question, we have developed four sub-questions:

1   What impact will full automation have on social development?
2   What impact will mass unemployment have on social development?
3   What impact will a universal basic income have on social development?
4   What impact will "living for free" have on social development?

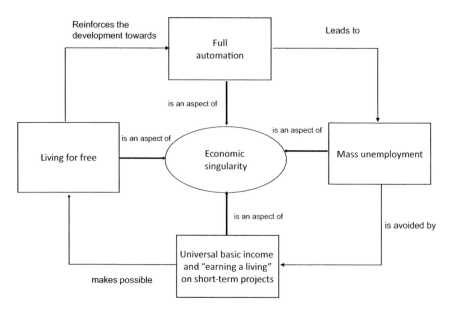

Figure 2.1 Economic singularity.

We have summarized the introduction in Figure 2.1. Figure 2.1 also illustrates how we have structured this chapter.

Full automation

The question we are investigating is as follows: What impact will full automation have on social development?

Economic singularity will promote ideas, understandings and notions that will permeate all strata of the economy, i.e. production, distribution and consumption. One of the most obvious results will be full automation of production, distribution and consumption, as well as of information processes within organizations (Locke & Wellhausen, 2015). Another particular characteristic of full automation will be the emergence of clusters of innovations that will come in cascades (Johannessen, 2017; Janeway, 2018). In this way, full automation will change all of our ideas about the meaning of work. When new technologies have been put into use in the past, there have been revolutions in our ways of thinking and behaving, for example in the First Industrial Revolution. It is here that the First Industrial Revolution has practical relevance. We must remember, however, that the First Industrial Revolution had its origins in around 1712, when the first practical steam engine was developed by Thomas Newcomen.[2] In other words, the First Industrial Revolution has been underway for more than 300 years. Automation has been a result of the First, Second and Third Industrial Revolutions. Our point here is that the Fourth Industrial Revolution will not only boost the automation of production processes, but will also automate information processes (Janeway, 2018; Johannessen, 2018b).

The Third Industrial Revolution was the start of digitization and the beginning of the automation of information processes in organizations, institutions and society as a whole. The Fourth Industrial Revolution will involve increased digitization, namely, intelligent robots and artificial intelligence that will be globally connected to other intelligent robots. To make a distinction between intelligent robots on the one hand, and, on the other hand, intelligent robots that are connected to other intelligent robots globally, the term "informats" is used here for the latter type of intelligent robots (Johannessen, 2018a). Once info-structure, digitization, intelligent robots and informats are in place, we will have developed fully automated production, distribution and consumption (Janeway, 2018). It is at this point in time (although obviously there is no specific "point" in time) that change processes will accelerate and the usefulness of our current knowledge will completely collapse, because intelligent robots and informats will take over the work and operations previously performed by people.

For those who are unable to adjust to the unknown and uncertain future, the past will represent a safe haven. It seems reasonable to assume that nostalgia will flourish amongst these people. "Back to the past" may quickly evolve into political movements that will hamper technological developments. This is what we will call here Trumpism, i.e. the philosophy and politics espoused by Donald Trump. But reactionary dams that are unable to regulate the flow of new ideas will at some point break, resulting in cascades of innovations sweeping away the nostalgia (Johannessen, 2017).

When, not if, full automation becomes limitless and incorporates all the processes in organizations and society, productivity will increase enormously (Janeway, 2018). In the thought experiment described at the beginning of the chapter, none of the workers will be left in the factory to demand higher wages. Therefore, it is uncertain that a future increase in productivity will lead to higher wages. In such a case, we will have to organize society and the distribution of value creation in a completely new way. With full automation, the traditional bargaining and negotiation between employers and employees will completely break down.

Artificial intelligence, full automation of businesses and organizations, and global digitization in integrated networks will together mean that we will have to completely change our current business models and think anew. For instance, the organization of Amazon, Google, Uber, etc. is an indication of future trends (Libert et al., 2016: 3–27). Full automation applies not only to new entrepreneurial businesses, but will completely change established businesses. The banking and finance industry is just one example where the question has become: How few employees can we have and still operate effectively? Sales, the number of employees and profits will all be affected by full automation. In this picture, change will be the new norm and the basic business model will have to integrate the free flow of innovations. Already today, there are companies

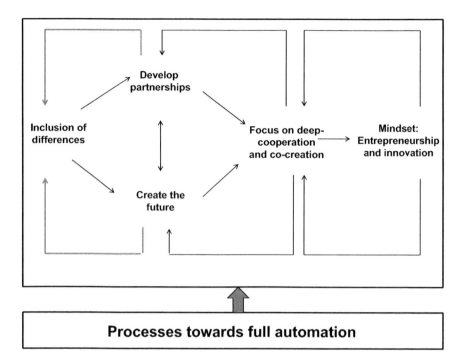

Figure 2.2 Central processes towards full automation.

focusing on digitization, automation and the sharing of profits with employees, as well as developing co-operation models with customers and suppliers leading the market. They grow faster than the market, have higher profits than average and also lower marginal costs than the average in the same industry (Libert, et al., 2016: 3–27). By reviewing 1,500 businesses, Libert et al. (2016) have developed ten principles that can be used in all industries to increase growth and profits.

We have abstracted these ten principles to reduce complexity, and designed a five-step model, as illustrated in Figure 2.2. Figure 2.2 can be used to develop businesses and organizations towards "full automation".

Mass unemployment

The question we are investigating is as follows: What impact will mass unemployment have on social development?

The major debate about innovation concerns the extent to which intelligent robots and artificial intelligence will bring about either work-free lifestyles, or an era dominated by mass unemployment (Hansen, 2016; Franklin, 2017: 76–87; Johannessen, 2019). The truth will no doubt be somewhere in between. But, even at the central point between these two extremes, working life will be so characterized by unemployment that our understanding of these concepts will change. The debate about universal basic incomes has already started (Gordon, 2018). In addition, many people will have short-term jobs that they use to supplement government benefits (Chace, 2016:4–6).

While the first three industrial revolutions led to increased productivity, higher wages for workers and improved living standards, some writers believe that this will not be the case in the Fourth Industrial Revolution. Gordon (2018) writes that so far digitization in the United States has not led to higher salaries for employees. On the other hand, income inequality has increased significantly in the US, but to a lesser extent in Europe.

The richest 1 per cent have swallowed up the largest part of the increase in wealth creation (Dorling, 2015). This is an indication that the power structure is changing to the advantage of the absolute richest. Neither intelligent robots, artificial intelligence nor a formidable productivity increase can change this picture. Consequently, new innovations do not seem able to deliver the same advances for workers as innovations did between 1750 and the mid-1900s.

Productivity and value creation will increase, but economic inequality will also increase formidably and take on apocalyptic proportions (Avent, 2016). In addition, demographic trends in the industrialized countries indicate an increasing proportion of the population are older than before, which will further enhance the aforementioned developments, if the elderly stop working and become retirees (Ainley, 2016).

There is a current debate on innovation which may be characterized as being between the optimists and the pessimists. The optimists believe that the new technology will lead to the same increase in prosperity for most people as did previous technological innovations. The pessimists say that this time it will be different. We take a third point of view here. We are of the opinion that new technology and innovations in the Fourth Industrial Revolution will be of such force that they may lead to a work-free life for most people. This is similar to the optimists' view. However, we must not forget the interaction between innovation and technology on the one hand and the political system on the other. As long as the political system does not actively promote a more equal distribution of value creation, mass unemployment will be the result and an explosive increase in economic inequality will be the consequence. This is in line with the pessimists' view. Thus, our perspective is that we are optimistic with regard to technology and innovation, but pessimistic with regard to the political system.

Our perspective is based on three assumptions (Johannessen, 2017, 2018a, 2018b, 2019):

1 In the short term, all innovations will lead to small and large economic crises. This may be the reason why Gordon (2018) and Brynjolfsson and McAfee (2014) suggest that digitization will not result in economic growth.
2 However, in a longer perspective, innovations will promote value creation, increase productivity and, through social structures, distribute value

creation according to the social balance of power, through negotiation between employees and employers. This pattern emerges as a consequence of most innovations throughout history (Johannessen, 2017). The argument is that the old will first be destroyed, leading to various types of crises. This will be followed by the new technology being put into more effective use, resulting in a cascade of changes throughout society. It is at this point in time that innovation will lead to increased value creation. However, it may take between 20 and 40 years before innovations impact society in this way (Johannessen, 2017).

3   The prerequisite for the distribution of value creation is not present to the same extent today, because employees are less organized than before (Chomsky, 2016a), while capital has acquired political and opinion-making power (Chomsky, 2016b). Therefore, inequality will increase and some form of mass unemployment will be the result. Before this happens, the political environment will probably force the introduction of some form of universal basic income.

For most countries in the OECD, there has been a decline in inflation-adjusted earnings (OECD, 2015). The decline has not been large, but is still noticeable. The decline has varied between –7 per cent in Estonia and –0.2 per cent in Australia. Only a few countries have had an increase in per capita earnings, such as Germany, Japan, Chile and Poland. Overall, digital innovation has benefited the few, primarily the richest 1 per cent. On the other hand, many employees have experienced a fall in the real value of their earnings (OECD, 2015). The great increase in inequality we have witnessed from 2000 up until today has led to a call for the regulation of earnings in order to promote greater economic equality. In this connection, historian Walter Scheidel's book *The Great Leveler* (2017) makes interesting reading. He has examined economic inequality through history, moving from the Stone Age to today. The book concludes that there are only three processes throughout history that have led to significantly greater economic equality: war, revolutions and epidemics. However, one objection against Scheidel's ideas is that the Nordic countries have developed more equality than many other countries, including the USA, without war, revolution or epidemics. Of interest in this context is the fact that trade unions and the political labour movement have been very strong in these countries, partly explaining why there is relative equality in the Nordic region. Another interesting conclusion of Scheidel's is that voting rights, democracy, regulations and education only have a limited effect on equalizing economic inequality.

Technological mass unemployment is not necessarily a bad thing. If a restructuring of society is carried out to enable an increase in productivity, and the consequences of this increase are dealt with equitably, we may witness a similar development to that which occurred in the late 1800s and the early 1900s in the industrialized countries: working hours were shortened, and the increase in wealth creation benefited wage earners. However, the necessary preconditions for this to occur are a strong political awareness among wage earners, a strong trade union movement and a strong and progressive political system. If these preconditions are present, mass unemployment may be avoided (Chace, 2015, 2016; Ainley, 2016;).

Mass unemployment can also be avoided by treating part-time jobs as if they were full-time jobs, for statistical purposes. Technological unemployment has already led to the situation where many amongst the middle classes, as well as unskilled workers, have taken on temporary short-term project-like work in the United States (Chace, 2016: 26–28). Of course, this does not represent mass unemployment, but may be an early warning signal about what awaits us when intelligent robots are used on a large scale in production, distribution and consumption (Hanson, 2016; Gordon, 2018).

Other early warning signals may be seen in those industries where established companies have lost their leading positions. They have been pushed away by businesses that are characterized by having fewer employees than the established businesses. One such example is the case of Kodak vs. Instagram; Instagram flourished with only around a dozen employees (Johannessen, 2018a, 2018b). Innovation largely reduces costs.

The trend towards mass unemployment in various forms and degrees is also emphasized by Brynjolfsson and McAfee (2014). They point out that the speed and depth of development and spread of the new technology will make technological unemployment unavoidable. Innovations emerge in situations where costs are relatively high (Johannessen, 2017, 2018a). This can explain the outsourcing of industry to, inter alia, China and India. This may be called organizational innovation, where the value chain is globalized and not bound by the geographical location of a factory.

Mass unemployment will not only affect workers in production and administration. Susskind and Susskind (2017) argue that the professions will also be transformed, with many of their functions taken over by intelligent robots. For instance, this will apply to lawyers, doctors, nurses, teachers, architects, and so on. In the first part of this scenario, the professions will work closely together with the new technology. In a slightly longer time perspective, by 2040, the intelligent robots will have taken over most of the functions of the professions (Weeks, 2014; Hanson, 2016; Gordon, 2018).

As mentioned, there are both optimistic and pessimistic views regarding the development of economic singularity. However, if we assume that mass unemployment will be the result of singularity, then future prospects look dismal. Yet, Federico Pistono's book *Robots will steal your job, but that's OK* (2012) takes an optimistic view of the future, although he predicts unemployment will be widespread. In this context, one might ask: Is it not better to spend your life doing something you really burn for, something you want to be good at, and something where you gain experience slowly, but which ultimately you are able to master, rather than struggling with a job which makes you unhappy?

The optimists defend their argument historically by referring to the Luddites who smashed the new innovative textile machines during the First Industrial

Revolution (cf. "the Luddite fallacy").[3] The optimists and pessimists agree that economic inequality will increase. The pessimists assert that this is not morally defendable, while the optimists believe that inequality, in favour of those who are richer, is a necessary incentive to ensure an increase in wealth creation, which will ultimately benefit everybody (Chace, 2016: 48–53). The optimists claim that while the future looks gloomy to many, it is not apocalyptic. Our perspective is somewhat in line with the optimists, although over a longer time perspective. In the short term, it is highly probable that only minor changes will occur. When innovation, i.e. intelligent robots and informats, becomes commonly used in most work functions, the consequences will be of an apocalyptic nature to many. In a slightly longer perspective, society will not be able to function properly with such a breach in the social cohesion, thus prompting the creation of a future where everyone will improve their standard of living. No one can predict specifically what the future will hold, but there are several scenarios, such as the establishment of a universal basic income, a 4-hour working day, or well-paid project positions in short-term engagements or other forms of new organization of work. However, if people do not have an adequate income they can live off, then the crisis will likely lead to chaos, social dissolution and revolution. We have seen this occur before in history, when great social upheavals have caused pain to many and unfulfilled lives for long periods of time. Those in power are of course aware of this, and they will therefore change the organization of society before this occurs. Therefore, in the long run, the comprehensive use of intelligent robots will be of benefit to all, although it will lead to extremely large differences, where the 1 per cent class will govern by means of their representatives (Dorling, 2015; Johannessen, 2018a, 2018b, 2019). There are important reasons why the optimists do not think there will be any rebellion against apocalyptic economic inequality. Firstly, people with different income levels will settle in geographical clusters (Abrahamson, 2004), and consequently, the poor will not witness the extravagant wealth of the 1 per cent elite. Secondly, an argument derived from the saying, "religion is the opium of the people", states that relatively free entertainment (Netflix, Viaplay, etc.), as well as social media, functions as "opium" for the masses. In other words, people are reluctant to do anything that might disturb their leisure time in front of some form of screen. Historically, this may be viewed as being similar to the Roman's bread (universal basic income) and circuses (free entertainment on the internet), i.e. pay and entertainment being offered as a means of pacifying discontent.

Universal basic income, and earning a living from short-term projects

The question we are investigating is as follows: What impact will a universal basic income have on social development?

During the next few decades, or perhaps before, most jobs will be taken over by intelligent robots. Up until now, the transition to an economy based on knowledge resources has been relatively unproblematic. An important point here is that when one is in the eye of a storm, everything seems calm, changes take place slowly, and few people notice the turbulence of the storm out at sea. This is also one way of viewing the current situation with regard to intelligent robots, artificial intelligence and digitization. It is only when you are no longer in the eye of the storm that turbulence and chaos occur.

Perhaps we will have to rethink the nature of jobs and work, as intelligent robots will be taking over most functions in the workplace. If many, or most, jobs are taken over by intelligent robots, then we will have a choice between developing a society with many oppressed individuals, which will reduce social cohesion, or instead developing a society where individuals are allowed to use their abilities to pursue their burning passions and can do what they are (or want to be) good at, for the good of society and the individual. The alternative can be described at its extreme as a choice between feudal capitalism or a democratic society (Johannessen, 2018b, 2019).

If we want to maintain the social contract between individuals and society, we must ensure that most people experience their lives having meaning, even though they are unemployed, i.e. they do not have income from work (Gordon, 2018). One strategy could be a universal basic income, while working on short-term contracts to ensure an adequate level of income.

The universal basic income is intended as a guaranteed minimum wage for all citizens, without any form of needs testing. The Basic Income Earth Network[4] has been working to promote a universal basic income since 1986. In those countries that have launched basic income pilot projects, the level of the basic income varies, but is usually close to the so-called poverty line. We have described some examples below in this section.

The use of a universal basic income may be understood as part of a strategy to dampen a potential social rebellion at the start of the Fourth Industrial Revolution – a new type of "sedative drug" to pacify the poor. If the extensive use of intelligent robots and artificial intelligence results in unemployment for most people, Western societies will probably have no other choice than to implement some form of universal basic income. The alternative, when most people are threatened with unemployment, will be the possible collapse of the social system.

Basic income projects have been implemented and tested already in several countries such as Finland, France, etc. There is also opposition to basic income in the US, amongst other countries (Chace, 2016: 5); however, this opposition will probably disappear or diminish when the social consequences of technological mass unemployment become more evident.

Brynjolfsson and McAfee (2014) argue against a universal basic income, because they believe it may lead to boredom and a lack of participation in social life. However, a possible social rebellion will be anything other than "boring", and will create major problems for the 1 per cent class; we thus believe, if only for this reason, that a universal basic income will be established. On the other hand, we have offered direct and indirect arguments against the universal basic income in this book and earlier books (Johannessen, 2018a, 2018b). The reason for this view is that the cohesive force of society will be undermined, and that many people's lives will be violated, if a majority of the population have to live off a universal basic income and random part-time jobs. In such a situation, it seems reasonable to assume that society in the long term will break down if many people have to live on a universal basic income near the poverty line. Of course, the alternative is a fairer distribution of the wealth creation that will most probably result from the extensive use of intelligent robots, because productivity will increase enormously (Karabarbounis & Neiman, 2014; Goertzel & Goertzel, 2015).

Although a basic income may be universally introduced in the future, this will not reduce economic inequality. It may prevent miserable conditions, but it would still not reduce the experience of failure and of being violated for those receiving the basic income, because the feeling of not being able to cope in such a situation would be strong. The reasons are simple. The 1 per cent elite who own 90 percent of the wealth (Bauman, 2013; Weeks, 2014) will distance themselves from the other 99 per cent, both economically, cognitively, psychologically and even physically, i.e. they will have no physical contact with the others (Chace, 2016: 5–6). If this happens, it will strongly resemble the period before the fall of the Roman Empire, and the period before the First and Second World Wars (Scheidel, 2017).

Can a society function if a large proportion of the population finds that they are economically and socially violated over time? The answer is probably no. On the other hand, a universal basic income will keep people from reacting, because they may risk losing the little they already have, something that the prospect theory has argued (Kahneman & Tversky, 1979, 2000). Thus, a universal basic income is one way of maintaining the status quo: extravagant wealth for the few, and a miserable violated life for the many. Ford (2016) suggests that the universal basic income will be about US$10,000 per annum. This may be enough to survive on, but it is not enough to live a worthwhile life. That is why there will be an incentive to find part-time jobs and short-term contracts to supplement the basic income. This at least is a major argument that has been given for adopting a universal basic income in those places where it has already been tried out (Ford, 2016).

The following is an important reason why the universal basic income and other social mechanisms may be introduced: the 1 per cent may manage to convince the other 99 per cent that they have something to lose in a potential rebellion – the prospect theory suggests such a scenario (Kahneman & Tversky, 2000). The theory proposes that one will exert more effort in preserving what one has already achieved than acting to change social conditions when one is unsure of the outcome. Figuratively, this may be illustrated by the saying, "a bird in the hand is better than two in the bush".

Several basic income pilot projects have been launched in several places around the world.[5] Some of these, and their results, are listed below.

Manitoba, Canada (1974–1979)

- 8.5 per cent more people finished high school.
- More women took longer maternity leave.

Namibia (January 2008 to December 2009)

- Dropout from school was reduced from 40 per cent to less than 1 per cent.
- The crime rate fell by 42 per cent.

India (17 months around 2011)

- A reduction in cases of illness.
- Improved school attendance.
- Increase in the production of food from own land.
- More people applied for part-time jobs.

Brazil (2003 to the present day)

- Poverty in Brazil was reduced by 10–26 per cent.
- School attendance increased by 5–19 per cent.

London (2010)

- Large reduction in "street kids problem".

New York City (2007–2010)

- Reduction in prevalence of hunger.
- Increased use of dental care services.

There have also been projects tested out in Alaska, Seattle, Denver, North Carolina, Uganda, Kenya and Iran.

Living for free

The question we are investigating here is as follows: What impact will "living for free" have on social development?

It is perhaps the case that asking which jobs will disappear as a result of new technology is not particularly relevant. It may be more relevant to ask which functions, and which activities within these functions, can be performed by intelligent robots. The reason for this is that many jobs will continue to exist, but they will be transformed, so that – at least during a transitional phase – intelligent robots will be able to assist people in doing these jobs. But by asking this question, we can also address the issue of what kinds of additional competences need to be introduced into most professions.

We can determine with certainty three things:

1   There is no consensus concerning whether the use of intelligent robots will result in unemployment.
2   Nobody knows what will happen if intelligent robots automate and informatize[6] most work functions and activities.
3   We can all help to create the desired future.

"Living for free" may be understood in relation to a simple scenario of a possible future where full automation has become the reality. In this scenario, it is not who we are that is important, but who we want to be and how we wish to present ourselves. One can present oneself through various social media, or through the platforms that are available in our community. In this network of like-minded people, we can present ourselves and create our own identities without being bound by the influence that our history and experiences may have on others' perception of us.

The time frame for this scenario is that it is set to occur in 2040, because several authors believe this to be a realistic prediction of the date by which biotechnology, information technology, nanotechnology and artificial intelligence will be integrated into super-intelligent robots (Kurzweil, 2005, 2008; Levesque, 2017; Russell & Norvig, 2013). Figure 2.3 does not aim to predict the definite reality for this situation, but rather to offer input to a debate about what kind of future we want, given the widespread use of artificial intelligence

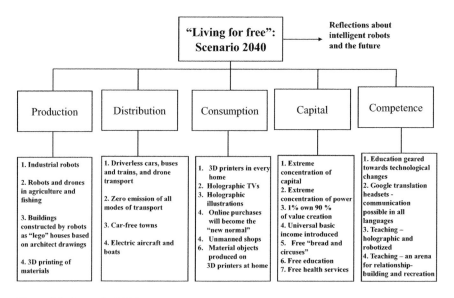

Figure 2.3 Scenario 2040.

and intelligent robots. We choose to focus on five main elements of this 2040 scenario: production, distribution, consumption, capital and competence.

A more in-depth exploration of scenario 2040

Production

New technology can be understood as a tool that will allow us to become, actually or conceptually, what we want to be, do what we are good at, or make a difference. Intelligent robots will help us with this transition from where we are to where we want to be. While we felt ourselves previously to be limited by our abilities, our pasts and our experiences, this new intelligent technology has the potential to liberate us from these limitations. Industrial robots, drones and 3D printers are examples of technologies that can increase productivity and create extraordinary value. The true consequence of this new technology is that we will be liberated from our own limitations, our own IQs, our intellects, our abilities to reason, our poor memories, etc. In short, we could say that intelligent robots will allow us to be better versions of ourselves.

Living for free basically relates to the fact that we have become free from our own limitations that have been determined by our inheritance and the environment. Figuratively, people are like insects that have been given wings by the new technology, and are able to orient themselves in the world in a completely different way from before. Traditionally, we have been largely limited by our history, our experiences, our childhood and socialization. The new technology frees us from our limitations, but at the same time it makes us more dependent on everyone else, because technology is intertwined in a global network.

In the tension field between living free and dependence on the new technology, distractions, tensions and crises will be created. The extensive use of intelligent industrial robots, 3D printers and intelligent drones will result in many people losing their jobs. At the same time, there will be a need to develop new skills, and maintain and create new functional areas for these intelligent machines. However, we must also be aware of the fact that although the machines and robots will possess logical intelligence, they will lack most of everything else that constitutes being human.

"Living for free" will not be synonymous with either a utopian society or its opposite – a dystopia. It will not be technology in itself that will affect economic equality/inequality, it will rather be human decisions that are decisive in this context. Economic equality is an objective element that can be measured in various ways, such as by the Gini coefficient. Perceived fairness, however, is a subjective element, which can vary from individual to individual. However, if economic inequality increases, it is not improbable that perceived fairness will be reduced.

The new production technology will not create a happy work-free society, or one characterized by total mass unemployment and great suffering. The reality concerning 2040 will be rather more mundane – constituting what may be called *status quo ante* (protopia); in other words, a society in which most people will experience improved living conditions, but where a smaller part of the population will be much worse off than today. Future society will be characterized by continuous changes and cascades of innovations. For this reason, people will have to continuously upgrade their professional and techno-logical skills. Developments towards 2040 will be characterized by quality improvements of production equipment, incremental innovations and some radical innovations, but few revolutionary innovations (Brynjolfsson & McAfee, 2014; Avent, 2016; Colvin, 2018).

Imagine a future where your intentions, habits, wishes and routines are revealed through your searches online, in social media and the like; to a certain extent, this already exists. These searches can then be analysed by different types of big data analytics (Marr, 2017; Mayer-Schønberger & Cukier, 2013; Mayer-Schønberger & Ramge, 2018). Imagine that intelligent search engines can give you answers before you have even made an enquiry, because they know your wishes and dreams through your previous search history.

Which technology will change all other types of technology? How will the production of goods and services develop, if technology is able to adapt itself? The answer to both questions is the super-intelligent robots that are linked to other super-intelligent robots in a future AI network. These super-intelligent robots will be able to code themselves according to the demands that exist at any one time. They will have contact with people's dreams, wishes and needs, through access to users' search histories on various types of global networks. Consequently, they will be able to create new products before customers will be aware that they need them. Let's imagine that the internet is free, as it is today. Let us further assume that what we call artificial intelligence is as freely available and understandable as the internet is today. What will our everyday lives be like then? We will definitely be smarter than we are today. We will have access to artificial intelligence that can make decisions for us in a way we will be able to review, as with blockchain technology. "Stupid" people will become smarter and "smart" people will not be as clever as before in rela-tion to the "stupid" people. Mental similarity between people will increase, and will even out, but at a much higher level of intelligence. In such a "free" world, we will not only have free access to information, but also to the artifi-cial intelligence (AI) that can utilize this information. This may be compared to the situation today, where some people have access to "inside information" when making decisions. It's not because those with inside information are smarter than us, but rather because they have access to something to which we don't have access. If access to all information, and to artificial intelligence that can maximize the usefulness of this information, becomes available, then even the "stupid" person will be able to increase his/her intelligence.

In this scenario, everyone will have access to artificial intelligence at home in their living rooms. They will be able to take this artificial intelligence with them wherever they are, because it may be inserted in a pair of glasses, a shoe, planted inside their earlobes, and so on. The point is not where it is, but what it does: it will contribute to the vast majority of people experiencing being able to cope with life in a completely different way, and at a completely different level, than they can today.

We can further imagine that the internet is expanded with a network that has artificial intelligence built into its functions. Kelly also has a similar vision of a future AI network[7], without being as explicit as we are in this scenario. Kelly (2016: 38–41) argues that this AI network will emerge due to three existing breakthroughs: cheaper parallel computing power, big data and improved algorithms. One can only imagine what the integration of these three elements and a powerful quality improvement in each of them will lead to. This may result in a situation where everybody has access to artificial intelligence. If the AI network can improve our intelligence, how will it affect production in hospitals, schools, factories, offices, law firms and consultancies, as well as skills acquisition for pilots, firefighters, road workers, school teachers, nurses, service workers, professors, and so on? The answer is that in scenario 2040, the specialists of today will become the super-specialists on par with the best in the world tomorrow. If this is correct, imagine how this will affect the development of, for example, super-hospitals, major universities, large shopping malls, and all the debates that focus on the importance of size for gathering expertise and reducing costs for the benefit of the patient, student or user, etc? The latter point concerning the importance of size with regard to gathering competence and reducing costs is, however, an argument that falls flat. It is possible there may be other "good" reasons why size matters, such as accumulating power and increasing influence over people; but postulating that size is important for competence and costs is not a viable argument concerning this future vision.

In a conceivable future, one can imagine that all production will be done via a "super-net". This super-net will consist of an interconnection between the internet and the new AI network. For the individual user, the interface will be as simple to use as googling a city is today. The general user of the internet has little knowledge of the technology or the processes that enable them to google a city, or use Google Maps to orientate themselves in the narrowest streets of a remote mountain village in Ukraine. Similarly, we can also imagine a similar situation concerning future access to the AI network. An abstract visualization of this super-net is shown in Figure 2.4.

This super-net will affect how we produce in 2040. On the basis of this simple scenario, the work done by people today will in the future be done by intelligent robots that will do it even better. It is a misconception to imagine that such robots will resemble humans. These future robots may take various forms and may even be completely invisible in, for example, an AI network, an implant in the finger, in the ear lobes, and so on. It is not difficult to imagine some of the jobs these future robots will be able to perform, but it is more difficult to imagine all the functions that they will be able to do.

There are also some jobs people are not able to do, which robots will be able to perform. For instance, entering a burning house can be an impossible task for a firefighter in some situations, but a robot constructed using heat-resistant material will be able to tackle it. Another example concerns

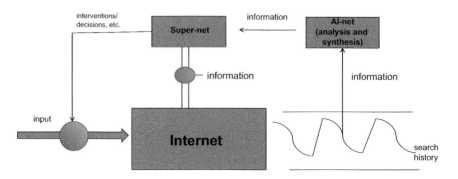

Figure 2.4 Super-net: the interconnected internet and the AI-net.

deep-water exploration. Deep-water environments present all kinds of difficulties for humans, whereas future robots, adapted to such an environment, will be better suited. This may result in greatly increased production of minerals and metals from seabed mining.

There are also many tasks of which we were not even aware, that robots will be able to do. For instance, a sophisticated Google translate earpiece that can enable us to communicate in foreign languages. For example, when we travel to Spain, we'll be able to understand what Spaniards say with such an earpiece, and, similarly, they will also understand what we are saying, if they are using such a device. All we'll have to do is connect to the super-net, so we'll become linguistically competent all around the world.

Finally, there are those jobs in which, at least initially, people will not be replaced by robots, but the robots will be able to provide a supportive role to improve the quality of performance. For instance, this will concern jobs in communication, and jobs involving relations, empathy, creativity, problem definition, collaboration skills and innovation, to mention a few of the most important areas. In these jobs, human skills will be invaluable, but AI and super-intelligent robots will also be of help in improving performance.

Distribution

It is probable that the internet and artificial intelligence networks will be the largest distributors of information, knowledge, competence building, competence application and many types of goods and services. As intelligent 3D duplicating machines are developed, the same trend will apply increasingly to the distribution of goods. In such a scenario, what businesses own will be their intellectual property. The owners of intellectual property will license code to a customer, who will use this intellectual property to produce an item. This is not unlike the situation with the software that we purchase online today. The difference is simply that AI networks will include large-scale 3D printers close to the customer. The customer will buy a licence to use code to have an item produced by one of these large-scale 3D printers. These printers may be located in various urban areas, so that customers are always close to places where large items can be produced and distributed. We can envisage the same procedure being applied to small items, but simply with the difference that customers have access to smaller 3D printers in their own neighbourhoods, or even in their own homes.

The digital economy, intelligent robots and artificial intelligence will drive the new "distribution highway". To exaggerate the point somewhat, it might be said that the trend is that the distribution channels will become the production channels. This integration of distribution and production is referred to here as *distriduction*. *Distriduction* may quickly evolve into the innovative new in the near future. Processor power, storage capacity, artificial intelligence and invisible super-intelligent "robots" may well be located in the distribution network, and not physically located, as the "old" factories were.

Hospitals will also be able to create new values by delivering services with the help of a link between intelligent robots and the new distribution system that will be globally interconnected. In practice, this means that all new medical knowledge in a global context will also be available in the intelligent robots at the local hospitals in the cities. The competence concept will thus acquire a different content from before. The specialist expertise will not necessarily be located among doctors and nurses, but in the connection between super-intelligent robots and the new distribution-production network, which has access to the new super-net where both the AI network and the internet are interconnected via an interface.

This *distriduction* system will be able to create values in a completely new way. Today, our thinking concerning wealth creation is based on a traditional industrial production logic, i.e. where the goods are produced in factories at a particular geographical location, near a source of energy. However, when globalization took off in the 2000s, the factory walls were literally blown away and wealth creation was distributed according to a cost, quality-expertise and innovation logic. In this wave of globalization, the traditional industrial workers lost their jobs to workers in countries such as China, India and Malaysia, because these countries are able to produce goods at a much lower cost. However, the new *distriduction* logic will bring production "back", although not necessarily to the specific locations where the industrial workers lost their jobs, but at least to the individual worker wherever he/she happens to have their workplace located. Thereafter, the goods are sent as information, data, or the like, to the customer requesting the product or service. The customer will have close access to small and large 3D printers. In this way, the customer will receive the goods faster, while transport costs will be reduced to almost zero. Like today, behind the whole of the process will be the overall design of the product. The difference, of course, will be that production will not be located according to costs, because the distribution will be relatively cheap. It will be the overall design that will be the decisive wealth-creating element in the new wealth *distriduction* logic. The physical distance will be of less importance. One can imagine that large 3D printers will be located in the rural areas around the cities. This will create a new relationship between the rural and urban areas.

The values created in the *distriduction* system will make sense both to those who produce and distribute goods and services and also to those who demand the goods and services. The common denominator for the new value creation will be products and services that have meaning regarding needs and wants. For example, if the individual, business or society has no need of the product or service, then it will have no value. Products and services that have meaning for the customer will be the fundamental element of value creation in the *distriduction* system.

"Meaning" may be created by connecting to our history, thus creating our identity. Meaning may also be related to how we wish to appear in the present, or how we wish to be perceived in the near future. The meaning dimension in value creation will especially emerge in what is called "the internet of things". Here we will be able to create ourselves through how we connect to the internet and the global space. In this 2040 scenario, we will be able to extend the idea of "the internet of things" to the AI network. Having full access to the world's best expertise in our areas of interest will give both value creation and meaning a new dimension.

At the beginning of industrialization and far into the 1980s, the starting point of distribution was large warehouses where goods were stored before they were sent to customers. Eventually the goods stored in warehouses came to be stored in container trucks on the roads ready for delivery when customers demanded them (just-in-time system). However, in the future, the storage of goods will be moved away from warehouses and roads and into homes by using small 3D printers, with large 3D printers located around the cities.

Customers will request a product; they will then be assigned a code, and print out the product on their intelligent 3D printer at home or on a large 3D printer located outside the city. This will be both time-saving and cost-saving, as well as easing the pressure on the infrastructure and environment.

The most important thing for customers is to save time and costs, so the product is available exactly when there is a need for it and at a lower price than otherwise would be the case. For example, if you order a book from Amazon, you will be given a code; the code can then be keyed into an intelligent printer, and exactly the same book that was previously sent by mail or other vendors can be produced where it is needed. The customer will thus have saved time, fewer emissions will be released into the environment, and there will be less of an impact on the infrastructure. If you cannot afford such an intelligent printer, one may be accessible in the city's library. In this way, the function of libraries will also be re-established as the importance they previously had, that is, providing free or cheap reading materials for everybody. Instead of having to wait one week for a book, you will be able to pick it up at the city's library in the time it takes to get there. It is probable that the *distriduction* system will be able to function in this way for the delivery of many types of products. The city's libraries will thus acquire a new function, not only related to books and reading materials, but also to the delivery of many types of goods that can be produced on their intelligent 3D printers.

For individual businesses, it will be the codes on which they earn money that create value. Therefore, competence in relation to intellectual property rights will also be sought in the future. Anything that can be copied freely will give no value to businesses. Therefore, they will have to protect their codes and integrate copying restrictions into the codes. What will also create value will be the individualization of products. The customers will pay for this individualization, and thus create value for businesses. In the future, intellectual property rights will be the central value creation element.

Consumption

Consumption is geared, not only towards goods and services, but also towards culture. Culture was originally linked to language and narratives; later the written word was revolutionized by the emergence of new technology in the form of book printing,[8] and the mass production of books. Eventually, one of the consequences of this cultural consumption was the emergence of newspapers and libraries. Books and book printing also affected culture in other ways, such as our thinking: it became linear. Like the words in a sentence with a beginning and an end, we began to think in terms of linear logic, as if all sequences had a linear cause and effect.

When everyone can read, and, in principle, everyone can publish what they write on various self-publishing platforms, what will then be the next step in the development of technology that will result in books becoming redundant and our culture changing from one that is book-oriented into something new. The digital age will witness the mass production of books being replaced with digitized texts, printed when a customer or multiple customers request the book; the printing of the book will be done on a 3D printer located near to where the customer lives. There is an ongoing transition taking place, from the written word in books to the written word on screens. In the future, it is probable that something like a Google reading "robot" will allow you to consume any text by reading it aloud, so you can read or listen to books written in all the languages of the world.

The new digitization technology makes it possible to copy everything that can be copied, and everything that can be reproduced and which has a value for the consumer is thus reproduced, such as music, opera, paintings, etc. With the new copy and reproduction technology, what was previously reserved for the few is now available to everybody.

It is not so long ago that the digital culture first saw the light of day. In the 1950s, the first TVs appeared in people's homes. Some time later, in the 1990s, computers began to be used in people's homes. After this, developments were more rapid – emails, cell phones, smartphones and so on became available to everybody. The digital culture was born, but the consequences had not yet begun to manifest themselves.

It used to be more common that people sat in cafes reading a newspaper while drinking a cup of coffee; however, it is now more common to see people using their smartphones, perhaps searching on Google, possibly reading some news, but most of all reading about what they are particularly interested in; for instance, by surfing the websites of various newspapers, news organizations and other websites. Thus, from being a print culture, we are slowly turning into a digital culture, where our information is collected across various newspapers and news organizations. In the near future, it will probably be common to enter into subscription agreements for individualized news packages or portals that collect, say, 10 to 100 newspapers in one package, at the same price we now pay for one newspaper.

One of the consequences of the development of digital culture and information-gathering across newspapers and websites is that our opinions, perceptions and belief systems will change (Van Quine et al., 2013). The print culture provided a stable framework for the written word, and for how things should be done. This culture was stable, predictable, and was experienced as being relatively safe, even for those who did not have much to contribute, or who did not consume much printed matter. Books and other printed matter slowly developed a culture of knowledge; in around the year 2000, we can say that the industrial society was replaced by the knowledge society with its focus on an innovation economy.

On the other hand, the digital culture does not have such a fixed framework: everything is floating; even the words on screens may be changed to big, small, black, blue, red, at the touch of a key. The digital culture is change- and innovation-oriented. Nothing is fixed and predictable, everything is possible, and everything is flowing and moving.

The stable element of the book and print culture was the law book, either the laws of the state, the constitution and its interpretation by legal authorities, or religious law, such as that written in the Bible, the Quran, the Torah, etc.; the latter books are interpreted by various types of priests and religious authorities.

When stability is threatened, it seems reasonable to assume that many professions attempt to maintain the status quo. There is a wish to return to the known and established, to the linear culture where the rules and boundaries were known. The digital culture, where everything is floating and innovations change people's everyday lives, is perceived by many as being unsafe and uncertain. Therefore, in current times, we are witnessing various types of Trumpism, both large and small. Trumpism may be understood as a wish to return to things as they once were, to an industrial logic and linear thinking. However, in this context, it may be said that the wheel of time rolls only one way – into the future; although the wheel of illusion can move in all directions.

The digital culture is technology-optimistic. Problems, of no matter what type, are solved by technology, and by technological innovations. Thoughts become words through programs that translate from speech to text and from text to speech; the spread of ideas and thoughts increases. The digital culture differs from the print culture, in that "texts" are not necessarily edited to the same degree by editors or other specialists who check structure and content. The digital culture results in all such "middlemen" becoming redundant, through, amongst other things, the new blockchain technology (Werbach, 2018). Consequently, in the digital culture, more and more middlemen are disappearing, not only in relation to the movement of ideas and "texts", but also in relation to the movement of money, where blockchain technology affects banks and financial institutions. Blockchain technology also leads us to ask: What are the functions of managers and leaders? Do we need managers as "middlemen" between those who provide services and products and those who pay for them? The answer is both yes and no. We do not need today's directing and controlling managers, but we do need managers who think strategically and who can motivate their employees. We need managers who focus on what the employees are passionate about because this is what will motivate them. We need managers who help an employee become skilled in the areas that he/she has the prerequisite for being good at. We need managers who develop the work processes of the individual employee, so that he/she is continuously able to master skills. It is these managers who are our future managers (Hansen, 2016).

The print culture has literally exploded into thousands of pieces, like an explosion in slow motion. This culture is being replaced by the broken pieces that are continuously moving, and our past experiences are no longer meaningful. When the usefulness of our experiences collapses, there will also be a search for various types of Trumpist ideologies that promise to go back to the past, so that those who have lost what they once had will feel safe again.

In the digital culture, we literally choose what we want to see and listen to, as well as where and when. One of the consequences may be that the linear logic, the authority of "authorship", as well as the authority of structured rule-based hierarchies in organizations, nations and other social systems, will all be eroded and disappear. Even the book and other digitized products will soon be included in a network of linked ideas. In this way, consuming a novel or a textbook will enable us to be in touch with all the existing and developing ideas, concepts and theories of a phenomenon in a global context.

A large part of our consumption now goes via the internet, looking at, for instance, music, opera, concerts, movies, books, blogs, tweets, experiences, dating and relationships, and so on. It is becoming continuously easier to form various types of relationships through the internet, and sometimes the relationships remain entirely online. In a short time, we will be able to read any text in any language on the internet, through some type of "Google translate". In this way, we will in theory be able to consume more of say, Roman literature, than did the most well-read Romans in their time. As storage capacity increases, prices fall and storage units become smaller, we will have instant access to everything we want at the moment we want it. The possibilities are expanding and a literally boundless consumption culture is emerging. When everything becomes possible, we need to make choices all the time.

This opportunity and choice culture will create a situation where everybody makes his or her own decisions, without middlemen. It will be possible to make investments by accessing intelligent robots – one will be able to choose a level of risk, and the robot will do the rest. Studies will be tailored to suit the interests of the individual student, where it will not be necessary to choose one particular school or university. The student will be able to choose a series of courses from various universities throughout the world, and eventually his/her CV and examination certificate will be printed and include an expansive heading rather than the logo of a specific university. In such a situation, location will mean little or nothing, while quality, reputation and service will mean everything.

Capital

Companies such as Facebook, Uber, Google, Apple and Alibaba are just a few examples of concentration of capital and the power that goes with that. Capital is being concentrated in fewer hands (Dorling, 2015). The new technology has also resulted in changes to the way in which capital functions. For instance, Alibaba has no stock – it is distributed in a completely different way than before. Uber does not own that many cars; similarly, Airbnb is not primarily an owner of the property but instead offers accommodation, such as apartments and houses, for rent. Companies such as Netflix, Viaplay and HBO allow users to stream movies for a monthly subscription fee. It was only a few years ago that we had to buy the actual physical product, such as a DVD disc, so that we "owned" the movie. Today we rent it for the time we need to view it. The same is the case with the rental of music via Spotify, and with Amazon's Kindle that gives us access to books, without us having to own them. Photoshop is not owned as a product, but we purchase the right of use when we need it. Volvo is developing a concept whereby you will be able to subscribe to a car, such as a Volvo XC40. This brief description illustrates the fact that ownership and intellectual property rights are changing.

Why should we own something in a world where the right of use seems to be the new trend? Why should we own a house or apartment in Spain, Florida or anywhere else for that matter, when we can rent it? Why should we own the house or apartment we live in? The development and growth of the right of use seems to be changing the way we think about ownership. The trend seems to be that we lease cars, rent houses or apartments, rent movies and so on – there are virtually no restrictions on what we can rent, rather than own.

It is not the property rights that are essential but the right of use, so that we have access to what we need. Capital costs for the individual will be reduced when we do not need to borrow large amounts to purchase houses, cars and the like. Neither will we need to spend money on maintenance and insurance. More and more products that we previously owned will be made available with the rights to use when we need them.

Access will be obtained through the internet and the World Wide Web; the right of use will be obtained through insurance schemes and agreements. With such a development, the insurance industry, brokers and legal professionals will find new opportunities for expansion.

Digital technology is changing the concentration of capital. The tangible in many cases is being overrun by the intangible. The capital that is based on immaterial services is swallowing up the material capital that is based on physical products. As a consequence, information processes in social systems are gaining more importance than physical production processes. This is also reflected in social status and salaries. For instance, a finance analyst can expect to demand a higher salary than a nuclear physicist, although the latter has a more comprehensive education than the former.

Even the automobile is not what it once was. The modern automobile may be primarily a physical means of transport, but it has become increasingly reliant on powerful computing to operate. The automobile's key functions are being increasingly controlled by computing power, online connections and an emerging AI network. Thus, in the automobile as well, the symbol of freedom and individual identity, information processes are becoming more important than actual physical processes.

These developments are also changing how we think. More and more, we want what we ask for when we ask for it, not tomorrow or the day after. Instant access without time lags will be a competitive advantage for all goods and services.

While capital is becoming centralized, decisions, production, distribution and consumption are being decentralized. Due to the global network, the flow of information is becoming the most important element in all production, distribution and consumption. However, the concentration of capital does not mean that property rights will end up in fewer hands. It is rather the major share of value creation that will end up in the hands of a small part of the population, not property rights, which is the central factor in this development. Therefore, it seems reasonable to assume that a majority will protect their property rights, even though capital will be concentrated in increasingly fewer hands. Property rights as such will be less important, both for the users and for the small part of the population that will mainly gain access to the flow of cash. The seeming paradox that emerges is that the decentralization of decision-making will lead to a centralization of capital.

In the innovation economy, economic growth is driven by innovations. However, innovations are often the result of linking old ideas together in new ways (Arthur, 2009). Having an understanding of this insight makes it possible to create literally endless innovations. As new innovations are created, the basis for developing even more increases. So far in 2018, China has made twice as many patent applications as the United States.[9] If the statement that it is innovation that drives economic growth is correct, then the number of patent applications is a clear indication that China will overtake the US in economic power in the near future.

Competence

The new technology must continuously be focused on, so that it does not fall off and lead to stagnation. This requires a completely different competence development from the one we are used to. According to the logic of the industrial society, you first developed your skills, then you put them into use. Maintaining skills will be demanded on a large scale, precisely to maintain and further develop the intelligent robots.

The continuous renewal of technology means that continuous competence development will become the basic educational philosophy. You will acquire some basic skills and knowledge at school and university, but you will need to develop these skills and knowledge throughout your life. It is in this context that one may speak of an integration between working life and education.

The basic skills needed to keep up with technological developments may be called co-operation, information-sharing and distribution. This is not unlike what happened in the hunting and gathering culture. The group of hunters shared information about possible prey and co-operated in hunting and trapping the animal, then distributing the meat according to certain rules, so that just the one or those who felled the animal did not take everything for themselves.

Sharing, collaborating, co-creation and distributing will go down a completely new road when the new technology makes it possible to see, hear and feel by interacting with intelligent robots. Today, it is possible to "see" over long distances by using drones, or by using CCTV cameras in urban areas, or find other uses, such as home security at your house or cabin in the countryside. We can already listen and communicate with others at a distance using telephones. However, the new technology will make it possible to use long-distance listening devices, which will become as common as viewing at a distance using drones. As of yet, there is no mass-produced technology available that makes it possible to "feel" at a distance. However, it is not difficult to imagine something like a thin vest equipped with various sensors that respond when we speak or see someone who is not at the same location as we are. "Feeling" at a distance will undoubtedly present unique situations, such as being able to feel what someone caught in a war zone is feeling, or someone starving in a famine zone; or, also in another context, in relation to intimate relations and sexual experiences. Figuratively, one can imagine a type of "diving suit" equipped with sensors that allow you to feel the joy and pain of others. One can further imagine that instead of wearing a "diving suit", the sensors are built into the clothes you are wearing or implanted in your earlobe. If the technology is developed to make this possible, then in all likelihood this reality will emerge in one form or another. Virtual reality in such a scenario will possibly become more "real" than reality. Of course, it is not difficult to envisage the dangers of such a development – the danger of people escaping into an artificial reality. There will, though, also be advantages, because we will be able to feel the suffering or happiness that we may cause others. Moreover, there are those millions of people who today want to "escape" from loneliness; virtual reality will make this possible, even though it will not be "real". Loneliness can be lethal, and if technology can help to cure loneliness, it will be perceived as an advancement, at least for those who emerge from their loneliness.

At the level of the individual, the new technology will enable comprehensive use of self-tracking health devices. It is common today that athletes and others concerned with fitness measure their heart rate (max and average heart rate), calorie consumption and so on. In scenario 2040, a whole new type of lightweight and powerful instruments will be able to measure everything that can be measured. For instance, it will become common to measure the skin temperature, blood composition, blood sugar, sleep patterns, body fat, cholesterol levels and composition, ECG functions, cell division rate, content of faeces, urine and sweat, breathing rate and so on.[10] In this way, one will experience having control of one's own body and be able to understand how the consumption of various types of food affects different elements in the blood and faeces, etc. This data may also be used by insurance companies to specially design life and health insurance for individuals. This body competence may be used for many other things, ranging from areas related to health, personal productivity, dating, etc. Today, having such a detailed focus concerning the functioning of one's own body may be perceived as indicating some type of neurosis; however, in a future scenario it is probable that having such a focus will be considered a valid competence in relation to job hiring and job promotion. This information may also be perceived by the individual as part of a personal security network. Moreover, it is probable that such information will be utilized by insurance companies to design the cost profile of individual users.

Instead of visiting the doctor every six months or once a year in order to measure one's blood pressure, this will be continuously measured by an intelligent robot that will propose measures, for instance, to reduce blood pressure. In this way, the individual will gain insight into what causes the rise in blood pressure and correct his/her behaviour accordingly. The same will apply to blood flow, blood composition, condition of the heart, etc.

Some will argue that this will lead to anxiety and depression. Perhaps this may occur in some cases. However, it seems reasonable to assume that the majority will be given the opportunity to change their behaviour and improve their health, thus getting a better life, when they receive up-to-date information about what they need to do to bring about improvements.

Personal treatments will be more specific when the doctor has this data available. One can also imagine that individualized medicine will be designed, based on this data. Instead of the mass production of medicine, specially designed medications will be tailored to the individual's needs.

Such new approaches to medical data will also change how research is conducted. Instead of an average measure, research may be more directly oriented to the individual, thus tailoring treatment and medication. The diagnoses will be more precise and thus the individual may receive better treatment. Instead of meta-analyses where N is, for example, 100,000, one will be able to use a much lower figure, for instance, where N is 5,000. In this way, innovations will become more individual-oriented and target people better than more general innovations in medical research.

However, the point here is that it is not necessarily a case of whether N = 100,000 or N = 5,000. For the individual, the most relevant research focus will be the case of one. In this context, an intelligent robot will be able to continuously scan the data about the individual. In such a scenario, when deviations occur, long before the individual notices anything, the intelligent robot (which may be a medical nano-submarine in the blood vessels) will be able to perform an intervention, so that the development of a medical condition is hindered before it even occurs.

Conclusion

The question we have investigated here is as follows: What impact will economic singularity have on social development? There is one positive aspect and one negative aspect to economic singularity.

One result of economic singularity will be an extreme increase in productivity. The negative scenario will be mass unemployment and an extreme increase in productivity. Our point is simply that this increase in productivity, rather than translating into higher wages, as we are accustomed to, will have quite the opposite effect. Capitalism will ensure that demand continues through the continual adjustment and differentiation of the new universal basic income.

The positive scenario is that mass unemployment will not occur. Society will be organized so that everyone will benefit from the extreme growth in productivity that will follow on from full automation.

We can choose to organize our society so that full automation becomes a question of providing security to those who lose their jobs. From this perspective, there will be the question of different types of universal basic income. In such a situation, everyone will be assured of a minimum income. This will be the goal of capitalists, because it will serve their interests. A system with universal basic income will create further inequality and a society where feudal capitalism is maintained with a kind of master-and-serf logic.

A positive outcome for most people will be that society will be organized so that tax on income is zero. All taxes will be taxes on value creation. Thus, taxation can contribute to creating greater economic equality.

"Earning a living" can be replaced by "living for free", if the productivity increase that will come with full automation is divided between all the country's inhabitants. For this to occur, however, the entire economic system that we have built up since the sixteenth century – the capitalist system (first trade capitalism and then industrial capitalism) – must be replaced by something qualitatively new. For this to occur, there must be shifts in the tectonic plates of society. The likelihood of such shifts happening is minimal. It is much more likely that capitalism will maintain the capitalist system and that inequalities will increase, because capitalism and its "boys in blue ties" have the political, cultural, economic, ideological and technological power. They use this power to maintain their positions.

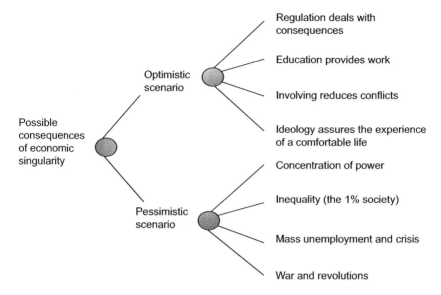

Figure 2.5 Two views of economic singularity.

A common feature of both the optimistic and pessimistic views of economic singularity is that both camps believe that it will affect unemployment, but disagree as to the extent of that, and what form society should or must take.

We have summarized these two views of economic singularity in Figure 2.5.

Notes

1 Daniel Kahneman was awarded the 2002 Nobel Prize in Economic Sciences for his work with Amos Tversky on decision-making under uncertainty, including, among other things, prospect theory.
2 https://en.wikipedia.org/wiki/Thomas_Newcomen.
3 https://en.wikipedia.org/wiki/Technological_unemployment.
4 https://en.wikipedia.org/wiki/Basic_Income_Earth_Network.
5 www.reddit.com/r/basicincome/wiki/studies.
6 Informatization may be understood as a type of automation of information processes. Automation is the situation where all production processes will be done by machines and intelligent robots. In practice, we are talking about automation of both production processes and information processes.
7 We provide a more detailed description, analysis and different scenarios about a future AI network in Part III on institutional innovations.
8 As a result of Gutenberg's innovation, c. 1450.
9 www.wipo.int/edocs/pubdocs/en/wipo_pub_941_2017.pdf.
10 Faeces and urine will be measured by the installation of small computers in restrooms. The sensors installed in the restrooms will measure the composition of

the individual's faeces and urine. These analyses will then be sent directly via the wireless network to your health device, which then collates this information with other types of measurement analyses. The compiled information will then be sent to an intelligent robot, which may be online, in the cloud, or a local server.

References

Abrahamson, M. (2004). *Global cities*, Oxford University Press, Oxford.

Ainley, P. (2016). *Betraying a generation: How education is failing young people*, Policy Press, Bristol.

Arthur, W.B. (2009). *The nature of technology: What it is and how it evolves*, Free Press, New York.

Avent, R. (2016). *The wealth of humans: Work and its absence in the twenty-first century*, Allen Lane, New York.

Bauman, Z. (2013). *Does the richness of the few benefit us all?* Polity, New York.

Brynjolfsson, E., & McAfee, A. (2014). *The second machine age: Work, progress and prosperity in a time of brilliant technologies*, W.W. Norton, New York.

Chace, C. (2015). *Surviving AI*, Three Cs, New York.

Chace, C. (2016). *The economic singularity*, Three Cs, New York.

Chomsky, N. (2016a). *Who rules the world?* Hamish Hamilton, London.

Chomsky, N. (2016b). *Profit over people: War against people*, Piper, Berlin.

Colvin, G. (2018). *Humans are underrated: What high achievers know that brilliant machines never will*, Nicolas Brealey, New York.

Dorling, D. (2015). *Inequality and the 1%*, Verso, London.

Ford, M. (2016). *The rise of the robots: Technology and the threat of mass unemployment*, Oneworld, London.

Franklin, D. (2017). *Megatech: Technology in 2050*, Economist, London.

Goertzel, B., & Goertzel, T. (2015). Introduction, in B. Goertzel & T. Goertzel (eds.), *The end of the beginning: Life, society and economy on the brink of the Singularity*, pp. 6–31, Humanity+ Press, Los Angeles, CA.

Gordon, E. (2018). *Future jobs: solving the employment and skills crisis*, Praeger, New York.

Hansen, M. (2016). *Great at work*, Simon & Schuster, New York.

Hanson, R. (2016). *The age of EM: Love and life when robots rule the Earth*, Oxford University Press, Oxford.

Janeway, W.H. (2018). *Doing capitalism in the innovation economy: Reconfiguring the three-player game between markets, speculators and the state*, Cambridge University Press, Cambridge.

Johannessen, J.-A. (2017). *Innovations lead to economic crises*, Palgrave Macmillan, Cham.

Johannessen, J.-A. (2018a). *Automation, robots and crises: How to survive the Fourth Industrial Revolution*, Routledge, London.

Johannessen, J.-A. (2018b). *The workplace of the future: The Fourth Industrial Revolution, the precariat and the end of hierarchies?* Routledge, London.

Johannessen, J.-A. (2019). *Institutional innovation: From democratic capitalism to feudal capitalism in the Fourth Industrial Revolution*, Routledge, London.

Kahneman, D., & Tversky, A. (1979). An analysis of decision under risk, *Econometrica*, 47(2): 263–292.

Kahneman, D., & Tversky, A. (2000). Prospect theory: An analysis of decision under risk, in D. Kahneman & A. Tversky (eds.), *Choices, values and frames*, pp. 17–43, Cambridge University Press, Cambridge.

Karabarbounis, L., & Neiman, B. (2014). The global decline of the labor share, *Quarterly Journal of Economics*, 129(1): 61–103.

Kelly, K. (2016). *The inevitable: Understanding the 12 technological forces that will shape our future*, Viking, New York.

Kurzweil, R. (2005). *The singularity is near*, Penguin, London.

Kurzweil, R. (2008). *The age of spiritual machines: When computers exceed human intelligence*, Penguin, London.

Levesque, H.J. (2017). *Common sense, the Turing Test, and the quest for real AI*, MIT Press, Cambridge, MA.

Libert, B., Beck, M., & Wind, J. (2016). *The network imperative: How to survive and grow in the age of digital business models*, Harvard Business School Press, Boston, MA.

Locke, R.M., & Wellhausen, R.L. (2015). *Production in the innovation economy*, MIT Press, Cambridge, MA.

Marr, B. (2017). *Big data in practice*, John Wiley & Sons, New York.

Mayer-Schönberger, V., & Cukier, K. (2013). *Big data*, John Murray, London.

Mayer-Schönberger, V., & Ramge, T. (2018). *Reinventing capitalism in the age of big data*, John Murray, London.

Miller, J.G. (1978). *Living systems*, McGraw-Hill, New York.

OECD (2015). *Employment outlook 2015*, OECD, Paris.

Pistono, F. (2012). *Robots will steal your job, but that's OK: How to survive the economic collapse and be happy*, Create Space, New York.

Russell, S., & Norvig, P. (2013). *Artificial intelligence: A modern approach*, Pearson, London.

Scheidel, W. (2017). *The great leveler: Violence and the history of inequality from the Stone Age to the twenty-first century*, Princeton University Press, Princeton.

Shanahan, M. (2015). *The technological singularity*, MIT Press, Cambridge, MA.

Susskind, R., & Susskind, D. (2017). *The future of professions: How technology will transform the work of human experts*, Oxford University Press, Oxford.

Van Quine, W.O., Churchland, P.S., & Føllesdal, D. (2013). *Word and object*, MIT Press, Cambridge, MA.

Weeks, J.H. (2014). *Economics of the 1%*, Anthem Press, London and New York.

Werbach, K. (2018). *The blockchain and the new architecture of trust*, MIT Press, Cambridge, MA.

Part II

Social singularity

Introduction

The core ideas discussed in this Introduction are as follows:

- An AI network is being developed that will become a distinct, albeit linked, part of today's internet.
- Technology will become part of all education.
- In the Fourth Industrial Revolution, being able to code will be as important as being able to read.
- Social robots will be developed that have artificial emotions.

The concept of social singularity was first proposed by Vinge (1993). In his article, Vinge proposed two scenarios. One scenario envisaged artificial intelligence being of enormous significance for all social systems. The other scenario envisaged artificial intelligence technology also having a biological component that would affect every individual human being. Today we know that both these scenarios will occur in the relatively near future, by around 2040 (Kurzweil, 2005, 2008).

Intelligent robots and artificial intelligence distributed via all digital networks will develop what we could describe as a new network, going above and beyond the internet. Here we refer to this network as the artificial intelligence network ("AI network"). Everyone with access to a computer will have access to this network. Instead of having just one internet, we will have the additional AI network. Use of the AI network, however, will require certain basic skills. One such skill is coding, which will be necessary for making use of the AI network (Franklin, 2017; Gordon, 2018). For this reason, coding will become an integral part of all educational subjects in the very near future. A doctor, for example, will be a tech-doctor, a nurse will be a tech-nurse, a teacher will be a tech-teacher, and so on (Libert et al., 2016).

In order to find information and knowledge in a library, one has to be able to read; and in order to find information and knowledge in an English library, one has to understand English. The same applies to the AI network. Effective use of the AI network will require one to have coding skills (Russell and Norvig,

2013; Aoun, 2017). In all probability, a new kind of skills divide will develop over the next few years – similar to the way that people who are illiterate have traditionally been excluded from most kinds of work. Just as a transition from illiteracy to literacy is very important for both an individual and society, the transition from being coding-illiterate, to being able to write and understand code, will be very important.

This artificial intelligence will not simply be logical and rational: it will also have a capacity for digital empathy (Dumouchel & Damiano, 2017: xi). At first sight, digital empathy seems like a cold, frightening concept. However, social robots will be able to assist with many needs. When these AI social robots enter our homes, they will create social innovation.

It is extremely likely that social singularity will occur in the care sector, education, the legal system, the healthcare system and, not least, in the political system. Social singularity may mean the end of representative democracy, because everyone will now be able to participate in the decision-making process via their intelligent computers. This may open the way for a more direct form of democracy, with individuals representing themselves, without elected representatives or middlemen. One factor that will promote the move towards direct democracy will be blockchain technology. An important purpose of this new technology is precisely that of encouraging trust in social systems, without requiring the presence of a middleman.

When social singularity is achieved, politicians and bureaucrats, in the sense we know them today, will become things of the past; on the other hand, elites will emerge, who will manage and control developments. The financial elite, those who own capital, and the knowledgeable elite, those who own knowledge, will constitute the highest levels of the social elite. The rest, who are in paid employment, will depend for survival on four crucial competencies: coding, communication, collaboration and problem-solving skills (Nørskov, 2016; Atkinson, 2018). In addition to this, it will be important to understand and adapt to the power structures. The reason is that those who do so will gain an advantage over those who do not adapt (Brown, 2017). Another aspect of social singularity is that it won't be necessary to have paid work in order to survive; it is most probable that various forms of universal basic income will be developed, ensuring that people can meet their basic needs. However, economic inequality will not be reduced, but will become qualitatively greater (Dorling, 2015).

It will probably be difficult for most of us to accept the idea that we will be able to emotionally relate to intelligent robots, and vice versa. On the other hand, most people will agree that tiny toy dogs and hairless cats are cute, and that it is possible to become emotionally attached to them. What is it about them that makes them cute, or that makes one become emotionally attached to them? Is it the dog's fluffy fur? The cat's gentle purring? The dog's mournful eyes? Whatever it is, it is surely only a matter of design, and the development of new synthetic biological materials, that will enable the construction of intelligent robots that are gentle and "pet-like". Such a development will lead to social innovation in the social system.

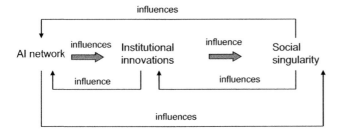

Figure PII.1 Social singularity.

Societal singularity as described above will be established by AI networks, institutional innovations and the emergence of various types of elites.

The question we are investigating here is: How will singularity affect the development of societal institutions?

To answer this question we have developed two sub-questions:

1 How will the AI network affect societal institutions?
2 How will institutional innovations affect societal institutions?

The Introduction is shown figuratively in Figure PII.1, which also shows how this chapter is organized.

References

Aoun, J.E. (2017). *Robot-proof: Higher education in the age of artificial intelligence*, MIT Press, Cambridge, MA.

Atkinson, A.B. (2018). *Inequality: What can be done now?*, Harvard University Press, Cambridge, MA.

Brown, R. (2017). *The inequality crisis: The facts and what we can do about it*, Policy Press, London.

Dorling, D. (2015). *Inequality and the 1%*, Verso, London.

Dumouchel, P., & Damiano, L. (2017). *Living with robots*, Harvard University Press, Cambridge, MA.

Franklin, D. (2017). *Megatech: Technology in 2050*, Economist, London.

Gordon, E. (2018). *Future jobs: Solving the employment and skills crisis*, Praeger, New York.

Kurzweil, R. (2005). *The singularity is near*, Penguin, London.

Kurzweil, R. (2008). *The age of spiritual machines: When computers exceed human intelligence*, Penguin, London.

Libert, B., Beck, M., & Wind, J. (2016). *The network imperative: How to survive and grow in the age of digital business models*, Harvard Business School Press, Boston, MA.

Marr, B. (2017). *Big data in practice*, John Wiley & Sons, New York.

Mayer-Schønberger, V., & Cukier, K. (2013). *Big data*, John Murray, London.

Mayer-Schønberger, V., & Ramge, T. (2018). *Reinventing capitalism in the age of big data*, John Murray, London.

Menary, R. (ed.). (2010). *The extended mind*, MIT Press, Cambridge, MA.

Menne, I.M., Schnellbacher, C., & Schwab, F. (2016). Facing emotional reactions towards a robot: An experimental study using FACS, in A. Agah, J-J. Cabibihan, A.M. Howard, M.A. Salichs, & H. Hongsheng (eds.), *Social robotics: 8th international conference, ICSR 2016, Kansas City*, Proceedings, pp. 372–381, Springer, Cham.

Misselhorn, C. (2009). Empathy with inanimate objects and the uncanny valley, *Minds and Machines*, 19(3): 345–359.

Nørskov, M. (ed.). (2016). *Social Robots*, Ashgate, Farnham.

O'Neil, C. (2016). *Weapons of math destruction*, Penguin, New York.

Pavia, A., Calvo, L., & Ribeiro, T. (2014). Emotions modelling for social robots, in R.A. Calvo, K. D'Mello, J. Gratch, & A. Kappas (eds.). *Oxford handbook of affective computing*, pp. 296–308, Oxford University Press, Oxford.

Redstone, J. (2016). Making sense of empathy with social robots: A new look at the "imaginative perception of emotion", in M. Nørskov, (ed.). *Social Robots*, pp. 19–38, Ashgate, Farnham.

Russell, S., & Norvig, P. (2013). *Artificial intelligence: A modern approach*, Pearson, London.

Vinge, V. (1993). *The coming technological singularity, Vision-21 Symposium*, www8.cs.umu. se/kurser/5DV084/HT10/utdelat/vinge.pdf.

3   AI network

Introduction

The main ideas discussed in this chapter are:

*   Artificial emotions are being designed into intelligent robots.
*   Artificial relationships are being designed into intelligent robots.
*   Revolutionary innovations as the result of the development of agora robots and agora informats.

An AI network is a kind of internet that has AI linked to the actual network. While the internet provides information to a person searching online, the new AI network will provide relevant knowledge to a person who needs it, in some cases even before the person tries to find it. This phenomenon will be made possible by big data. The AI network will function like a type of social robot. We can imagine the AI network metaphorically following us around like an Akita Inu dog – constantly loyal once it has got to know us. Before it gets to know us, we exist for it only in the same way as do a door, a window or anything else nearby. The Akita Inu must get to know and respect us before it will really follow us "like a dog". We can envisage a social robot behaving in much the same way. It would get to know us online, finding out about our needs and desires through our search activity. This sounds very strange and fantastical, but in fact it is completely logical and rational, because all our search patterns, buying patterns and behaviour patterns on the net are stored in big data, and generate what are basically our digital selves. It is our digital selves that will know, before we are aware of it, what we are searching for, what we want, what we desire. Our digital selves know this, because they are generated using big data analytics that are focused, personally, on us. In this way, we could say that the social digital robots that exist in the cloud will develop our relationships in the cloud with the help of big data.

An AI network will not simply be more of the same internet as we know it today, because AI will create "the innovative new", which will exist as a separate network "outside" the internet. From a technical point of view, of course, the two networks can exist together, but they will have two different functions. The internet produces information, while the AI network will produce knowledge. The internet provides an individual with information when he/she searches for that information. An AI network will give us knowledge before we have asked for it.

An important purpose of the AI network is that it will help the user to achieve goals, even when the external world changes. A driverless car avoids a collision, even if the driver attempts to override the functions of the car. A driverless boat changes the course that has been set if the wind changes and the waves become too challenging for both cargo and boat, even if the "captain" attempts to change the course back. The AI network will have a greater logical rational intelligence than the people who designed it. Therefore, the AI network will be able to make decisions that may seem paradoxical to the individual, but that are in fact rational, because the AI network has greater insight into the possible consequences than the individual. An important point regarding artificial intelligence and intelligent robots is that, in the same way as humans, they will be comprised of different combinations of intelligence types, such as musical, logical–mathematical, spatial, linguistic, emotional, social, relational intelligence, and so on (Gardner, 2006; Chace, 2016: 54).

Through the AI network, intelligent robots, and not least intelligent informats, will be able to develop a type of super-intelligence. This super-intelligence will be developed by providing the intelligent robot or informat with the ability to perform at a high level in relation to several specific intelligences (Johannessen, 2018b).

The question we will investigate in this chapter is as follows: How will the AI network affect social development?

In order to answer this question we will ask the following three sub-questions:

1   How will artificial emotions be constituted in the AI network?
2   How will artificial relationships be constituted in the AI network?
3   How will big data be constituted in the AI network?

We have illustrated the AI network in Figure 3.1, which also shows how the chapter is organized.

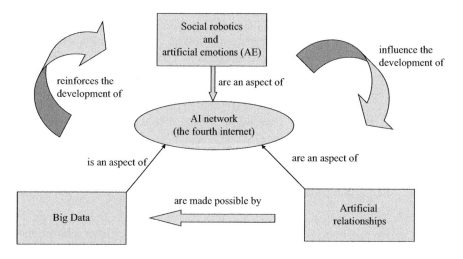

Figure 3.1 The AI network.

Social robotics and artificial emotions

A social intelligent robot will have a very highly developed logical and rational intelligence. In addition, a social robot will be able to develop artificial emotions (Valleverdú, 2009). In the same way as artificial intelligence simulates the functions of the human brain, artificial emotions simulate human feelings and empathy. Artificial emotions can be understood as a form of simulated emotion and simulated empathy. These are emotions that one can describe as being staged or apparent. The feelings are not real, but the recipient of these emotions will experience them as genuine.

Social robots may seem daunting; but then people were also apprehensive about the first cars and aeroplanes. If we think of social robots as an extension and a reinforcement of our emotions, then they may not seem so daunting. They can help us to become more empathetic, more socially aware, and better enable us to take care of those who are lonely or suffering emotionally. The counter argument is that social robots may make us feel more complacent and that we may withdraw into ourselves, shunning relationships with others.

One thing we know with great certainty is that the consequences of social robots will be profound and affect most aspects of human life (Nørskov, 2016; Dumouchel & Damiano, 2017). It seems reasonable to assume that the moral behaviour of these robots will reflect the ethical norms of the environment in which they operate.

Empathy and social robots have become a theme that interests many, far beyond the specific research field. The empathy and feelings we have for individuals of flesh and blood are real, while the empathy and feelings we may have for robots in the future, regardless of design, will be artificial. This is the distinction we use in the following section. Artificial emotions can occur in the interaction between a human being and an intelligent robot. The intelligent robot may have artificial emotions built into its design. How are artificial emotions experienced? A starting point may be the ideas of Misselhorn (2009), who expresses the view that these emotions are created as an alternation between perception and imagination. One could extend this thinking and say that artificial emotions lie in the interaction between perception, imagination and illusion. We have shown this figuratively in Figure 3.2.

Just as artificial intelligence is not the same as human intelligence, artificial emotions are not the same as human emotions. Having said this, we now know that artificial intelligence and intelligent robots will be of great help to many people. Similarly, we believe that artificial emotions, based on perception, imagination and illusion, can be of great help to many in the encounter between a human being and an intelligent robot with artificial feelings.

Social robots will be able to imitate human sociality in an intelligent way, says Breazeale (2002). Such intelligent social robots will be able to interact with a person, and the person in question will quickly imagine or experience that this is another "person". Social robots will be able to interact, understand, communicate, acquire information, be a coach and teacher, be a "mini" physician

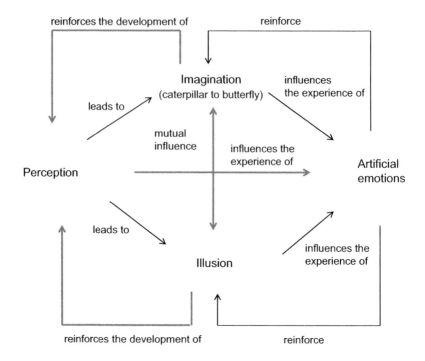

Figure 3.2 Artificial emotions.

and nurse, a caregiver and an empathetic "other person" to whom you can relate. Breazeale (2002: 1) goes so far as to say that they can become our friends. We would rather say that these intelligent social robots with artificial emotions will be able to fill a need for many people, who, for various reasons, find it hard to relate to others. Instead of further developing relationships in the cloud, these people will acquire a substitute that can fulfil human needs in a similar way to that of a pet. It is my personal experience that my two dogs certainly cover some of my needs, in that they give me the opportunity to be close to wilderness and nature, even though I live in a city. Similarly, the emotional robots will be able to meet the needs of people not met by other people. In other words, it's better to be close to a pet such as a dog, or, in the future, a social robot that is designed with similar qualities, than to be lonely.

It has been shown that it is possible to develop emotional ties with social robots (Breazeale, 2002, 2003). However, it is not the robots that have emotions for humans, but vice versa. The reason, as we argue here (Figure 3.3), is our ability to imagine, and illusion. The last element in Figure 3.3, perception, may also be an ability which intelligent robots can possess. The robot's artificial emotions are really our experience of the emotions we attribute to the social robot, not that the robot itself has emotions. However, if we attribute emotions to a social robot, a form of attachment or something similar, that is because

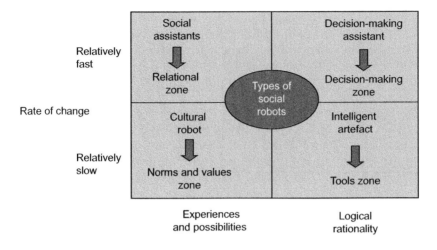

Figure 3.3 Various types of social robots.

we transfer our emotions to the social robot and receive a mirror image back. The question that arises is whether social robots have emotions, artificial or not, or whether it is only a matter of transferring our own emotions to the social robot? The question may be interesting, but it may not be relevant to the person who experiences an emotional bond to a social robot, even if it may be the result of the fact that the person has attributed emotions to the robot which they feel themselves. It seems reasonable to assert that the experience is real, even though the emotions are artificially produced. Is it not possible to experience emotional attachment to other people, although their feelings are simulated? Is it not likely that most of us experience this simulated feedback as real? The examples are many regarding such simulated feedback situations, both in communicative situations and intimate relationships. Most people who have experienced such situations will probably say that the emotions were experienced as real. What is the difference between simulated feedback and so-called artificial emotions, where a social robot is involved? We claim here that if the experience feels real, then the emotions are real in their consequences. This reflection was first developed, but with a different conclusion than ours, by Catrin Misselhorn (2009). The phenomenon we refer to is called the "uncanny valley".[1] This phenomenon describes a person's attraction and emotions towards an object that resembles a human being. The greater the similarity, the greater is the emotional energy, and at the same time the feeling of eeriness. This phenomenon is thus described as resulting in an eerie, mysterious or remarkable feeling. However, why would this feeling be more eerie and remarkable than simulated feedback from another person?

Both simulated feedback and artificial emotions are an imagined perception of emotions. Why one should be more eerie than the other is difficult to understand. One can say that both forms of emotional feedback are simulated, one being possibly more advanced than the other. A social robot can no doubt give a person an *experience* of compassion and sympathy, as well as other emotional expressions. It is more doubtful whether the feeling goes the other way, that is to say, that a person can feel sympathy and compassion for a social robot. That one can feel compassion for a pet that is suffering is beyond doubt. But, can a person feel compassion for a robot? Russell and Norvig (2013) have shown in an experiment that people felt a kind of sympathy for a social robot called Pleo; thus, it may also be possible to feel sympathy for a social robot. It is also the case that children can feel sympathy, sometimes strong sympathy, for inanimate objects, such as dolls and stuffed animals. Emotions, it seems, may be felt by a person for something inanimate such as an object or machine, but the individual perceives the object/machine as being something else. In the following discussion, we assume that sympathy, compassion and other expressions of empathy are constituted by the relationship between perception, illusion and imagination. In relation to this understanding, Figure 3.3 aims to explain figuratively how emotional expressions towards a social robot are possible. Considered the other way, that is, from a social robot to a human, this concerns an expression of artificial emotions and simulated feedback. There are, therefore, no real emotions expressed by a social robot for a human being, but real emotions can be expressed by a human for a social robot.

Is it at all possible to feel empathy for an inanimate "object"? If the "object" triggers an emotional experience in a human being, that is to say, the human being experiences it, one can say that the person feels empathy for the "object". This is the position expressed by Misselhorn (2009: 351–352).

Various types of social robots

There are various ways in which social robots can be used in people's lives; these may include, for instance, a robot that is a skilled chef/kitchen machine, pet or a learning assistant for children with autism spectrum disorder, and so on. It will be the purpose of the social robot that will determine its appearance and scope. However, it must be emphasized that social robots are artefacts that will not be able to detach themselves from the functions they are designed to perform (Dumouchel & Damiano, 2017: 12). Thus, no matter how intelligent social robots are, and regardless of their artificial emotions, they will never be able to live an autonomous and independent life as if they were free individuals. On the other hand, future social robots will differ from mere mechanical tools, due to their functionality and their behaviour as personal social assistants, for instance, as a type of care assistant for children with autism spectrum disorder. When social robots act as social assistants and imitate human expressions, they will be viewed as being much more than mere mechanical tools, such as a hammer, saw or the like. Their function as "social assistants" will mean that they will be viewed as more than just mechanical tools; thus, the social robots that function as social assistants will cross over into the relational area and be differentiated from the area one associates with tools and machines. Another type of social robot will most probably be used as a support for making complex decisions, for instance, in relation to automobiles, rockets, drones, financial transactions and so on. These robots will function as decision-makers. It may also be imagined that "cultural robots" will be developed; these will be able to work together with visitors and immigrants to a region or country, providing advice on what the prevailing norms and values are in the region or country. A typology of the various social robots is shown in Figure 3.3.

The future is created by seeds sown in the past

The new AI network is not an improvement on the internet, it is something innovative and new that cannot be compared to today's internet. If we meta-phorically compare the internet with an aircraft that is developed over time so it is able to fly faster and faster with the goods (i.e. "information"), the AI network may rather be likened to a helicopter that is able to land at the precise spot where it is needed to solve the tasks that require attention, and then when the problem is solved, take off again for a new place.

Innovative developments are often based on something that has existed before, but on a smaller scale. Thus, the landline phone existed long before the smartphone was developed; the calculator existed long before computers were developed that could solve mathematical tasks; other forms of energy existed long before the development of nuclear power and wind energy. In other words, the future lies like seeds that were sown in the past. It is just a question of finding out which seed should be given the best fertilization, and it does not necessarily have to be the seed that seems to have the greatest potential. The history of innovation has taught us this. For instance, consider the Qwerty keyboard on typewriters, which was later utilized in personal computers. If one is to look into what may develop in the future, one should have a very good overview of the innovative ideas and competing technologies in the past and present, as well as insights into which mechanisms there are in nature that can act as substitutes for the technology on which one is most focusing.

Historically, it may seem that the acceptance of technology is a function of the technology's functionality. This is not simply a rewriting and simplification of what goes under the name of "uncanny valley". In an early stage of techno-logical development, there appears to be a high degree of expectation towards technology. When technology starts to change many aspects of working life, a phase of technology "smashing" emerges. This progresses to a phase where the fear of technology is replaced by optimism towards technology. The perceived functionality is the function that controls the extent to which technology is accepted, which we can find in the "law of accelerating returns" (Kurzweil, 2001) or, simplified, the functionality law (Kurzweil, 2008). This law states that

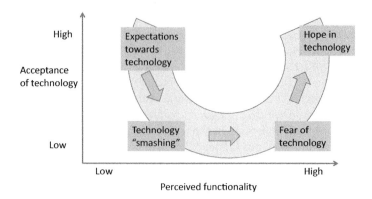

Figure 3.4 The acceptance of technology as a function of functionality

the technologies that have the highest functionality for users develop exponential growth.

We have shown this development in Figure 3.4.

Empathetic robots

Can robots display empathy? If we include artificial emotions and artificial relationships within our definition of empathy, then the answer is yes. Are there theoretical and philosophical problems arising from such a perspective? Yes, definitely. People who advocate what is known as methodological solipsism[2] distance themselves from this kind of idea. In brief, this methodology is based on the idea that the only starting point for thinking is an individual person. The clearest example of methodological solipsism is Descartes' assertion: I think therefore I am. Research into empathetic robots exists however at the interface between many different disciplines (Dautenhahn, 2007: 103–108; Harmelen et.al., 2008; Asada, 2015: 19–33).

Social robots can have numerous applications within areas such as education, medicine, entertainment, health and care, therapy and various service industries. These social robots should not be confused with production robots, where the purpose is increased productivity and cost reduction. The social robots will have enhanced well-being as their focus of operation, both individually and collectively.

An indication of whether a social robot is functional can be linked to the statement: Being present, and also being present in the moment when a person needs it. Being present in the moment, as well as perceived closeness, are the two criteria we use here to define a social robot.

A high degree of presence in the moment and a high degree of perceived closeness are defined here as the features of a social robot that can provide a form of companionship. These social robots may be similar in appearance to a human being, and have an artificial social competence that is expressed through artificial relationships and emotions.

A robot with a high degree of being present in the moment, but a small degree of perceived closeness, is defined here as a social robot that provides service to a person without the person experiencing any companionship. These robots will also have artificial emotions and relationships, but their shape and exterior will be completely different from human beings. These robots will therefore be perceived by the individual as being like any other machine, such as a robot vacuum cleaner. Of course, no one in his or her right mind would consider such a robot as having anything to do with companionship. These robots are referred to here as service robots.

A high degree of perceived closeness, but a low degree of being present in the moment, is defined here as a social robot that figuratively may be perceived as a pet. These are social robots that are present, but not necessarily present in the moment. They may be compared to a cat or guinea pig. These robots are referred to here as pet robots.

A small degree of perceived closeness, together with a small degree of being present in the moment, are the features of a social robot stripped of both artificial emotions and relationships, but which may have a high degree of artificial intelligence. These robots are rational, logical, instrumental, but without the ability to connect to a person in any way other than cognitively. We call these robots cognitive robots.

We have shown this typology in Figure 3.5.

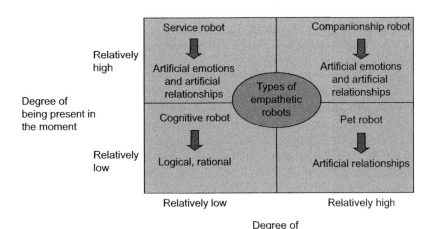

Figure 3.5 Empathetic robots.

The cognitive robot has the ability to decode verbal messages and provide an adequate and appropriate response. However, this does not qualify as an emotional or social response. In communication, the verbal part of the message is only a small part in comparison to body language. Body language, on the other hand, is part of the emotional and relational component of a communicative act between two people, or between a person and an agora robot.[3]

Emotional expression has become part of the research on social robots (Pavia et al., 2014: 296–308). The research on empathetic robots has implications beyond the design of the robot itself. It also reinforces the research on emotions in psychology, the mind–body problem of philosophy and cognitive psychology, as well as research on emotions in neuroscience, to name just a few areas.

Artificial relationships

What may seem alarming to many, from a relationship perspective, is the fact that human relationships are being reduced to shorter and shorter physical meetings. Relationships are increasingly taking place in the "cloud"[4] (Eden et al., 2012). It is here that relationships are being created, which may be partly defined as artificial relationships. This is perhaps more alarming than the fact that robots will start to resemble people, a fact assumed by the phenomenon "the uncanny valley" (i.e. that this may elicit feelings of strangeness). Today, if you go into a restaurant, a fitness centre or the like, you'll see people using their smartphones, computers, iPads and so on, keeping in touch with other people who may even be geographically located near to them. In other words, even based on this general observation, it would seem that at present face-to-face contact is being reduced and relationships in the cloud are on the increase. Perhaps relationships between people are becoming more superficial. If such a trend continues, it seems reasonable to assume that we will become less empathetic towards people's loneliness, despair, dreams and hopes, because these are emotional expressions with which we become familiar through face-to-face communication or observation.

The accelerating development of new and disruptive technology is speeding up the trend of having relationships in the cloud. These relationships are not so much supplementing existing relationships, but rather replacing them. This development will, many researchers claim, completely change human civilization (Eden et al., 2012: 1–12). The assumption is that, just as the use of artificial intelligence and emotions are exploding, and being used to an increasing extent, relationships in the cloud will increase to such a degree that they will in the future constitute the preferred type of relationships (Eden et al., 2012). We can already witness this trend today if we look around us. Walking along the street, it's often the case that you risk bumping into someone, because they're busy on their phones – perhaps playing a game of chess, writing text messages, or communicating with other people using social media. It is not difficult to imagine that in the not too distant future, they will not necessarily be communicating with friends and acquaintances, but rather with social robots in

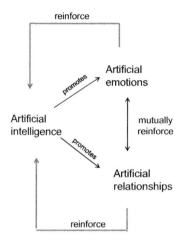

Figure 3.6 The artificial cycle.

the cloud. These social robots may constitute the most important relational contacts, regarding everything from sexual questions and love to despair, loneliness and human rejection.

This development will be possible because we will have a new internet, that we call here the AI network. This network is intelligent, consisting of thousands of intelligent robots that are globally linked. The individual who uses this network will experience the development of artificial relationships.

We have shown this development in Figure 3.6.

Artificial relationships or relationships in the "cloud" are already part of our communication today. It may be said that this relational development began as early as when the phone and telegraph first came into popular use. However, in the not too distant future, it will not necessarily be another person with whom we are communicating, but instead an intelligent social robot. This robot need not be visually present in your living room, but could be located in the AI network; alternatively, it is also probable that the social robot will be able to manifest itself as a hologram, for instance, in your living room; in this way, you'll feel that it is actually present in your own house or apartment. It may also be imagined that one can subscribe to this intelligent robot. This is not necessarily any more abstract than when you subscribe today to a newspaper, magazine, car and so on. The difference is only in the complexity of the technology. Whereas before you had to visit the library if you wanted to borrow a book, it is now possible to borrow the book from the same library by downloading the book to your own computer. One can imagine something similar in the case of a social robot. The extent of the artificial relationships will probably be one of degree, i.e. when we have contact with a social robot via the AI network, the degree of the artificial relationship will be relatively low. However, if the artificial robot resembles a human being, and manifests itself as a hologram in our living room, then the degree of the artificial relationship will be higher. It may further be imagined that the social robot will be able to act as a mentor, coach or the like, for the person in question. In this way, the social robot will be able to help the individual to develop their knowledge in the direction that he/she wishes. Artificial relationships, which may on first reflection seem intimidating, can, however, have relational benefits for many. The robot will be able to take on the role of a teacher for the individual, regardless of what he/she wants to learn or improve.

Artificial intelligence is the mechanism that triggers artificial emotions and artificial relationships. The hypothesis is that the more that artificial intelligence is developed, the greater the likelihood that artificial emotions and artificial relationships will also be developed.

If this hypothesis is correct, it will also mean that many of the values we cherish today will be history in a few years' time, when artificial intelligence has reached the level of singularity.

While technological developments, such as the harnessing of fire, the wheel, the steam engine and today's status of computer technology, took thousands of years, it is possible that the development of artificial emotions and artificial relationships may occur during the period of one generation. The challenges of adapting to such a development will be enormous, and a plausible hypothesis may be that the technology "smashing" and fear of technology shown in Figure 3.5 above will assume apocalyptic dimensions, because all known values will change.

Social robots: Two scenarios

The production and distribution of goods and services, as we know it today, will change completely when intelligent robots are introduced. At the individual level, emotional and relational values will take a different direction. The opposite of loneliness is not necessarily fellowship, but intimacy. On the other hand, one can assume that loneliness and intimacy can be graded on a scale where you can talk about a high degree versus a low degree for both elements. In such a gradation, it seems reasonable to assume that companionship may become a function of moderate loneliness and moderate intimacy. The point of reflecting on loneliness in this context is that social robots may be able to function as a substitute for social companionship, even if they will not be able to satisfy the intimacy criterion for most normal people. Social robots that have developed both social emotions and the ability to form artificial relationships may very well be of help to lonely people in the future. It can be imagined that this will apply to the spheres of both intimacy and companionship.

Once intelligent robots with technological singularity have been designed and put into operation, a complete transformation of the economy will occur, because costs will drop and functionality will increase (Chace, 2018). This will, in turn, lead to an explosion in artificial emotions and artificial relationships.

This may be described as the artificial cycle. The artificial cycle will be self-reinforcing, because the acceptance of technology will increase when people experience increased functionality due to technology (Kurzweil, 2008).

> The artificial cycle will develop as follows: *Let a super intelligent robot that is connected to other super intelligent robots globally (informats) be designed to help people and their relationships in the most beneficial manner. Let these super-intelligent informats be designed with artificial emotions and the ability to handle artificial relationships. Let us call these informats with their three main functionalities, artificial intelligence, artificial emotions and artificial relationships, agora robots.[5] Such an agora robot would also be able to improve its own design; and, through 3-D copying, produce an improved version of itself.*
>
> (Kurzweil, 2008)

Scenario I

Humans, with an evolutionary history that spans millions of years, will, in the near future, encounter agora robots with an evolutionary history that spans less than one generation. The agora robots will be connected through the AI network, so they can continually improve themselves. They will literally be like the phoenix bird that rises from its own ashes, but now in an improved version of itself. These agora robots will be able to speak all the world's languages, so they can communicate with all the peoples of the world, as well as with other agora robots.

The individual will experience a greater degree of autonomy and absence of repressive mechanisms, as all work is redefined to creative activities. The reasons are simple: agora robots and other industrial robots perform all the work, which was done before by people, wearing them out physically and mentally.

Such a development could lead to the individual being able to clearly see the social mechanisms that sustain inequality. This could easily lead to a threat to the prevailing ideology that creates the 1 per cent society, where 1 percent of the population takes 80 percent of the wealth created (Dorling, 2015).

A Boudon-Coleman diagram for this scenario is shown in Figure 3.7.

Scenario II

It is not difficult to imagine that the innovative new intelligent robots will lead to mass unemployment. This will result in turn in the share of value creation that goes towards wages being severely reduced and capital income increasing, because the intelligent robots will increase productivity. At the same time, it is probable that the intelligent robots will take over the functions that people did before (Brown, 2017; Atkinson, 2018). In such a situation, it is probable that a universal basic income will be established in one form or another, and become the new source of income for most people. Economic differences will increase, because the idea of a minimum universal basic income will also

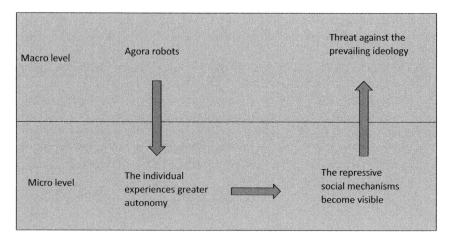

Figure 3.7 Boudon-Coleman diagram of intelligent robots: Scenario I.

encourage the unemployed to take on part-time jobs to supplement their income (Standing, 2018). However, the intelligent robots and informats, as well as the AI network, will have taken over many of the functions in the workplace that were previously performed by people, so there will be few extra jobs available. In order to support themselves and their families, individuals will most likely show loyalty to any employer, working for lower wages than they used to earn. In this way, the cocktail of intelligent robots and universal basic income can push down wage levels. This will further reinforce the individual's dependence on the state and employers, because one must have bread to survive; in this situation, being submissive like a dog will be viewed as better than starving. In this way, one can imagine that intelligent robots will reinforce the prevailing oppressive ideology that maintains and reinforces the status quo.

We have shown Scenario 2 in Figure 3.8.

Agora robots and agora informats: a revolutionary innovation

Agora robots will be a revolutionary innovation, because they will shift the tectonic plates of economics, technology, politics, culture and social relations. This singularity innovation will be on a par with the invention of the wheel, steam engine, internal combustion engine, electric motor and nuclear energy. Agora robots that are connected globally through the new AI network will become agora-informats. These informats will artificially develop the most basic emotions found in any known culture (Brown, 1991): happiness, sadness, disgust, anger, fear and surprise. The facial expression of these six emotions is largely very similar in different cultures (Ekman & Keltner, 1997). These six

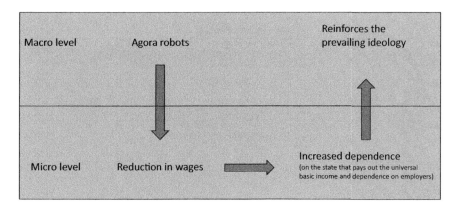

Figure 3.8 Boudon-Coleman diagram of intelligent robots: Scenario II.

emotional expressions will then be shaped in relation to context and situation, so that the agora robot and agora informats have sufficient variation in their emotional expressions to cope with any emotional situation. These artificial emotions will then be used to form artificial relationships. In this situation, we will have agora robots and agora informats that possess artificial emotions and that are able to form artificial relationships.

One can assume that the basic relational skills found in all known cultures can be expressed as follows: listening, fairness, helpfulness, good-heartedness, generosity, forgiving.

We have illustrated the agora robot in Figure 3.9.

With the emergence of the agora robots and agora informats, global culture will change. The myriads of complex cultures that exist in the world will, with the advent of the agora robots, merge into a singular universe of cultures. Figuratively, you might say that cultures were developed on many islands around the world over a long period of time. With the advent of the agora robots and informats, bridges will be built between these islands. Over the years, the people of the islands will – via the bridges – create common norms and values. When this occurs, cultural singularity will be a fact.

Agora robots, with their clear logical rationality, will enable us to make good decisions, instead of making decisions that make us look good. The fact that we make decisions that make us appear good, and often better than we are, may be related to the fact that we are basically social beings who wish to present ourselves in our social universe as better than we really are. This assumption, of which there are thousands of examples (Simler & Hanson, 2018), is an important factor that makes our decisions less good than they could be. Of interest in this context is Ralph Waldo Emerson's aphorism that "Every man alone is sincere. At the entrance of a second person, hypocrisy begins".[6] The agora robots, with their logical rationality, artificial emotions and artificial relationships can help us to

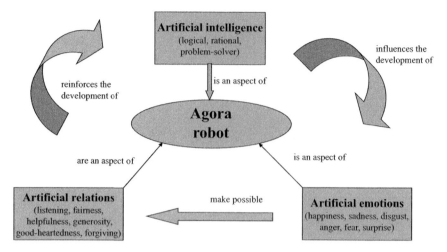

Figure 3.9 The agora robot.

avoid these decision-making traps. Simler and Hanson, in their book *The Elephant in the Brain*, say that people often act on the basis of hidden motives, for example they wish to appear better than they are (2018: 4–5). We think and act largely on the basis of selfish motives, but try to hide this from others. Consciously or unconsciously, we strive to present a better version of ourselves. If the assumption of Simler and Hanson is correct, and a lot of research suggests that it is, then the agora robots can be a way to overcome this evolutionary defect in humans.

The agora robot is a social robot that thinks, feels and relates to the people on whom the robot has focused its attention. The agora robot's thinking is a system of cognitive, emotional and relational processes, even though the three elements are artificial.

We present the view here that the agora robot is a practical variant of the extended mind thesis. The thesis states that the mind is not skull-bound, but extends into the environment to which the person relates (Menary, 2010: 64). The extended mind thesis answers the question: Where is the mind located? The answer is, according to the extended mind thesis, that the mind extends into the environment, that is, to what our attention is focused on in the external world. This incorporates both space and time, as we have shown in Figure 3.10.

The common answer to the above question is that the mind is in our brain (Dumouchel & Damiano, 2017: 92). Our view here, as shown in Figure 3.10, is that the mind focuses on the past, present or future and extends into space related to where our attention is directed. For instance, our attention may be directed at something geographically near or distant, as well as along a temporal axis of past, present or future.

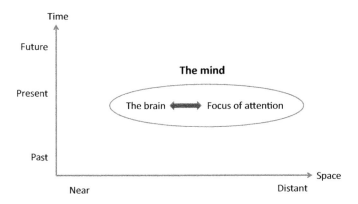

Figure 3.10 Where is the mind located?

If the agora robot arm stretches out for an object, and retrieves information about the object from other agora robots, which are located at completely different locations around the globe, then the agora robot's mind is a function of (1) time, (2) space, (3) attention and (4) the processes that constitute the thinking. This thinking can be influenced by artificial emotions and artificial relationships.

If we conceive the mind as a function of the four elements above and we assume that the agora robots have been developed, then the AI network will act as an extended "mind". This does not mean that agora robots take over from people. On the contrary, the agora robots will enhance human thinking.

One can further imagine that agora robots can really free people from the burden of paid work, as expressed by Aristotle: *All paid work drains the soul and makes it wither.*[7] Thus, the days of wage labour may be numbered, once the agora robots become comprehensively established. If the goal of paid labour is to buy free time so we can do what we want, then the agora robot can help us in that direction.

Big data

The question we are investigating here is: How does big data constitute the AI network?

Many people assume that big data is processed by "neutral" algorithms. This is further assumed to lead to "objective" science. This thinking has also led many to believe that big data can finally lead to "true" politics. The quotes around "neutral", "objective" and "true" are meant to infer what the author thinks about this development. We will show here how big data works in society, affecting our lives as well as the development of businesses and organizations.

In the near future, we will no longer need to select a sample from the entire data, and then, through statistical analysis, find the probability that something is correct. We now have access to all the data about many phenomena in society. Therefore, we can use this access to big data, and analyse the results from the entire data, not from just a small sample of it.

Instead of probability, which is used when we take a representative sample from a complete dataset, the concept of complexity is brought into the understanding of big data. While we previously collected "small data" based on a problem, big data is not collected based on any specific problem. The complexity of big data may be described using four constructs (Holmes, 2017: 15–19):

- *Volume*: There are huge amounts of data collected.
- *Variation*: The data is not located in shared computers. The data is contained in the thousands of computers, networks, social networks, web, internet, etc.
- *Speed*: Data is created in incomprehensibly large amounts every second of the day.
- *Truth of the data*: This refers to the quality of the data collected.

The complexity of big data is a system consisting of the four constructs above. The purpose of big data is to use very large amounts of data to improve the processes that already exist (Marr, 2017: 1). In addition, businesses use big data in innovative ways, to improve business performance.

There is no rigorous definition of big data that has been agreed on (Mayer-Schønberger & Cukier, 2013: 6).

An *abstract definition*: Big data may be described as a system consisting of the four constructs described above: volume, variation, speed and truth.

A more *concrete definition* could be: "research that is made possible by means of the capture, aggregation, and manipulation of data about a given phenomenon on an unprecedented scale and scope" (Schroeder, 2014: 165).

A *formal definition*: Big data may be described as the collection, storage, analysis, application and presentation of giant datasets. Such large amounts of data may be collected from various places, for example the data collected in the particle accelerator in Cern;[8] or in the Human Genome Project; people's search activities on, for example, Google; astronomers' telescopes collecting data in New Mexico and Chile; all the health data in a nation and later throughout the world, as well as credit card data, etc.

Big data is an information revolution that changes much of how we think today about information processes and information technology. When we talk about big data, we are referring to the literally astronomical amounts of data that are collected.

The collection of large amounts of data everywhere in society can be used to analyse individual and collective actions. It can be used in a positive way to find causes of illnesses, undesired behaviour, crime, etc. But – and it's a big but – there are also looming negative aspects, such as the use of big data as part of a control mechanism, where the "big brother sees you" syndrome will become a reality. Orwell's

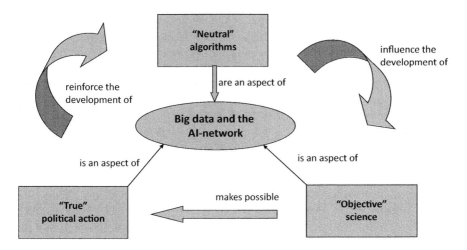

Figure 3.11 Big data and the AI network.

novel *1984* is just an introduction to the possible negative consequences of using big data. In practice, every one of us has experienced a few of the consequences of using big data. When shopping online, you will often receive offers of other products and services that you may be interested in at a later point, when you are online again. This is the marketing aspect of big data. This is part of the trend that big data makes possible, namely the transformation of those data tracks that we leave when we shop, search or interact online, into information to be used in a consumption process. Today, big data's analysis techniques are so effective that they can focus on the individual and his/her needs. Google and Amazon are examples of how this analysis technique is used in relation to the individual.

When big data is connected to artificial intelligence in a new AI network, we will probably witness a development where people in positions of power will be able to steer and control people's opinions, action patterns and behaviour. In Figure 3.11 we present a model showing our understanding in this book of the relationship between big data and the AI network

"Neutral" algorithms

Data from search engines, health data and data from our credit card transactions are often viewed as neutral data that is completely harmless and only for the benefit of the individual and society. The quantity of data created is astronomical and impossible for a single person to relate to. For this purpose, algorithms, mathematical models and analytical tools are needed. The algorithms, mathematical models and analytical tools are not "neutral"; they are constructed for one or more specific purposes. Anyone who knows a little about the design of algorithms knows that they are set up with inclusion and exclusion criteria.

IF–THEN is the simplest form of an algorithm, and this form is also the basis for most algorithms. The IF part of the algorithm specifies something, by excluding something else. It is these features of an algorithm that mean that algorithms are not neutral in any way. The algorithm is bound up with what you want to know, and it is a specific strategic action, not a neutral act. It is where the specifications of the algorithm lead that provides guidelines for how we should use the large amounts of data which the algorithm processes. When these algorithms are linked to artificial intelligence and then to a global intelligent network, we will have developed an agora robot that, in all logical and rational functions, surpasses human cognitive intelligence.

Why is big data special? The answer is simple. Today, and in the near future, we will have the possibility of utilising and analysing large volumes of data to which we did not have access before. Many are of the opinion that big data is a new industry (Mayer-Schønberger & Cukier, 2013; Holmes, 2017; Marr, 2017).

Big data can prove to be the solution to many of the transformations that are the product of automation via intelligent robots (Schroeder, 2014). Data mining can be done in many ways, but one of the main purposes is to discover patterns, as well as patterns of patterns, in the large amounts of data.

The storage process of big data follows Moore's Law, which briefly stated says that processing power and the storage capacity of microchips will double about every 18 months. One of the practical consequences of Moore's law is that computers become cheaper, faster and more powerful roughly every 18 months. In order for this development to continue, there are many reasons for new technology, such as nano-computers and quantum computers, to be developed (Holmes, 2017: 27–29).

Big data analytics uses algorithms, mathematical models and analytical tools to solve problems and answer questions. A general methodology used when analysing big data is to divide it up into smaller pieces, and then analyse them. Figuratively, it may be imagined that you have a map of a terrain. To get to know the terrain, the area is divided up into smaller areas on the map, so that you can become familiar with the terrain bit by bit. The rule here is to pay attention to the map first, and then the terrain. The process may also be likened to how archaeologists examine an excavation site by dividing it up into grids, in order to reveal what is concealed in the earth. However, the difference from the archaeology metaphor is that in the case of big data, large machines can analyse large amounts of data in a microsecond, a process that would take a very long time if done manually.

In recent years, we have witnessed the rapid development of smartphones. At present, we are also seeing the development of big data and AI networks, which will lead to "smart" homes, "smart" schools, "smart" health, "smart" stores, "smart" entertainment, "smart" clothes, "smart" cities and so on.

Neutral algorithms are not so "neutral" when they have been shown to have contributed to the financial crisis that was triggered in 2008, when people had to leave their homes, institutions collapsed, unemployment increased and many countries, such as Greece, Spain and Italy, are still struggling with the consequences of the crisis. Cathy O'Neil, a mathematics professor, has shown

(2016) in detail how algorithms and mathematics played an important role in the run-up to the financial crisis. She argues for the establishment of a panel that can regulate how algorithms are used, and also public access to how they are used. Being on the wrong end of a biased algorithmic decision, victim of an errant driverless car, a skewed financial operation and so on, can have catastrophic consequences for individuals, organizations and even nations.

O'Neil has a name for these algorithms and mathematical models that control our lives: "Weapons of MATH Destruction" (WMD), which is also the title of her book. The algorithms and models can very easily have a values-bias in their IF-THEN structures. For instance, imagine a manager of an HR department who is responsible for hiring people. Suppose he/she reasons as follows: If you do not pay your bills promptly, then the likelihood is that you will not follow the rules in the workplace. A simple algorithm may be designed for the purpose. The HR manager is then able to request credit information about the job applicant. The point is that the algorithm does not provide information about why any bills were not paid. For example perhaps the applicant did not pay the bills, because he/she was sick; or because they were unemployed. There may also have been errors in the computing system, so that the real financial situation of the applicant was not reported correctly, and so on. Despite the negative credit check, the job applicant may be the one best suited and qualified for the job, but this information will not be given by the algorithm. The applicant was never interviewed, because he/she was excluded in the first round of interviews by the "neutral" algorithm. This example shows that an algorithm is not necessarily "neutral", but can contribute to social exclusion, poverty and unemployment.

Marr (2017) has shown 45 examples of how big data can be used in practice. Some of Marr's examples clearly show that big data is not a neutral and objective application of large amounts of data. For instance, Marr shows how banks and retailers use big data in their business models, which are in no way based on neutral and objective assessments.

An important point for the individual businesses using big data analyses, whether this is Wal-Mart or a small pizzeria in a small town, is that they can tailor the marketing and sales to the individual customer. The marketing is perceived as relevant to the individual and is not segmented for a group. The data is collected and analysed for the individual customer, and big data and data analytics are used to make decisions about the individual based on that data.

O'Neil (2016: 71) has shown how a business using big data can identify people who feel isolated and lonely. They then offer specific products to these people, resulting in the business earning six times as much as other businesses that sold the same product to a more general customer group.

The example shows that ethics should be an important consideration in the application of big data. While Marr (2017) mainly shows examples that are positive regarding the use of big data, O'Neil reflects more on the negative aspects of where its use may lead, if society does not closely monitor developments.

Other examples of the selection process of persons targeted by marketing are given by O'Neil (2016: 71–73). In one example, marketing was aimed at pregnant women who are on social welfare support. Using data analytics, the business in question found that the pregnant women had low self-esteem, were in low-paying jobs and had recently experienced the loss of a close person. They also participated in drug abuse programs. The example may seem somewhat staged; however, O'Neil reports that the product marketed and sold to these people resulted in the business earning a lot of money. Why were these people chosen? asks O'Neil. The answer is simple and cynical: Businesses are able to reap large profits in targeting vulnerable groups.

Using big data, you can find out where people are vulnerable, where they can be violated, the areas where they feel they can't cope, and so on. When they know this, big data and data analytics can focus on a person's special needs and target sales directly at them. Thus, it is possible to find the person's "Achilles heel", which may be loneliness, appearance, vanity, social rejection, etc. The next stage is to entice them into the market of dreams, to get hold of the small amount of money these people have. However, when there are many such people with small amounts of money spending in the market of dreams, businesses can earn a lot of money.

Did someone say "neutral" algorithms?! They are as far from neutral as it is possible to be. If neutral means being impartial or balanced, algorithms as they are applied to big data are about as balanced as a seesaw with a mouse at one end and an elephant at the other. Algorithms used for analysing big data are biased, and they can be exploited by those who profit from the distress and problems of others. On the other hand, it must also be emphasized that big data has many positive uses, such as in research, for instance, in cancer research. In such applications, it is difficult to see any negative aspects of using big data.

"Objective" science

When data analytics are used to automate and speed up work, for example in banks, this is perceived as being objective and neutral. There are no human prejudices in the picture that can distort decisions. The point is simply that conditions are built into the so-called neutral algorithms; human bias is nothing by comparison. It is impossible for a nonprofessional to uncover these conditions. Not only is an expert required to uncover the conditions, but an expert who is able analyse each of the premises of the algorithms in a software program. Who is capable of doing this?! The complexity of the algorithms and mathematical models make it possible to build small, apparently insignificant "prejudices" into the IF-THEN structure of the algorithm. In their social and economic consequences, these small embedded "prejudices" can have catastrophic consequences for individuals, not to mention organizations and nations. O'Neil writes: "many of these models encoded human prejudice, misunderstanding, and bias into the software systems that increasingly managed our lives" (2016: 3).

The mathematical models used in computer systems when processing big data are opaque. They are impossible to unravel for anyone who is not an expert in precisely this area of mathematics. Once a decision is made, there is no possibility of appeal. In this situation, the individual has no legal protection when faced with "neutral" algorithms and impenetrable mathematical models. The individual's perception of fairness and justice is put strongly to the test in this situation, to put it mildly.

From a positive viewpoint, big data can be used in research, among other things, to identify complex causal chains of diseases. What is the new aspect of using big data in the social sciences? The answer is simple. It concerns a transition from probability calculations on the basis of a selected data sample, to understanding the complexity of enormously large amounts of data. The questions that can be asked are completely different, because big data can investigate questions about relationships that were previously not linked together. One can find patterns, as well as patterns of patterns, about which it was previously not possible to know anything. The traditional research approach in the social sciences before the advent of big data took as its starting point a research question, and one or more methods of collecting data were then used to find the answer to the question. With big data, the research process is transformed. One has the data available and then you dig into this data, hence the term data mining. The mining process is concerned with finding relationships, indications of patterns, and possibly an overall pattern. One then develops questions, to which one finds answers by using data analytics. In other words, big data has thus turned the research process on its head.

Digitization and big data force us to rethink our relationship to science. With access to big data, transaction costs are also reduced when conducting major scientific projects. Research projects will be carried out to a greater extent by large businesses, which will need to tailor their products and marketing. Science, with the help of big data, can quickly become a social mechanism for large businesses.

When scientific research is conducted it is crucial that the right questions are asked and that we develop and apply models we can trust. If this is not done, we cannot rely on the results we obtain. However, this was the scientific mindset before we had access to big data. With big data, we can ask a question; to address the question, access will be given to all the historical data to which the question relates, without having developed any models or hypotheses. In big data, a pattern shows us how the answer to the question has evolved over time. This may concern anything, such as purchasing patterns, online search patterns, health information, travel patterns, etc. Not least important will be the connections between the various registers that create a pattern in which businesses may be interested. By connecting registers, patterns may appear of which we were not even aware beforehand. By accessing these patterns, businesses can increase the probability of sales, as well as have a better understanding of how product development should progress, in order to satisfy the individual customer.

From a mass market and mass production, big data makes it possible to develop "the market of one". This means in practice that businesses can develop tailor-made products for the customer, before the customer even demands the product. Thus, it is not a matter of "mass-customization" (Gilmore et al., 2000), but rather a matter of tailoring the product to the individual customer. The price in "the market of one" will be in line with the price of mass-produced goods, as the variable costs will drop, because intelligent robots will perform most of the production.

The models used to extract patterns from big data are mathematical models with which most researchers are unfamiliar. Thus, researchers are using models without a full understanding of how they work. They will know even less about the functioning of the algorithms used in the models. With this development, science will become less objective than we would like, because we do not even know which premises are built into the algorithms and models being used.

By studying patterns in large amounts of data, businesses and institutions can turn a negative situation into a winning one. There is nothing wrong with becoming a winner, but what is problematic is that science will no longer be an ethical project, where truth is the goal. With the emergence of big data, science may quickly become just a tool that big businesses can use to achieve goals.

Big data connected to intelligent robots interconnected to global AI networks will turn science into technology and technology into ideology. In such a context, science may quickly become a tool for both large and small businesses, enabling them to profit from science. When science and big data are connected, it may quickly prove to be the case that science moves away from the quest for truth, towards a search for profit.

In the past, when a bank manager in a small town needed to assess whether or not a customer should be given a bank loan, a meeting was usually held at the bank between the bank manager and the loan applicant. The bank manager would have acquired as much information as possible about the person beforehand, such as his family, his prospects and other variables that were of importance for making a decision. The loan applicant, wishing to make a good impression, would come to the meeting dressed in his best suit. Today, with the use of big data, our experience is that the decision-making process when applying for a loan is more objective. Yet, how do we know if it actually is? What conditions are built into the models? What information is selected and used in the algorithm? In the bank in the small town, we were able to discuss and present our case to the bank manager, but we cannot discuss or present our case to the models used in conjunction with big data. We don't really know if the loan application process is objective; we don't know, because we don't have the skills or the possibility to do anything about the models that govern the decision-making processes. Are there any assumptions used in the models that score fewer points for various groups, such as women, immigrants, older or younger people, ethnic minorities, specific religions, left-handed people and so on? We hope there aren't, but we don't really know. Big data has made both science and democratic processes more opaque. One can of course say that the processing of personal data in registers is regulated by law; this may be correct, but it is problematic to reveal which premises are built into the algorithms and models used to retrieve data from these registers.

Using big data, it is not difficult for insurance companies to cost-risk assess clients. The point is, however, that such analyses often confuse correlation and causality. Correlation concerns something that is strongly associated with something else. But correlation is not concerned with cause and effect; one must identify causal relationships in order to establish causality. If you mix up correlation and causality, big data can be used to get the desired answers to the questions asked. Both insurance companies and banks can end up making the same mistake, namely, confusing individuals with classes of individuals. Consequently, this is why we need a scientific method, even when we use big data to find answers to our questions. Using big data, it is easy for anyone with access to resources and large datasets to find answers to questions. The fact that the answers may be distorted does not necessarily mean that those who ask the questions have the expertise or the interest to discover this, as long as they can use the results to generate profits. This may result in considerable negative consequences for many people in the future, and has already caused problems for people today (O'Neil, 2016).

"True" political action

The algorithms generated and used by the major search engines, and the large social media sites such as Facebook and others, can have major consequences for where people focus their attention. The new algorithms can determine the outcome of democratic elections. These algorithms can also affect how we think and act (O'Neil, 2016: 179–183). For instance, using big data, you can identify the interests and preferences of an individual citizen and then target him/her with a specific mail, presenting a certain politician in a way that corresponds to the citizen's expectations. With the help of big data, the politician can show that aspect of himself that corresponds to the individual citizen's expectations, although other citizens would not necessarily be shown this aspect of the politician.

Using big data, politicians can gain access to people's wishes, fears, hopes and what can get them to change their behaviour. In addition, when they can directly contact the individual with a tailor-made message for him/her, democratic elections will have gained a different content. The "true" political action will have become "the politics of one". In concrete terms, this means that one delivers what the individual wants to hear.

In practical politics, individual politicians cannot, of course, fulfil all the wishes and needs that they promised to. Nevertheless, the politician is elected on the basis of their "true" political policy. In such a situation, politics starts to resemble the sale of "discount" goods in a supermarket. The more you lower the price of the product that the customer wants, the greater the likelihood you'll keep the customer in your store; the customer will also purchase other items, making up for your "losses" on selling the discount item. However, the "discount item" which is sold to everyone through intelligent networks, and as the result of searches in big data, ultimately becomes politics' Achilles heel, because you cannot deliver what you have promised to everyone.

If we disregard how elections can be tailored to the individual, and investigate how politicians can use big data once they are in office, then big data can be seen in a more positive light. For instance, big data and the AI network can be utilized in the health care sector to deal with many of the diseases that have caused millions of people misery, such as cancer, AIDS, malaria, and so on. Science will also be able to use big data, intelligent robots and the AI network to find relationships which one could barely imagine before. When such relationships are shown to exist, governments can then use resources to inform the public about which behaviour can promote their health, or identify the best medical treatment for the individual patient.

The core of big data is in being able to predict what is going to happen. This may include political elections, political actions, the development of a patient's illness or the possibility of behavioural changes, etc. The most important thing is not big data in itself, but how big data can be linked to intelligent robots and AI networks. It's when this connection becomes a fact that big data as an information revolution will certainly result in unimagined consequences, positive and negative. The positive aspects clearly include how the individual patient's sickness can be diagnosed and treated.

The science-fiction-like aspect of big data and big data analytics is, amongst other things, the ability to identify criminals long before they have committed their first criminal act. The point is, however, that this can become a reality, although today it may seem unthinkable. Figuratively, this can be viewed as a pre-emptive attack (in military terms); that is, an attack to prevent a perceived future attack. The imprisonment or treatment of a potential criminal before the criminal action is carried out may seem absurd to many, but many also support this approach concerning pre-emptive attacks.

It is the link between big data, artificial intelligence and the AI networks which will affect value creation, innovations and the political system. This development will also affect employment and our understanding of political processes.

If democracy is to be defined as government by the people, then why should the people not be able to have direct influence, instead of influence through representatives elected by others? One might imagine that in the same way as the goods and services market has been literally moved away from the marketplaces in cities to online stores on the internet, such as eBay, political decisions can be shifted away from established political forums, such as Congress, to decisions made via the individual citizen's computer. An individual will have access to analysis of big data and the AI network, and will be able to make decisions that he/she thinks are the best for himself/herself and others. The "true" political action will thus be transferred from a representative democracy to direct democracy. Just as eBay and other online markets never close, it may be imagined that the political system will work in a similar way.

Just as the market was an effective social innovation that was established several thousand years ago (and has now changed), the political system, which is also millennia old, will be able to change and become a new social innovation, where people can experience direct influence on political choices and actions, and not just at the ballot box every four years. From only having the opportunity to influence politics every fourth year, big data, analytical tools and simple presentations of analyses, as well as the AI network, will make it possible for citizens to have influence 24/7.

The market is a social mechanism that allows the allocation of resources. Similarly, one can imagine that the political system will be transformed, allowing direct involvement in political decisions, without intermediaries. The links between big data, artificial intelligence, AI networks and the new blockchain technology will be able to play an important role in a social innovation, applied to the political system. With the emergence and widespread use of blockchain technology, political representatives will become redundant. Through such political innovation, all forms of corruption will become visible.

Imagine that a large industrial plant in the middle of a city is to be demolished, and one wishes to build something else there in its place. Who is the best suited to come up with the best proposals? Politicians or urban planning experts? Who is better suited to know what they want to build there than the citizens of the city? One allows the people to decide what they want, how it will be developed, and let the experts make suggestions. Citizens then decide through their computers what they want the area to look like. Such a development will transfer power and political decisions from a political class to the people who previously elected these career politicians. It seems simple and uncomplicated.

In such a new democratic system, the citizens will be assisted by big data, analyses and artificial intelligence in the AI network. If one is of the opinion that the citizens don't know what's best for them – then you're in good (or bad) company with the feudal lords throughout history who believed the same; namely, that the elite class knows what's best for the citizens.

Representative democracy was a development away from despotic and tyrannical forms of government. However, this does not mean that representative democracy is preferable to direct democracy. In a future direct democracy, the people will have the technological tools to decide what is best for themselves and their families, for others, and for the future.

One objection may be the issue of who will submit proposals for voting. The answer is simple. This is something everyone can do; the new technology will be able to process them into an abstract form, and organize and systematize the proposals, and then post them for voting at specific times, for example the first Sunday of each month. It is possible that the city centres will take on a new function, similar to the old agoras in the ancient Greek world; one will be able to discuss the proposals in the agora before each citizen accesses his/her computer to decide what's going to happen.

Representative democracy has been useful and has worked well in modern history, but this is not a valid argument that it is an optimal democratic system. It's only better than what it replaced, tyrannical forms of government. Direct democracy, now possible with the new technology, will enable each individual citizen to be involved in what is happening in their local community, and in other areas.

Who should determine tax levels, health investments and military budgets? Who should decide if the nation should go to war or not? Those who will be the victims of the war, and their mothers and fathers, they should be the ones with the most influence when deciding this! They would be able to do this in a direct democracy, not in a representative democracy.

Accessibility to intelligent computers, big data, intelligent robots and AI networks will make direct democracy possible. Of course, career politicians and political leadership in the established parties will oppose such a development, because they will lose influence and prestige in such a democratization process. However, it makes more sense that a majority of the population determine their own future by direct access to decisions, rather than leaving this up to political horse-traders behind closed doors.

Just as we have electronic markets today, it will be easy to establish an electronic democratic system. The digital innovation that has taken place since the late twentieth century, the development of intelligent robots, AI networks and increasing digital skills in the population, will make the economic system and the political system more receptive to institutional innovations. In the financial system, the digital markets are today transforming the business models we know into various forms of digital markets. In the political system, we have not yet seen any evolution towards digital political systems that will supersede representative democracy. However, in the near future it will be possible for all citizens in a geographical area to participate actively in democratic processes. The reasons for the development of institutional innovation within the political system are as follows:

1   It will lower costs. We know from innovation theory that when the costs are relatively high compared to other similar processes, the probability of the emergence of innovations is also high.
2   The quality of the decisions will be better, because those directly affected will be able to participate in the democratic process. We also know that where the relative quality is declining, the probability of the emergence of innovations is high.
3   If we consider the contempt for politicians that has spread across the United States and Europe, the digitization of political processes will give power back to the citizens. This may be considered as a productivity improvement when understood in relation to the idea that productivity is linked to the relationship between output/input. We also know from innovation theory that where relative productivity is falling, the likelihood of the emergence of innovations is high.
4   Innovations have spread very rapidly in what can be termed the global economy, the innovation economy or the knowledge society. We know from innovation theory that when the spread rate of innovations is high, the likelihood of the emergence of innovations is also high.

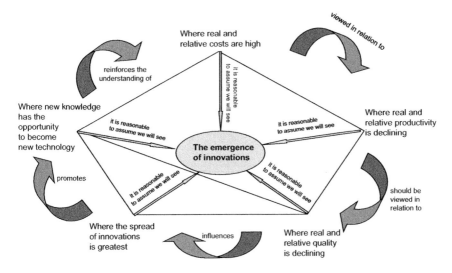

Figure 3.12 Where innovations will emerge.

5   Digital development has created a higher level of competence with regard to digital solutions. This increasing competence has made it possible to develop a technology for digitizing the economic system. The opportunity to also use this competence within the democratic processes is now present. We know from the theory of innovation that when new knowledge has the potential to become technology, the likelihood of the emergence of innovations is high.

We have illustrated the above discussion in Figure 3.12.

In view of the above discussion, and the visualization of the discussion in fig. 13, it seems reasonable to assume that the political system will soon witness a development towards digital solutions for democratic processes. A transition from representative democracy to direct democracy is now technologically within reach.

Conclusion

This chapter has explored the following question: How will the AI network affect societal institutions?

Research into the future will always be disappointing for people who think it is about making accurate predictions. On the other hand, those who look to nature to get ideas and who see possible applications derived from analogies from nature, may generate ideas for "the new". "The new" is not a given, someone has to design and develop it. Such people look to nature in order to design the new, which has not existed in the world before then.

The AI network, artificial intelligence and intelligent robots will develop what we refer to here as agora robots. These agora robots will develop artificial intelligence, artificial relationships, artificial emotions and the ability to empathize. Ideally, an agora robot would be able to participate in every kind of communication scenario. Such scenarios are characterized by shifts in perspective, paradoxes, emotional outbursts and other irrational behaviour. The development of the agora robot, although this is still some way off in the future (2035–2040), will give rise to a robot that simulates human behaviours. Already we are seeing the development of social robots with anthropomorphic characteristics.

No human interactions occur in the absence of any kind of emotions. It is our ability to recognize and react to emotions in other people that makes us empathetic. We recognize facial expressions, body language, verbal expressions, tiny signals and so on. We can also immediately understand the other person's situation, or at least some aspects of it. If we exhibit the basic emotional states of joy, sadness, disgust, anger, fear or surprise, an agora robot will be able to recognize this. A more complex example – but a common one, especially in emotional situations – would be where we use a range of coordinated expressions, composed from these six basic emotional states. An agora robot would have to be designed so that it can uncover the emotional coordination that a person uses to express a particular emotion.

This relational aspect of an agora robot will play on relational expressions: listening, fairness, helpfulness, generosity, kind-heartedness and forgiveness. In addition, the agora robot will be able to use its logical, rational problem-solving artificial intelligence in a relevant situation.

The answers we have arrived at to the question being examined in this chapter can be summarized as follows:

1   A new type of robot, the *agora* robot, will see the light of day. These robots will have *artificial intelligence*, will be able to express themselves with *artificial emotions* and will relate to people with the help of *artificial relationships*.
2   Like an information revolution, big data will transform our economic and political systems. In the economic system, there will be a transition from physical to electronic markets. In the political system, it seems reasonable to assume that there will be a transition from a representative democracy to an *electronic political system*, from which genuine democracy will emerge.

Notes

1 https://en.wikipedia.org/wiki/Uncanny_valley.
2 https://en.wikipedia.org/wiki/Methodological_solipsism.
3 We describe the agora robot a little further on in the chapter. The short version here is that the agora robot is a social robot with the ability to portray emotional and communicative expression.
4 The "cloud" refers to data which is stored on remote servers accessed from the internet.

5 The agora was the innermost square in ancient Greek cities, where trade, communication and relations were conducted. "The agora was the center of the athletic, artistic, spiritual and political life of the city". (https://en.wikipedia.org/wiki/Agora).
6 Cited in Simler and Hanson, 2018: 4.
7 This is not an independent citation, but a paraphrase of comments in the Danish newspaper *Politikken*.
8 https://no.wikipedia.org/wiki/CERN.

References

Agah, A., Cabibihan, J.-J., Howard, A., Salichs, M.A., & He, H (eds.). *Social robotics: 8th international conference, ICSR 2016*, Kansas City, Proceedings, Springer, Cham.

Asada, M. (2015). Towards artificial empathy: How can artificial empathy follow the developmental pathway of natural empathy? *International Journal of Social Robotics*, 7(1), 19–33.

Atkinson, A.B. (2018). *Inequality: What can be done?* Harvard University Press, Cambridge, MA.

Breazeale, C. (2002). *Designing social robots*, MIT Press, Cambridge, MA.

Breazeale, C. (2003). Emotion and sociable humanoid robots, *International Journal of Human-Computer Studies*, 59(1/2), 119–155.

Brown, D.E. (1991). *Human universals*, McGraw-Hill, New York.

Brown, R. (2017). *The inequality crisis: The facts and what we can do about it*, Policy Press, London.

Chace, C. (2016). *The economic singularity*, Three Cs, New York.

Chace, C. (2018). *Artificial intelligence and the two singularities*, CRC Press, Boca Raton, FL.

Dautenhahn, K. (2007). Methodology and themes of human–robot interaction: A growing research field, *International Journal of Advanced Robotics*, 4(1), 103–108.

Dorling, D. (2015). *Inequality and the 1%*, Verso, London.

Dumouchel, P., & Damiano, L. (2017). *Living with robots*, Harvard University Press, Cambridge, MA.

Eden, A.H., Moor, J.H., Søraker, J.H., & Steinhart, E. (eds.) (2012). *Singularity hypothesis: A scientific and philosophical assessment*, Springer, Berlin.

Ekman, P., & Keltner, D. (1997). Universal facial expression of emotions: An old controversy and new findings, in U. Segerstrale & P. Molnar (eds.), *Nonverbal communication: Where nature meets culture*, pp. 27–46, Lawrence Erlbaum Associates, Mahwah, NJ.

Gardner, H. (2006). *Multiple intelligences*, Basic Books, New York.

Gilmore, J.H., Joseph-Pine, B., & Pine-Illinois, B.J. (2000). *Markets of one: Creating customer value through mass-customization*, Harvard Business School Press, Boston, MA.

Harmelen, F., Lifschitz, V., & Porter, B. (2008). *Handbook of knowledge representation*, Elsevier, Amsterdam.

Holmes, D.E. (2017). *Big data: A very short introduction*, Oxford University Press, Oxford.

Johannessen, J.-A. (2018b). *The workplace of the future: The Fourth Industrial Revolution, the precariat and the end of hierarchies?* Routledge, London.

Kurzweil, R. (2001). *Law of accelerating returns, Lifeboat Foundation Special Report*, https://lifeboat.com/ex/law.of.accelerating.returns.

Kurzweil, R. (2005). *The singularity is near*, Penguin, London.

Kurzweil, R. (2008). *The age of spiritual machines: When computers exceed human intelligence*, Penguin, London.

Nørskov, M. (ed.). (2016). *Social robots*, Ashgate, Farnham.

O'Neil, C. (2016). *Weapons of math destruction*, Penguin, New York.

Russell, S., and Norvig, P. (2013). *Artificial intelligence: A modern approach*, Pearson, London.

Schroeder, R. (2014). Big data: Towards a more scientific social science? in M. Graham & W.H. Dutton (eds.), *Society and the internet*, pp. 164–176, Oxford University Press, Oxford.

Simler, K., & Hanson, R. (2018). *The elephant in the brain*, Oxford University Press, Oxford.

Standing, G. (2018). *Basic income*, Pelican, New York.

Valleverdú, J. (2009). *Handbook of research on synthetic emotions and sociable robotics*, Information Science Reference, Hershey, PA.

Part III

Institutional innovations

Introduction

Social singularity is simultaneously terrifying and exciting. Throughout the history of innovations, we have experienced book burnings, machine breaking and house arrests. People have even been sentenced to death or shunned by society for discovering and applying innovations. Today's innovation – singularity – is no exception, with its intelligent robots, intelligent networks and debates about robots with artificial emotions and artificial relationships. The history of innovation can be expressed in a single statement: Adapt to the new or be crushed.

Not all innovations bring mankind forward towards a happier, flourishing society, however.

I grew up in a small fishing village (Mehamn), as far north as it is possible to get in Norway. The inhabitants of this fishing village had lived reasonably well from fishing for decade after decade. The institutional innovation that is globalization affected the village as though it had been hit by a bomb. Large trawlers took over from small fishing boats, and fishermen who had worked independently using their own boats became workers for the trawler owners who lived far away from Mehamn. When globalization reached Mehamn, it became cheaper to freeze the fish on board these large trawlers, and then send the fish to Rotterdam to be reloaded for the long voyage to China. Once the fish reached China, it was unloaded, thawed, filleted, packaged, frozen and sent all the way back to European markets, including the frozen fish counters in Mehamn. When the same fish was sold over the counter in Mehamn, it was approximately one kroner cheaper per kilo than if it had been brought onto land in Mehamn and filleted and processed locally. This shows how a simple global innovation had major consequences for a small fishing village with approximately 800 inhabitants. Unemployment increased, social problems exploded, and people began to leave Mehamn to live in other places where they could find work.

This situation is not unique to Mehamn, or to other fishing villages in Norway. We have seen the same trend in America: in West Virginia and in the Steel Belt, in fact in all areas where the economy is based on traditional industrial production. Detroit is an example of a place where the car industry experienced the same consequences of globalization.

All over the world, innovations are affecting our accustomed lifestyles. This is nothing new. The First Industrial Revolution, from about 1750 onwards, had a similar impact on individuals, families, organizations and society.

Machines took over young people's jobs in West Virginia, just as trawlers and globalization took jobs from young people in Mehamn. "Machine breaking" has a long history, but it always ends in the same way: Adapt yourself or join the "losers' community". Traditional industrial jobs moved to Mexico, India and China. Today they are moving to even cheaper areas, such as Bangladesh, Vietnam, Tanzania, Myanmar, Pakistan, several countries in Africa and so on. The people who didn't get on the "competence train" ended up on the train for people who lost out from innovations. The debate about a universal basic income is targeted at these latter people, because this train is already overloaded, and new coaches are continually coming onto the track. It is the millions of frustrated, angry and oppressed people who want to change society.

Many people say that this time it is different, referring to intelligent robots. But no, this time is pretty much like the other industrial revolutions. The difference is simply that now the innovation is singularity, and it's affecting the whole globe and all sectors, and it is not just thousands, but millions, of families that will be affected by innovation processes. The same thing is happening all the way from West Virginia to Mehamn. People who fail to join the competence train are left stranded on a siding. Gradually, the metaphorical train tracks are removed, and the people who were left stranded are unable to move on. They can risk being left in this economic and social impasse, along with their families, for their whole lives. When there are enough people in this position, they also start to have an influence on democratic elections, and can elect their own president, or their own people to government positions and so on.

Innovations have consequences for the whole of society. Not all innovations are experienced as a benefit for everyone affected, however. Some people will flourish, while others will flower and then experience autumn early in their lives, like many of the workers in West Virginia and in fishing villages like Mehamn.

The problem we are examining in this part is how technological and economic singularity generate institutional innovations that in turn transform social institutions. The general question we are exploring is as follows: How is singularity affecting social institutions? We have selected three important social institutions: democracy, working life, and higher education (universities). The three sub-questions that we investigate in order to answer the general question are as follows:

> How will singularity affect the democratic system?
> How will singularity affect working life?
> How will singularity affect higher education?

This introduction is shown figuratively in Figure PIII.1, which also illustrates how we have structured this part.

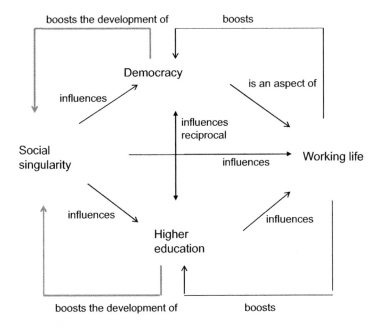

Figure PIII.1 Institutional innovations affecting institutions.

4 Democracy as the people's institution

Introduction

The main ideas discussed in this chapter are:

- The transformation of democracy from representative democracy to true democracy.
- New technology will make it possible to participate continually in democratic processes without any need for the middlemen characteristic of representative democracy.
- The two technologies that will make true democracy possible are artificial intelligence and blockchain technology.

Why should the type of democracy we have today be the final station on the path of democratic development? The birth of democracy in the Western world is considered to have taken place in Athens, in around the 6th century BCE. What has happened since then is that ever more groups in the population have become part of democratic processes. Despite this development, authoritarian tendencies are still emerging today. Historically, we have seen such trends in Europe in the 1930s and in Latin America in the 1970s, and today we are seeing them in many countries in Africa and Asia, including India.

The development of capitalism has clearly been significant for the development of democracy, but how? The political and economic aspects of democracy have experienced difficult times in many countries throughout the history of capitalism, as capitalism as a social system is not a sufficient prerequisite for a democratic system.

It seems reasonable to assume that social justice and co-operation are components of a democratic system. For the development of true democracy, we are assuming here that both political and economic democracy must exist. In addition, it is important that social justice and co-operation are decisive elements for the development of true democracy. We will describe and analyse what we mean by "true democracy" later in this chapter. In brief, we believe that true democracy is characterized by having all citizens in a country being able to exert continual influence on political processes, rather than only through elections, as is the case today. This will be possible with the new technology – intelligent robots and AI networks – that will emerge soon, along with a more intelligent internet.

Democracy can die in many ways, according to Levitsky and Ziblatt (2018). One of the ways democracy can die is through a lack of participation, together with an absence of political engagement. We assume here that in a true democracy, participation in democratic processes would be both a right and also an obligation, not unlike the right and obligation to attend school. Our point that participation is an obligation and not simply a right conforms precisely with the comment of Levitsky and Ziblatt (2018): democracy can die in many ways, including through a lack of participation.

A lack of participation is not the only thing that can be fatal for democracy: others include the destruction of democracy by authoritarian leaders. Such leaders may have been democratically elected, but then have chosen not to follow democratic rules. We have seen how 30,000 Black Shirts marched on Rome in October 1922, and how Italy's democracy collapsed when Mussolini took power.[1] Neither in Rome nor ten years later in Berlin was it a coup that brought, respectively, Mussolini and Hitler to power, but a fragile democracy that collapsed in the face of political parties that were determined to seize power.

Democracy is fragile and must be protected, but is representative democracy necessarily the best heir of the democratic concept? Or should the idea of government be conducted by the people, not by a self-appointed despot?

Freedom, equality and fraternity were the founding principles of the French Revolution (1789), and also of the American Revolution (1776). In general, these ideas have been the idealistic criteria underlying most Western democracies. One may ask oneself who has the most power in today's representative democracies, the people with economic resources, or those who are the people's elected representatives? The question of how much power remains with popularly elected assemblies is open to debate. The point is that there is not a true democracy, whereby citizens could participate in democratic decisions on a continual basis. This is what we see here as part of the innovative process brought about by singularity for democracy, at a time when technology will make true democracy possible.

The main question we are investigating is as follows: How will singularity affect the development of democracy?

The sub-questions we will investigate in order to answer the main question are as follows:

1   How will singularity affect the development of the relationship between democracy and capitalism?
2   How will singularity affect the development of political and economic democracy?
3   How will singularity affect the development of social justice?
4   How will singularity affect the development of true democracy?

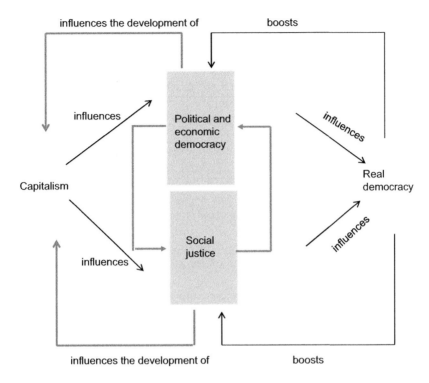

Figure 4.1 Development towards true democracy.

We have summarized this Introduction in Figure 4.1, which also illustrates how we have structured this chapter.

Democracy and capitalism[2]

The Western democratic system has been developed over more than 2,000 years, from Greek democracy to representative democracy. Originally, only people who were citizens of the cities of ancient Greece had the right to vote. Slaves and other people who did not own property did not have the right to partici-pate in elections. Right up until the nineteenth and twentieth centuries, people in various countries in Europe had to own property in order to be allowed to vote. In addition, women were not allowed into polling stations until well into the twentieth century. Today, most citizens in Western countries have the right to vote. The point of this brief summary is that the right to vote was the result of a long political struggle. In many countries, it has been lost and then regained.

Democracies have also been vulnerable to coups, where the right to vote has been removed and the military have taken control. This has happened in most countries in Europe, in wars and coups. It has also happened in Africa, e.g. in

Egypt. Other countries' resources have also been used to depose legally elected governments and national assemblies. This happened in Chile in 1973, for example, where the United States intervened. It also happened in Iran in 1953, where the United States was also involved, and had the Shah put on the throne. Both these examples could be described as coups where the United States was involved. The same has happened in Eastern Europe, where the intervening power was the Soviet Union, for example in Hungary in 1956 and Czechoslovakia in 1968.

On the other hand, democracies can die slowly, with fewer and fewer people getting involved in the democratic processes. The democratic processes with which most people are familiar include, amongst other aspects, an election, usually held every fourth or fifth year, in which people vote for representatives to a legislative assembly. When increasingly few people vote in these elections, this may be seen as a signal that democracy needs help if it is to survive.

Democracies can also die when people vote for authoritarian leaders who set aside democracy and promote their own interests. There are also many examples of lawfully elected leaders who transfer much of the value creation of the country to themselves, their families, and to the corrupt bureaucrats that keep such regimes in power.

Today, there are many heads of government with dictatorial powers who swear by "democracy". One of the reasons they can do so is that there is no commonly accepted definition of democracy. However, in the West, it may be said that the minimum qualification for a democracy is that it includes free periodic elections.

The first modern democracy was established in the United States during and after the American Revolutionary War against Britain (1775–1783). The fundamental principle of modern Western democracies is one person, one vote. However, this principle is undermined by uneven financial resources in politics, that is, when people with great wealth can fund candidates and political parties with their capital, then the probability of that candidate or party being elected increases considerably. The type of democracy controlled by people of wealth is called a plutodemocracy.[3] A plutocracy is a system of government where the rich govern by means of the capital they possess.[4] Today, such plutodemocracies are on the rise all around the globe. Consequently, although free democratic elections are a necessary condition for a true democracy, they are not a sufficient condition. In addition to the plutocrats'[5] direct funding of candidates and political parties, they also own newspapers, television and radio, and other forms of media, so they are able to influence people's opinions and attitudes; in other words, the plutocrats are able to greatly affect and control people's views and thoughts. The plutocrats and oligarchs[6] often hold common views, and their wealth also enables them to influence how people think and act through social technologies.

A democracy where the rich and wealthy have such an influence on the democratic processes is a democracy that is hollow and empty. It is not surprising that participation in democratic processes has fallen sharply, for instance, in the United States, where roughly only half of the eligible voters participated in the 2016 presidential election.[7]

Global capitalism has negatively affected many of the democratic institutions in several countries around the globe. Globalization really took off with China's entry into the global capitalist market around 1988 and the fall of the Berlin Wall in 1989. Already back in 1998, the investor George Soros warned of some of the negative consequences of global capitalism (Soros, 1998); amongst these, that democratic institutions would come under great pressure. One can ask whether it is possible for the institutions of democracy and capitalism to co-exist without the one being injurious to the other. If global capitalism is eroding democracy, why isn't democracy detrimental to global capitalism? Capitalism is characterized by private individuals who accumulate great amounts of capital. This capital gives these private individuals the power to influence the perceptions of political representatives and people, by means of cultural expressions. They do this through television, radio, public relations and, more directly, by influencing decisions in elected assemblies by lobbying. Can we speak of a true democracy, when a few very rich private individuals are able to utilize their capital to influence so-called democratic decisions? It is against this background that Joseph Schumpeter (1959) claimed that capitalism and democracy are incompatible, a view also held by the sociologist Benjamin Barber (2003).

Lobbyists, with access to great resources, can damage democracy in many ways. In the worst case, they can buy votes and thereby contribute to corrupting the democratic system. The ones elected, who are supposed to represent those who elected them, instead represent themselves by accepting such bribes. This type of corruption takes place in many so-called democratic countries around the world (Kroeze, et al., 2017). People with great financial resources can buy lobbyists who influence political representatives, who then adopt laws that hamper competition. This can facilitate the emergence of oligopolies and monopolies, and, at minimum, oligarchs of one type or another.

The major principle of capitalism is precisely the free market. However, when capitalists lobby to restrict competition in the market, not only do they influence "democratic" decisions, but they hamper democratic processes and the free capitalist system.

It can be argued that laws can be incorporated into the constitution that prevent lobbying, oligopolies and monopolies. The United States' antitrust law is one such example. Although this law has hindered capital concentration in many contexts, there is hardly any country in the world that has such large concentrations of capital as the United States (Chomsky, 2012). All legislation can be set aside by strong governmental alliances, so in the last instance, such laws are only "a piece of paper".

Ironically, those who apparently advocate the free flow of capital in free markets are at the forefront in influencing developments that lead to freedom disappearing through monopoly-like situations (Chomsky, 2012). We have seen this development in global capitalism, where it was cheaper to produce industrial products in China than in the US (Brynjolfsson & McAfee, 2014). This led to a deindustrialization on a huge scale of the industrialized countries, especially the United States and in Europe.

This deindustrialisation and unemployment occurred in West Virginia, in the car industry in Detroit and in many other places across the US. Although new jobs were eventually created, these did not provide the same level of income as the former industrial jobs. Workers are often employed on short-term contracts, working only a few hours a week. Frustration grew across much of the United States, and one of the consequences was that this development affected the US presidential election in 2016, when Donald Trump was elected president, partly due to his promise to create jobs by rebuilding American industry.

The logic of capitalism is simple: reduce costs and increase profits. This is done, among other things, by preventing too much competition, because then the prices will fall and, as a result, profits will fall too. To achieve this, capital interests will lobby legislative assemblies.

The free market requires a strong state that can intervene against restrictions on market freedom. An obvious consequence of the free market is that it leads to restrictive institutions and limits people's choices. The paradox is that the free market requires state institutions that are not only strong, but which also hamper people's freedom in order to preserve the freedom of the market. This paradox is solved by accepting strong capital concentrations and allowing the market to live its own life. In its consequences, this means that large capital concentrations take control − including over decisions made in legislative assemblies, through lobbying and corruption. In its consequences, large private organizations are protected by the state's power apparatus. This applies, for example, when a country needs to be rebuilt after a war that has been initiated by the said state, as in the case of the United States' second war against Iraq.

The free market is not just a paradoxical concept, it is a concept that in its consequences influences democratic processes. Some of the free market processes that affect national elected assemblies are linked to the consequences of the free market. We have mentioned some of the processes below (Bunge, 2015: 358–364):

a   *Overexploitation of natural resources*: Within the area of fisheries, we have seen how whales, herring populations, capelin, etc. have become endangered species. Increasingly, various types of plastic in the sea threaten our fish species. Large forests have been lost to deforestation, because huge profits can be made. The fact that these forests are vital to the balance of nature and to maintain the atmosphere is not a responsibility with which individual companies are concerned. Governments have been unduly influenced or corrupted and have permitted deforestation. We also see this in the way that some governments promote fossil fuel use, despite the fact that most scientists believe it is a major cause of global warming. The overexploitation of natural resources is, in its consequences, ecocide − an act of which later generations will suffer the consequences, while companies and their owners profit from it today.

b   *Profits before people*: Many private enterprises have substantial profits, although the social costs of production are high. Throughout history, we have seen that goods are sometimes destroyed to keep prices high. Food prices are also kept high in this way, even when people are starving. When the authorities do not understand the systemic connections, it can have dire consequences. Grain is shipped to people who are starving, which is basically a good thing. The issue, however, is that the farmers in the countries to which the grain is sent go bankrupt because they are not able to sell their own grain. This reinforces the hunger catastrophe and increases the necessity of continuing this vicious circle.

c   *The catastrophe industry*: War, catastrophes and disasters, which are tragic for those affected, can develop into profitable opportunities for private enterprises. We witnessed this in the Iraq war, where Halliburton made large profits rebuilding the country, after it had been bombed to smithereens.[8] We can also witness this in those regions where conflicts and violence rage and where private security companies are emerging. We see the same in war zones, where private "armies" take over more and more from the state military. When profit comes into warfare in this way, the motivation for ending a war also changes.

d   *Mass unemployment*: The many crises of capitalism, such as in 1870, 1939, 1980, 2007, have been accompanied by mass unemployment, where individuals, families and organizations, even nations, have felt the consequences. It might be said that industrial capitalism and mass unemployment are inseparable. Today we see a transition to a system based on knowledge and innovation – a development towards the Fourth Industrial Revolution. No one knows of course what this development will lead to. What we do know, however, is that technology, innovations and productivity gains will result in the old being destroyed and the new emerging. At a time when digitization, robotization and the emergence of qualitatively new intelligent networks and agora robots are emerging, it is reasonable to assume that we are on the threshold of a new era, with other forms of relationships to working life emerging from those we are used to. Project work, short-term contracts, universal basic income, etc. may mean that mass unemployment as a concept and phenomenon will disappear; however, the large majority of the population will experience other negative consequences resulting from completely different relationships in working life, where uncertainty will be the only certain factor (Johannessen, 2018a, 2018b). Previously, such technological advances and innovations were related to so-called technological unemployment, which was considered to be a transitional phenomenon until the market was able to regain balance. The new feature of digitization and robotization, however, is that there is much to suggest that the new types of relationships in the labour market will be of a more permanent nature. This is probably one of the reasons why so many are willing to experiment with various forms of universal basic income. We can also witness another trend as a result of the new form of mass unemployment, which is the emergence of co-operatives, especially in Europe.

e   *The war industry*: The symbiotic relationship between governments and
the war industry is not only a danger to democracy, but also to nations,
organizations, families and individuals. The war industry, also more politely
known as the defence industry, makes huge profits that they also use to
influence attitudes in legislative assemblies and in the population generally. Wars, and disasters resulting from the wars, create markets from which
private actors are profiting. It is not just the war industry that has objective
motives for testing and selling its weapons, but also the catastrophe industry
and entrepreneurs who live by rebuilding what has been destroyed by
wars. Where markets are limited, we have witnessed throughout history
that states have embarked on military actions to expand markets. The
Opium Wars in China are just one example of this. The colonial era is a
general example of the fact that markets create wars and that wars create
markets.

We have shown in Figure 4.2 some aspects of the relationship between capitalism and democracy.

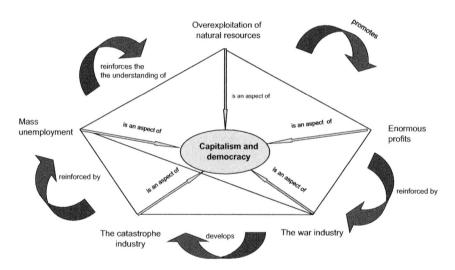

Figure 4.2 Capitalism and democracy.

Political and economic democracy

The effectiveness of political democracy has severe limitations, because it has little influence on the economic processes that are controlled by private actors. However, few criticize political democracy for being undemocratic. The perception of democracy in the West is that most people believe a political democracy is fully capable of performing the functions assigned to it. In most Western countries, the concept of democracy is usually equated with representative democracy, which includes, among other elements, a legislative assembly. However, Tilly (2007) believes this kind of political democracy to be too weak and formal. In order for democracy to become strong and durable, there must be meaningful and direct participation by citizens (Runciman, 2018: 1–9). Furthermore, participation requires equal access to resources, so everyone has the opportunity to promote their views. In addition to equal access to resources, a strong democracy assumes stability and social cohesion among citizens (Bunge, 2015: 365). These three social mechanisms of democracy – stability, social cohesion and participation – are the prerequisites for the development and maintenance of democracy. We have shown these three social mechanisms of democracy in Figure 4.3.

Nevertheless, representative democracy is still a weak form of democracy, as it does not *require* active participation. Representative democracy is founded on the idea that people vote for government representatives who then govern on their behalf. Historically, representative democracy marked an advance over medieval feudal forms of government, as well as other types of despotic and dictatorial government. Today, it can be debated whether representative democracy

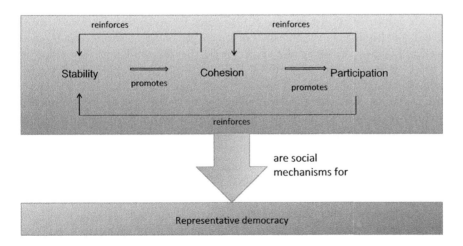

Figure 4.3 Social mechanisms for a stable and representative democracy.

is adequate at a time when technology has made it possible to develop direct citizen participation and thus enable the practice of true democracy.

Today, and through this post–World War II period, many elections only appear to be democratic, and there have often been democratically elected governments that have not been accepted by those who hold the real power. An example of the former is when the military takes over the power of governing, and then holds an election to give a veneer of democracy. This occurred in Egypt in March 2018. An example of the latter is when democratically elected governments are set aside, because those who hold the real power do not approve of the people's choice. This occurred in Chile in 1973. It also occurred in Iran, in 1953, when a lawfully elected government nationalized Iran's oil. In both Iran and Chile, the United States government and the CIA were heavily involved in bringing about a change of government in those countries, forcing democratically elected governments from power.

A relevant question today is: Why does political representative democracy go hand in hand with economic inequality? Further, why does economic inequality go hand in hand with political equal rights? The underlying question to both of these questions is: How do the economic elite manage to convince people in elections to accept economic inequality?

As far as I know, no one has been able to fully answer the above questions satisfactorily. Responses to these questions are often linked to ideology, the influence of the media and socialization processes (Dahl, 1985, 1989, 2000, 2005).

Historically, representative democracy evolved further into the welfare state in several European countries. The fundamental idea behind the welfare state is that the state has a duty to help citizens to "live the good life". The "good life" means that the welfare state ensures employment, education, health care and social welfare are provided for the unemployed, the sick and disabled, and so on. The fundamental ideas of the welfare state were first initiated in the late nineteenth century by the governments of Bismarck in Germany, Disraeli in Britain, Napoleon III in France and von Taaffe in Austria. The introduction of state welfare policies was partly aimed at curbing the development of socialism in Europe (Berman, 2006). The welfare state acts as a safety net to ensure that citizens maintain living standards and fulfil their basic needs. However, if current developments continue towards reinforcing the 1 per cent society (Bauman, 2013; Dorling, 2015), then it seems reasonable to assume the following eleven developments will take place:

1 A universal basic income will be launched as one of the strategies to avoid social rebellion. We saw how social welfare legislation was introduced in the late nineteenth century for the same reason, so we have good historical examples of such a development.

2 It seems reasonable to assume that representative democracy will be maintained, in order to curb the development of a more direct democracy based on continuous participation by citizens. The reason is that a direct and true democracy, which is argued for here in what follows, will

weaken the social position of career politicians and others who are served by the politicians who are persuaded to be spokesmen for the rich and the establishment.

3   It seems reasonable to assume that the welfare state will be further developed beyond the implementation of a universal basic income, in order to prevent social rebellion against the 1 per cent class, when society becomes increasingly unequal. In practice, this means that most representative democracies and the majority of political parties, at least in Europe, will dress themselves up in social democratic clothes to hinder social rebellion. This will result in the traditional social democratic parties being left without what they had thought was a unique political platform, because the other parties will have stolen their social democratic clothes. In other words, the social democratic parties will find it difficult to get into government, but government coalitions will adopt social democratic ideas. In our view, the only way in which the social democrats will be able to regain the political power they once held in Europe will be to distance themselves from the current "Bismarck" position adopted by many right-wing social-welfare parties. In other words, they should adopt policies that not only support "the poor", but also aim at social and economic justice for employees.

4   The rhetoric and practice of the right-wing parties regarding cutting taxes will be emphasized less and probably disappear, because the 1 per cent class will have no need for such policies anymore. Those who do not belong to the 1 per cent class, the other 99 per cent, will be less sympathetic to the policy of reduced taxation of the rich, when they see the 1 per cent class growing richer and richer at record speed. In turn, this will mean that the political differences between the right-wing parties and the social democrats in Europe will be even less than it is today. It is therefore probable that we will see more major coalitions of the type we have witnessed in Germany between the right wing and the social democrats, which will reinforce the ideological merger between social democracy and the political right.

5   Fifth, it seems likely that we will see a trend towards a stronger welfare state, and a more solid representative democracy, backed by alliances between social democratic and right wing populist parties, and simultaneously a further de-democratization of the economic system, where ownership of capital and property rights will become the "holy grail".

6   It seems reasonable that basic financial security will satisfy most people's wishes, because the 1 per cent class and their "men in suits" (Johannessen, 2018b) will use all available means to convince people that trickle-down economics works, that is, when the rich get richer the poor also get richer ("economic inequality is to everybody's advantage").

7   It seems reasonable to believe that a consensus will emerge in representative democratic governments that capitalism must be protected against itself. In practice, this will mean that any mechanisms that can damage a well-functioning capitalist system will be assessed. For instance, this may

involve preventing a further concentration of economic power. However, this will not be done to damage capital but in order to prevent capital from destroying itself through monopolization within the economy. In practice, this will mean that all social mechanisms that prevent competition will be removed. If capital is allowed to operate freely, it seems reasonable to assume that it will develop a feudal-like structure (Johannessen, 2018b).

8 It seems reasonable to assume that both the political right and left in representative democracies will support a free and strong trade union movement, because this will dampen the social storm that may develop when people see an extreme increase emerging in economic inequalities.

9 It seems reasonable to assume that the economic crises that have cleaned out the capitalist carburettor at regular intervals throughout history will take on new forms in the Fourth Industrial Revolution. In order to prevent social unrest, right-wing and social democratic parties will enter into alliances that further strengthen and develop the welfare state. In practice, this will mean that we will see major coalitions that develop a type of Keynesian economic policy to sustain capitalism and economic inequalities.

10 It seems reasonable to assume that representative democracy will be further strengthened to prevent a development towards true democracy. The reasoning is simple. True democracy will be able to do away with career politicians and promote both economic equality and social justice.

11 It seems very plausible that "the free market" will be maintained at all costs – a type of "military-like" diplomacy will be utilized to protect the 1 per cent class. The so-called free market is not possible without continual economic crises, which clean up the market so that it can repeatedly start afresh.

However, there are two paths that can be followed in order to avoid the developments described above (the eleven points). These two paths are social justice and the development of true democracy. We will describe and explain these paths in the following.

Social justice

The definition of social justice depends on one's political persuasion, that is, the political left and right have different views on what they believe to be social justice. The political right's view of social justice may be related to the statement: *What is good for the individual is good for society.* The political left mainly believe that social justice can be equated with economic equality, which can be measured using the Gini coefficient. The political left relate social justice to the statement: *The freedom and well-being of the individual is ensured through collective solutions.*

In this section, a strong democratic system is understood as being a system that aims to promote the well-being and economic equality of an ever-larger part of the population (Barber, 2003; Bunge, 2015: 369).

However, economic equality must not be understood to mean that everyone is equal or can become equal. There are no two people who are exactly alike. Everyone has different abilities, motives, intentions, desires, expectations, goals, backgrounds and so on. The point is that everyone should have equal economic opportunities to achieve well-being. Amongst other things, economic equality is related to free access to education and health, as well as to the right to an income sufficient to live on. Economic inequality based on race, religion, nationality, gender, sexual orientation and the like, is not conducive to the well-being of humanity and should be forbidden by law.

Just as slavery was justified by myths, religious doctrines and the belief that slaves had no souls, economic inequality is also defended by using ideology and doctrines that are believed to have "great insight", but which are not scientifically founded. The maintenance of the idea of economic inequality has a similar knowledge base to the maintenance of various mythologies and racist ideology, as well as other spurious ideologies, and is characterized by an absence of scientific foundation.

Racist ideology has an economic basis, that is, it was material interests that were the driving force behind the creation of racist ideology. Similarly, the maintenance of economic inequality has also spawned various ideologies (Bunge, 2015: 369–371). One of the main ideas used to explain inequality, in this case in relation to skin colour and economic inequality, is that it is "natural" or genetically based. Understood from this perspective, the logic is that one should not tamper with nature. However, if one discards such "natural" explanations, it may seem more "natural" that each individual should have a free choice with regard to education, work and so on, and thus be responsible for their own and their family's well-being.

Inequality, it is argued, may be explained by the choices made by an individual. Thus if someone "chooses" to live on a barren and outlying island, spending their days philosophizing, while living on a meagre diet of fish and potatoes, then it is their own free choice; they shouldn't then blame society for their lack of income at a later date. Of course, this may be a good rhetorical argument, but it hardly corresponds to reality. Those who argue that social inequality is a result of genetic differences or the free choice of the individual, choose to deliberately ignore social structure as an important social mechanism for creating and maintaining economic inequality.

Social structures determine how people develop and behave. If someone is born poor with poorly educated parents who live on social welfare, then it is highly probable that this person will also remain poor. Thus, it is only to a small extent that individual choices determine the future of the individual, even though we may all know examples of people who have managed to shape their own future in a way that contradicts social expectations. The point is that, in the main, social structures affect individual choices.

The three political ideologies of fascism, conservatism and neoliberalism propound that social inequalities are "natural" and determined by factors of genetics and free choice; in other words, it is these factors that determine what one achieves in life. Theoretically, this thinking is an extreme form of meth-odological individualism, i.e. the idea that "everything social is an outcome of individual choice" (Bunge, 2015: 369–370).

After World War II and up until the 1980s, social democracy flourished in Europe, and was characterized by a political debate that focused on social justice and economic equality (Brown, 2017). After this period, from the 1980s onwards, neoliberalism and free market ideas became a strong political force (Atkinson, 2018). Consequently, during this more recent period, economic and social justice were viewed as being less important as social mechanisms that strengthen social cohesion. After the fall of the Berlin Wall and the rising influence of neoliberalism on the political scene, social justice and economic equality were no longer key issues in the political debate (Hughes, 2018). The underlying argument against economic equality employed by the neoliberals was based on the idea of "freedom", "free" choice and the rights of the indi-vidual (Atkinson, 2018). These arguments echoed the ideas of classical liberalism advocated by academics such as Hayek (1944), as well as Narveson (1998) and Nozick (1974). The neoliberals and their academic allies overlooked scientific research that shows that the extreme inequalities we see evolving today pro-mote the disintegration of society, are harmful to public health and personally demeaning for the individual (Brown, 2017; Atkinson, 2018; Hughes, 2018).

It is interesting to note that the argument for economic and social inequality on political agendas is not only supported by the rich through the ballot box, but also by the poor. In other words, the poor also support policies that make the rich richer. Although Hayek (1944) claimed social justice to be a *Fata Morgana*, others have defended economic inequality by saying, in recent decades, that wealth is acquired. Neoliberal academics have by a masterstroke managed to sell their ideas to both the educated and uneducated. This smart neoliberal rhetoric caught the attention of many poor people, who later found themselves trapped in the precariat and "the working poor" (Johannessen, 2018b).

Another way of maintaining the idea that economic inequality is good for everyone is the concept of noblesse oblige, developed in the feudal society. This may be understood as a social mechanism that is effective in preventing social unrest. Noblesse oblige means that the nobility, or in a modern context the very rich (specifically the 1 per cent elite), have a social responsibility. This responsibility can be shown through charitable actions. For instance, generosity may be expressed through the building of hospitals, opera houses, sports facil-ities and so on. The argument is that the very rich should spend their money helping those in need. The question that then arises is: What is wrong with economic inequality, when the rich spend their money helping those in need? The simple answer, of course, is that charity allows social inequality to continue, and exacerbates economic inequality.

What type of egalitarianism or equality is possible, and which is desirable? Equality can be classified into two variants: a radical variant (Nielsen, 1985), and a moderate variant (Ackerman, 1980). The radical variant argues that everyone should have the same opportunities and rewards. In practice, this means that engineers, industrial workers, doctors, nurses and so on, should have the same working hours and the same wage. The moderate variant of equality argues that the social need for special competence and effort should be rewarded.

The position of moderate social justice is that everyone's basic physical needs, i.e. food, housing, health, education, right to work and so on, should all be covered; in other words, it should not be necessary to compete just to meet one's basic needs.

Further, the moderate position argues that competition beyond basic needs, namely to satisfy desires and dreams, will promote excellence, while the absence of competition will promote mediocrity (Miller, 1996).

One argument against the radical variant is that we are not born equal. People have different abilities, and some work hard to achieve special skills in an area needed by society. If they were not rewarded for this, then they would not have the same motivation to achieve this competence. However, the radicals disregard rewards in this sense, saying people should take responsibility (Atkinson, 2018); but the question of who will take responsibility is a question aimed at the radical variant. A second argument against the radical variant is that those who have hard physical work need more nourishment and more leisure time than say a teacher or professor. A third argument against the radical variant is that it focuses on rights but not duties; in society, we have both rights and duties, and therefore they should be considered equally. In other words, rights and duties should be equally important (Hughes, 2018). Moreover, why should we demand that everyone have the same duties, when individually people cannot fulfil them equally well? The objection is therefore that this equality of duties will only reduce society's productivity (Brown, 2017).

Elitism has many perspectives. The classic type of elitism is that of rule by king and nobility, justified as a necessity by historical arguments. Another variant of elitism related to the above is that of a meritocracy: those who govern should be selected according to merit, that is, those who have the necessary abilities and knowledge to govern. The more modern variant is that people should be elected into office on the basis of their popularity.

The systemic position is that the state's task is to promote social justice, where everyone has their basic needs covered. Individuals will then still need to compete to fulfil their specific wishes beyond their basic needs. In other words, the systemic position tends towards moderate equality (Bunge, 2015: 372–373). The reason for the systemic position is that one has to make that little extra effort to fulfil one's special wishes. The rationale for a more moderate variant of social justice in the systemic perspective is that people can easily become dependent on welfare assistance, and turn into so-called long-term welfare dependents, or worse still, transmit welfare dependency to their children – even over several generations. Such a development is injurious to the human dignity of the individual. Although basic needs may be met, people may still live in a state of relative poverty. If many become dependent on welfare, then it is those who are working who must pay for this inefficiency through their taxes. If such a development occurs unhindered, then a large parasitic welfare-proletariat may emerge.

Originally, state welfare is not a socialist invention, but a capitalist one designed to maintain power structures and unequal economic distribution. State welfare has its beginnings in the late nineteenth century with policies launched by national governments in Western Europe by political leaders such as Bismarck and Disraeli, together with others, as mentioned above. Therefore, in the future, it is probable that conservatives will argue for the establishment of "social justice" by means of a universal basic income; but it might be said that the real motivation behind such a strategy will not be to achieve social justice, but rather to prop up the capitalist system, by dampening the effects of social and economic inequality. Welfare society and a universal basic income are social control mechanisms that maintain social inequality and promote the idea that some people are more equal than others, and thus deserve to have their wishes fulfilled. This is why, in welfare states, we also see the concentration of wealth in few hands.

The systemic position indicates that social justice and economic equality cannot come from above in the form of governing instruments implemented by the state, but must instead come from co-operative and collaborative systems within the population. Thus, social justice should not be received as a "gift" from the state, but must be fought for through various co-operative systems.

True democracy

Freedom is a fundamental concept of any democratic society. But freedom is namely limited by the concentration of power that is held by organizations and people who are able to buy the most intelligent minds to defend their cause, so they can exert control over cultural, economic and political processes, by means of their access to material resources. In such a situation, the concept of freedom becomes distorted and only serves to keep power in the hands of the few, hands that have access to huge amounts of capital. In our view, freedom should mean some form of equality. By equality, we mean, among other things, economic equality, gender equality and so on.

Robert A. Dahl introduced the idea of "polyarchy", meaning rule by many, a concept he uses in relation to Western democracy.[9]

Dahl (1989: 221) developed seven necessary and sufficient criteria for a democracy to function well:

1   Elected officials
2   Free and fair elections
3   Inclusive suffrage of all citizens
4   Right to run for office
5   Freedom of expression
6   Alternative information
7   Associational autonomy

Dahl's definition of democracy includes elements that are controversial in the political debate on what constitutes a democracy. However, Dahl does not include aspects of governance and the application of political technology. Let us assume that a government is elected on the basis of the seven elements mentioned above, and governs for four years until the next election. During these four years, citizens do not participate in the governance processes, nor are they allowed to participate in political decision-making. In other words, the participation of citizens between the free elections is not part of Dahl's definition of democracy. It is the few who govern between the elections. Those who govern can make various decisions that go against the will of what the majority believe to be right, and yet this form of governance is still called democracy. Thus, a democratically elected government can rule undemocratically, and yet still be called democratic. With this analysis, democracy can hardly be said to function between the free elections. This is where the systemic position objects to Dahl's seven criteria (Bunge, 2015: 356).

Another objection to Dahl's criteria is related to "the agenda" – who sets the agenda for the political debate? Most frequently, the agenda is set by the party or parties that govern, not by the citizens who voted for them, unless they happen to be members of the party/parties that govern. The person who sets the agenda is also the person who creates the political space where action takes place. In a systemic understanding, citizens should be able to contribute to developing the agenda on all political issues at all times, because those who set the agenda also contribute to future policies.

In governance processes between elections, and participation in setting the agenda, the use of the new technology will be crucial. It will make it possible to expand Dahl's seven criteria and consequently develop true democracy, where all citizens can participate on a daily basis, and not just every fourth year in an election. Using the new technology, a more radical form of democracy, true democracy, will be able to question the effectiveness of representative democracy. Why should we elect representatives when the new technology will make it possible for people to be involved in decision-making every day and thus help determine a country's future. Further, one can imagine that this daily direct form of democracy will employ experts who can implement the choices and decisions made by the majority of the citizens at any given time. In order to maintain trust between the people and these experts, block-chain technology can be used. This technology will ensure transparency and thus that trust is maintained. By doing so, Dahl's concept of polyarchy could be discontinued and instead replaced by true democracy.

Strengthening the ties to the citizens, so that they experience a more direct participation in democratic decisions, will expand democracy. In this way, the representatives will gain greater access to the ideas of the citizens who have voted for them. Hutchinson (2005) believes that democratic processes should be based on participation, equality, decentralization and transparency. He quotes the adage that "the cure for an ailing democracy is more democracy". We believe this really can be achieved, by using the new technology that is emerging, i.e. blockchain technology, intelligent robots and AI networks.

The systemic definition of democracy, in addition to episodic participation in elections, includes the right of continual participation in decision-making as a crucial criterion. One objection that can arise against such a true democracy, where all citizens can participate via the new technology, is linked to issues of war and peace. Should the people decide whether the country should engage in a war or defend itself if it is attacked? From the systemic position, the answer is, of course, that those who will primarily suffer the consequences of a war should also be the ones who make the decision to go to war or not. Who else should decide? The generals, the plutocrats?

Conclusion

The question we have discussed in this chapter is as follows: How will singularity affect the development of democracy? The short answer to this question is that democracy will be transformed from representative democracy to true democracy, because new technology will make it possible for people to participate continuously in democratic processes without the need for middlemen. The two technologies that will make true democracy possible are artificial intelligence and blockchain technology.

The opportunity to participate in representative political elections, and the opportunity to participate in direct democracy, are only a necessary, not an adequate, criterion for the functioning of true democracy. Our point is that if an ever-larger proportion of the population fails to participate in democratic processes, in both representative and true democracies, then this will help to put tyrants and dictators into leadership positions. In practice, this means that indifference brings about something that really can make a difference by triggering a problem for everyone. We have seen this development in many Western democracies, namely the fact that fewer and fewer people are participating in representative elections. One of the reasons is that regardless of any particular political party, many people feel that career politicians are only fighting for their own interests. If this trend continues, then it may give rise to a particular kind of government: one that is democratic in its procedures, but undemocratic in its content.

One way of preventing indifference from becoming a component of democracy is to adopt the same strategy as with school education in the Western world. All children have the right – and also the obligation – to attend school. This idea of a right coupled with an obligation is something that one could also introduce in a true democracy. This would mean that every citizen would be obliged to participate in political decisions.

In Figure 4.2 above, we sketch out a definition of true democracy, and also show Dahl's criteria for representative democracy.

Notes

1 In fact, the situation was a little more complex. Mussolini had been asked to take over as prime minister before he allowed the Black Shirts to march on Rome. So the

Fascists did not seize power by means of an actual coup, rather they took advantage of a fragile democracy. The same was true of Hitler's rise to power. There was no coup, but a fragile democracy (the Weimar Republic) handed power to Hitler on a silver plate (Levitsky & Ziblatt, 2018:11–15).

2 We should emphasize that our discussion here is limited to capitalist countries, because these are the countries that have developed democratic processes.
3 https://en.wiktionary.org/wiki/plutodemocracy.
4 https://en.wikipedia.org/wiki/Plutocracy.
5 https://en.wikiquote.org/wiki/Plutocracy.
6 https://en.wikipedia.org/wiki/Oligarchy.
7 https://en.wikipedia.org/wiki/United_States_presidential_election.
8 www.ft.com/content/7f435f04-8c05-11e2-b001-00144feabdc0.
9 https://en.wikipedia.org/wiki/Robert_A._Dahl.

References

Ackerman, B. (1980). *Social justice in the liberal state*, Yale University Press, New Haven, CT.

Atkinson, A.B. (2018). *Inequality: What can be done?* Harvard University Press, Cambridge, MA.

Barber, J.B. (2003). *Strong democracy: Participatory politics for a new age*, University of California Press, Berkeley, CA.

Bauman, Z. (2013). *Does the richness of the few benefit us all?* Polity, New York.

Berman, S. (2006). *The primacy of politics: Social democracy and the making of Europe's twentieth century*, Cambridge University Press, Cambridge.

Brown, R. (2017). *The inequality crisis: The facts and what we can do about it*, Policy Press, London.

Brynjolfsson, E., & McAfee, A. (2014). *The second machine age*, W.W. Norton, New York.

Bunge, M. (2015). *Political philosophy*, Transaction, Somerset, NJ and London.

Chomsky, N. (2012). *How the world works*, Hamish Hamilton, London.

Dahl, R.A. (1985). *A preface to economic democracy*, University of California Press, Berkeley, CA.

Dahl, R.A. (1989). *Democracy and its critics*, Yale University Press, New Haven, CT.

Dahl, R.A. (2000). A democratic paradox? *Political Science Quarterly*, 115: 35–40.

Dahl, R.A. (2005). What political institutions does large scale democracy require? *Political Science Quarterly*, 120: 187–197.

Dorling, D. (2015). *Inequality and the 1%*, Verso, London.

Hayek, F.A. von (1944). *The road to serfdom*, University of Chicago Press, Chicago.

Hughes, C. (2018). *Fair shot: Rethinking inequality and how we earn*, Bloomsbury, London.

Hutchinson, A.C. (2005). *The companies we keep: Corporate governance for a democratic society*, Irwin Law, Toronto.

Johannessen, J.-A. (2018a). *Automation, robots and crises: How to survive the Fourth Industrial Revolution*, Routledge, London.

Johannessen, J.-A. (2018b). *The workplace of the future: The Fourth Industrial Revolution, the precariat and the end of hierarchies?* Routledge, London.

Kroeze, R., Vitoria, A., & Geitner, G. (2017). *Anti-corruption in history: From antiquity to the modern era*, Oxford University Press, Oxford.

Levitsky, S., & Ziblatt, D. (2018). *How democracies die*, Viking, London.

Miller, D. (1996). Two cheers for meritocracy, *Journal of Political Philosophy*, 4: 277–301.

Narveson, J. (1998). Egalitarianism: Partial, counterproductive and baseless, in A. Mason (ed.), *Ideals of equality*, Blackwell, Oxford.

Nielsen, K. (1985). *Equality and liberty: A defense of radical egalitarianism*, Rowman & Allanheld, Totowa, NJ.

Nozick, R. (1974). *Anarchy, state and utopia*, Basic, New York.

Runciman, D. (2018). *How democracy ends*, Profile, London.

Schumpeter, J. (1959). *Capitalism, socialism and democracy*, Harper & Row, New York.

Soros, G. (1998). *The crisis of global capitalism*, Public Affairs, New York.

Tilly, C. (2007). *Democracy*, Cambridge University Press, Cambridge.

5 Social singularity and work

Introduction

The main ideas discussed in this chapter are:

- Digitization is the necessary condition for work in the future. However, the sufficient conditions are intelligent robots, informats,[1] artificial intelligence and the new AI network.
- The development of informats will lead to the emergence of a "global brain".
- With the development of new kinds of artificial intelligence, and of technological devices that can be implanted in the brain, we are approaching personal singularity.

Any work, of whatever type and wherever carried out, reflects contemporaneous political circumstances and the level of technological development. This is as true today, on the threshold of the Fourth Industrial Revolution, as it was 10,000 years ago on the plains of Mesopotamia (Johannessen, 2018a, 2018b). Digitization, intelligent robots, the impact of artificial intelligence on most people's working lives, how one develops a good working life, and how informats will be developed into what can be understood metaphorically as a global brain: these are all developments that we must relate to in order to understand how singularity will affect working life (Kurzweil, 2006).

Much of what will happen when society has developed a form of singularity remains hidden for the majority of us. To understand the situation metaphorically, first imagine an old car engine from the 1950s, and then imagine a state-of-the-art car engine today. In the 1950s, anyone with a passing interest in cars could tinker around with the engine. In contrast, barely anyone is able to do anything to fix a hi-tech car engine today, because everything is hidden in codes, chips and the car's computer system, as well as in the car's connection to a larger computer, via an external network.

As with the high-tech car, society is becoming so technologically advanced that we just have to accept that we don't understand how everything works. We have the internet that is developing into a new internet, which we have called the AI network in this book. This intelligent network also comprises processing power that is integrated into the network itself. These emerging conditions mean that working life will be completely transformed in the future. Digitization marked the beginning of this development, just as the development of interlinking highway systems made possible the utilization of the newly invented automobile. Digitization laid the foundation for the Fourth Industrial Revolution, and may be understood as the first step on the road towards something qualitatively new, for people, workplaces and society. However, it is not digitization that is the main driving force of the Fourth Industrial Revolution, but instead intelligent robots, artificial intelligence and informats (Johannessen, 2018b). Digitization may be likened to the highways on which the automobiles drive, while the automobiles may be understood as intelligent robots, which are in contact with other intelligent robots and which are constantly updated by developments in the environment in which they travel.

Big data analytics, the internet of things and artificial intelligence are the prerequisites for a changing working life. In this future working life, we will not necessarily have to be physically present at the workplace, as long as we can complete the work we have been assigned.

Technological and economic singularity forms the basis for social singularity, and it is against this backdrop that working life will be shaped at the beginning of the Fourth Industrial Revolution (Goertzel & Goertzel, 2015a). The transition to working life in the Fourth Industrial Revolution will happen too rapidly for the human mind to comprehend, say Goertzel and Goertzel (2015a: 7). One of the consequences of this is that we will choose to focus on that which is right in front of us, and ignore those aspects of life not immediately related to our needs. However, when we narrow our attention in this way, we will become like atomized units without an overview of the big picture. It is in this context that intelligent robots and artificial intelligence will come to our aid, so we can avoid both "information input overload" (Miller, 1978), and also viewing working life and society as consisting of fragmented atoms. Intelligent robots will become our helpers in working life as well as in our leisure time, and artificial intelligence will enable us to understand relationships and to see part and whole in a larger context.

The new technology that is driving the Fourth Industrial Revolution has both positive and negative aspects. The negative aspect is that technology will take over most of the functions in the workplace, and capital will become concentrated in fewer hands. However, it is up to us which development we want and which development we believe will serve us best. Neither the logic of capital nor the logic of technology is an uncontrollable natural force. The philosophical foundation of this chapter is that we can create our future working life and the world we want to live in.

The question we will examine in this chapter is as follows: What impact will social singularity have on working life?

To answer this question, we have developed four sub-questions:

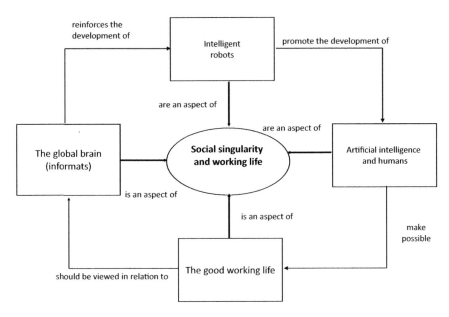

Figure 5.1 Social singularity and working life.

1   What impact will intelligent robots have on working life?
2   How will the relationship between people and artificial intelligence affect working life?
3   What will constitute the "good working life" when singularity becomes a reality?
4   What impact will "the global brain" (informats) have on working life?

We have summarized the introduction in Figure 5.1, which also shows how this chapter is organized.

Intelligent robots

In this section, we will examine the following question: What impact will intelligent robots have on working life?

The quote, "It's hard to make predictions, especially about the future", is both humorous and a paradox. It is attributed to the Danish poet Piet Hein.[2] Of more interest to us here, however, is a quote by Abraham Lincoln: "The best way to predict the future is to create it"[3] (which can also be found in Ackoff, 1981). In other words, it is important to create the future for oneself and others, rather than adapting to a future created by others. Regarding Piet Hein's quote – it is not absolutely correct. It may be true that it is difficult to predict the future specifically and in detail, but we know in general outlines what will occur in the future. For instance, in the natural world, we have data concerning sunrises and sunsets, as well as data concerning the ebb and flow of tides; in the human world, we roughly know the dates of future elections to national assemblies, the age composition of future populations based on present birth rates, and so on. Thus, statistically we can predict that "homes for the elderly" will be a topic of social and political debates in the years to come. Considering present energy consumption statistics and the current climate debate, it is highly probable that renewable energy solutions will be emphasized even more in the future. Against this background, we can also predict with great probability that when, not if, intelligent robots become commonplace, the labour market will be completely transformed. Of course, we do not know how, but we can say with great certainty that the old factory and office buildings will largely stand derelict in the future, because they will not be functional for a number of reasons. For instance, it will not be cost-effective, environmentally sustainable or rational to shuttle the entire workforce back and forth by car or other means of transport between the city centres and the suburbs every day. Therefore, the organization of work will be changed, revolutionizing how we manage and organize the labour market. Where costs are high and productivity is declining, innovations will most probably be developed (Johannessen, 2017: 208; 2018a). Consequently, cities will experience radical changes concerning workplaces and traffic solutions.

If we consider the development of civilization from a technological perspective, there has been a continuous accumulative and exponential technological growth from the invention of the wheel to the development of artificial intelligence. In parallel with this technological development, working life has also changed, although developments have not been continuous and regular. Consequently, we cannot predict with certainty the exact date when changes will occur. Nevertheless, we can be more certain about the overall trends that will develop. Therefore, it is not the precise prediction of dates, but rather trends and cyclical patterns that are of interest, regarding the relationship between society, technology and working life. Businesses, education and social life will be greatly impacted by future developments, so it is of interest to know something about the trends and cyclical patterns that will emerge.[4]

Robots, intelligent robots and other names that are given to the automation of production and information processes must not be confused with the avatars and human-like characters of science fiction literature. As a rule, intelligent robots cannot be compared to human beings at all. These intelligent robots are constructed using chips with enormous processing power, so powerful that they can be used to calculate collisions between atoms in the world's largest particle generator in Cern. Intelligent robots can be very small, in the form of nano-computers, which, although miniature, can still have very large processing power. When many writers, such as Alec Ross (2016: 15), write that we must learn to live side by side with robots, the reader may get the impression that this is like having an intelligent neighbour move into the office or apartment next door. Nothing could be more wrong. These intelligent robots and informats, if we disregard sex robots, industrial robots in the automotive industry and so on, are often hardly visible. They are often built into familiar devices, such as your computer, your shoe, your pants, or even implanted in your ear. Everyday life will become much easier when people can use such nano-computers, which are built into vacuum cleaners today, and into the new AI networks tomorrow. They will enable people to perform various functions at a much higher level than they are able to do today. This will apply to the individual's conversational skills, language competencies, vocabulary, technical competencies, thinking ability, work skills and so on. This will be possible because the nano-computers will have continuous access to information and processing power, without time-lag, and will be based on the latest evidence-based knowledge.

As the population grows older and there are fewer people who can contribute to society, there will be a change in the views about work, for both necessary and also logical reasons. The younger generation will find it difficult to understand why the older generation who, although healthy, and physically and mentally active, can travel around the world like tourists, while the young people have to foot the bill through their taxes. Moreover, the younger generation will have to work far beyond the current pension age, as the pension rules will most probably be revised in the future.

Such a change of attitude will mean that work and pension are not necessarily a linear journey over time, that begins when you are 30 years old after a long education and ends when you are 70 years old. This is the mindset of the industrial age that sets a beginning and an end to the production process. In the innovation economy and knowledge society, work for most people will not be a heavy physical process, or an exhausting mental one. The reasoning is simple. Intelligent robots will take over most of the physically and mentally stressful work activities. Moreover, it will not be necessary to carry out work in the factory or the office, when people can complete the same activity at their holiday cottage, lying in bed, on the beach, in a cafe or sitting at the kitchen table. With such an understanding, work will be viewed as a process related to personal development through producing, distributing and consuming. In such a context, why should it be assumed that individuals, when they are healthy, are ready to stop working at a predetermined age, be this 72 or 77 years? Such assumptions are based on an understanding of work as drudgery, which leads to the idea that the elderly should be stowed away in death's waiting room. Nothing will be more wrong when intelligent robots will have an active role in social life and production. From the kindergarten to the old people's home, each person will develop through producing, distributing and consuming. The linear industrial logic consists of first learning in school, then applying that learning in working life, and finally enjoying one's retirement as a "reward" for one's contribution to society, i.e. learning–producing–resting. This logic will change completely with the new working life. When the innovation economy and the Fourth Industrial Revolution become a reality, the linear logic will be dead, and circular understanding will become the dominant logic, that is, one learns, works and rests continuously in an interactive logic or a circular process, and in a circle there is no beginning or end.

A necessary prerequisite for achieving this is to put people before profit. This involves focusing on the individual in a lifelong working life, not the individual as part of an industrial logic of learning–producing–resting. In the new working life, the individual develops by creating what he/she is most passionate about, what she/he is good at and what he/she masters.

Future working life will not be a time-limited matter. Working life will be life itself. Of course, if you grow old or sick, you should be cared for and given help, and not have to work.

The hunter in the hunter–gatherer society became too old to hunt reindeer or buffalo when he reached 60–70 years old. Similarly, the farmer in ancient Mesopotamia would have a struggle tilling the land when he reached a similar age. The industrial worker was worn out by the time he/she was 70 years old. However, today's retirees who retire when they are 62–70 years old are often fit and healthy, although there are many cases where they are also worn out. Many of the fit and healthy retirees spend their time travelling, golfing, hiking in the mountains or sailing along the fjords, as if they were English lords of the nineteenth century. In tomorrow's society, intelligent robots will have taken over the vast majority of work tasks that are physically or mentally stressful. Therefore, it will also be important to change our attitudes about what working life consists of.

With the birth rate declining, and the population getting older, we will be forced into reaching a new understanding of what work and working life involve. The idea that the children should take care of the elderly belongs to the logic of the agrarian society, when poverty was common. In the new working life, a completely new logic will develop: Everyone will take care of those who need it. Sometimes it will be the elderly who take care of the younger, and in other contexts, the young who take care of the elderly. The point here is that in the future, working life and retirement will not necessarily be determined by a logic of linear time. In many countries today, when an individual passes the age of 62 years, he/she is able to retire with a state pension. In many cases, as mentioned above, they can afford to "live the life of an English lord", who considered all paid work to be an abomination. Thus, they can travel, play golf, hike in the mountains, sail along the fjords and so on. This is all well and good, but it is paid for through taxation, and in the future can become a financial burden on the younger generation.

Ross points out that in the future, when populations become older, there will not be enough workers to do the necessary jobs (Ross, 2016: 18). However, this reasoning belongs to an industrial logic of learning–producing–resting. Although Ross is one of the foremost authorities concerning the potential of intelligent robots, he disregards the fact that technological change will also result in a transition from an industrial logic to a new logic; this transition will occur precisely because of the technological changes he describes.

In other words, as mentioned above, you cannot use the logic of a hunter–gatherer society to explain how an agrarian society will take shape, or the logic of an agrarian society to explain how an industrial society will develop.

Thus, you cannot use an industrial logic to explain how the knowledge society, innovation economy and the Fourth Industrial Revolution with its intelligent robots, will all emerge.

An important point with all the transitions between the above-mentioned value-creating revolutions is that thinking from one mode of production survived long into the new age, when a new mode of production took over. Eventually, the logic of the new society would become dominant. In this context, one can say that our thinking is held back by the "anchor" of history, that is, our thinking has a tendency to remain in the past.

Ross makes the classic mistake of planning a future "war" using a past "war" as a starting point. War here, of course, is only figurative; you cannot exclusively use history as a starting point for understanding the future, because your thinking will be dragged into the past by the "anchor of history". This may be likened to driving a car with your eyes fixed in the rear-view mirror – we all know what happens in such a situation. It is a pity that Ross and many like him describe, analyse and plan the future with their eyes firmly fixed on the past. However, it is no wonder that Ross, who is the USA's leading innovation expert, and has been advisor to two presidents on this topic,[5] thinks in terms of industrial logic about the future. He is, after all, part of an industrial culture that has, for one hundred years or more, dominated the world with an ethos of putting its corporate profit before people.

If you are building the innovative new, then it is important to remember Schumpeter's concept of creative destruction. One has to destroy the old order in order to create the new order. Writers often use the phoenix bird to figuratively explain creative destruction from an industrial logic standpoint. When the phoenix dies, it leaves behind the phoenix egg, from which the new bird hatches. In other words, the old is not wholly eradicated. However, such a metaphor is inappropriate in our context, because the old will be completely destroyed, and future work and working life will be completely new. The new will be a transition from a linear thinking to an interactive or circular thinking. Therefore, the thinking of Ross and others – learning–producing–resting – does not apply.

The intelligent robots will have both general intelligence and specific operational intelligence. They will be ethical and reflective, as in the case of a self-driving car that makes an ethically informed decision (for instance, a self-driving car that has to choose between who should or should not be injured in the event of a collision that is unavoidable). Another example is an intelligent robot that helps a human in a mirroring activity[6] – such as suggesting a white lie to save face. The intelligent robot will also be able to diagnose a disease before the onset of an outbreak, and recommend necessary medication.

It is when the social tectonic plates begin to shift that the new developments become apparent. It is when the new logic becomes dominant that the new working life will emerge, and working will become part of continuous human development; that is, sometimes you learn, sometimes you produce and sometimes you rest, but not in a linear time sequence. The new logic is based on intelligent robots, artificial intelligence, nanotechnology, biotechnology, synthetic biology, etc. During past industrial revolutions, one waited until the new technology was introduced before one adapted to it. This was the case for the introduction of the steam engine, the automobile, the telephone and so on. However, in the case of the innovation economy, it will not necessarily be the best strategy to wait until the new has manifested itself before adapting. One can adapt already, because one knows that the new technology will change production, distribution and consumption. Thus, it will not be necessary to lock up capital in buildings, machines and administration, etc., but rather in talent that is distributed around various systems, and which can be connected as needed to produce a product or service. Therefore, global competence clusters will be crucial for value creation in the innovation economy.

Artificial intelligence and humans

In this section, we will examine the following question: How will the relationship between people and artificial intelligence affect working life?

One of China's political goals is to lead the development and application of robots with artificial intelligence (Huang, et al., 2017). While Japan is still at the forefront in terms of the robotization of elderly care (Ross, 2016: 16), China aims to take the lead in the export of human–robot interaction technology by the mid-2000s (Huang et al., 2017). In Japan, there are many companies and organizations that focus on the development and production of intelligent robots, especially those that will be able to help people; amongst these are Honda, Toyota, Tokai Rubber Industries, the research institute Riken, and AIST, a leading industrial automation company (Ross, 2016: 1–196). China and Japan differ in their approaches to the development of intelligent robots. Japan has a mainly commercial focus, while one of the Chinese government's policies is to become a world leader in the development and production of intelligent robots (Huang et al., 2017). However, at present, Japan leads the production and application of industrial robots (robotics) (Ross, 2016: 17). In Japan, robot development is largely demand-driven, as they have the most proportionally aging population in the world, and consequently, their industry demands technological productivity growth in various areas. As mentioned, China has an overall state strategic plan to develop intelligent robots. It is not difficult to envisage what China can achieve in this area of development and production with such a national strategic plan; for instance, consider what India achieved in Bangalore, when they developed a strategy to become a world leader in software production. Thus, it is also probable that China will be able to lead the development of intelligent robots and artificial intelligence in the future, when they have adopted an overall strategy with this aim in mind (Ross, 2016: 22–23).

Like Japan, the rest of the industrialized world faces an increasingly aging population, aged 65 and over. In order for the strain on the younger generation not to be too great, solutions need to be found to this upcoming challenge. Intelligent robots, artificial intelligence and new ideas about working life will all be needed to address this challenge. In the future, it will not be cheap labour that is the resource base for Chinese exports, but instead the demand for intelligent robots and artificial intelligence, that will come from, among other places, Europe. What was initially a strategic state plan in China will therefore quickly be replaced by demand from Europe and other regions. It is probable that intelligent care robots and intelligent artificial limbs will drive the demand; this applies to both China and Japan. In addition, there will also be an increasing demand for intelligent robots in the trade and industry sector as well as in the field of education.

To understand the development in China, it is worth noting that there are more than 100 faculties of automation in Chinese universities, while the United States has 67 (Ross, 2016: 22). It is usually thought that it is low-cost labour that drives the economic development of China. Although this is part of the picture, China is facing competition from other countries with even lower labour costs, such as Myanmar, Bangladesh, Pakistan and many African countries. However, the main driver of economic growth in China is government-generated innovation. At the strategic level, the state supports the development of both the automation faculties and the vision of the future possibilities regarding intelligent robots and artificial intelligence. The fact that the state is the strategic innovation driver gives China a leading role in the development of intelligent robots, because it can make long-term investments before demand is manifested.

On the basis of economic necessity and technological opportunities of the future, the industrialized countries will make use of intelligent robots that will be able to:

1   Take care of an increasingly aging population.
2   Facilitate some of the older population being able to continue participating in working life.
3   Enable the automation of existing industry.
4   Develop a fully automated industrial system.
5   Facilitate less stressful working conditions for the vast majority.
6   Develop the educational system.
7   Develop the health system.
8   Enable a more rapid economic development, as well as production that is safer, at lower cost and of higher quality, as well as perform functions and operations that people are unable to do, such as aiding the fire services in hazardous situations (e.g. entering burning buildings), and aiding the mining industry in hazardous deep-sea exploration.

Those countries with cultures that are able to quickly adapt to change and automation will have the least difficulty implementing the use of intelligent robots. In this context, it may be assumed that the Protestant work ethic of the United States and northern European countries will be well suited to facilitate change processes. On the other hand, the European industrial culture also has a built-in fear that machines and robots will take control and ultimately make humans redundant. The Luddite movement in the nineteenth century is an example of this. Also, the late physicist Stephen Hawking expressed scepticism concerning the development of intelligent robots based on artificial intelligence; there seems to be opposition to something being intelligent that is not human. The fear that we can lose control is highly developed in Western culture. This is despite the fact that it is exactly those same Western countries that have developed many of the world's most dangerous weapon systems based on advanced technology. Despite this reservation, we believe it is the Western countries that have the most suitable conditions for utilizing intelligent robots and artificial intelligence in order to increase value creation and solve the challenge of an increasingly aging population.[7] The strength of the Western economy is the many big businesses that have a long-term commitment to technological development and application of this technology, such as Google, Amazon, Facebook, IBM, etc.

To an increasing extent, people are orienting themselves towards the outside world via technological entities. Smartphones started some of this development. Smartphones have become an important resource and are used as a window to information and knowledge. As life expectancy increases and populations become older, we will see such technical entities being used to measure heart rate, blood composition, emotions, the "state" of the brain and so on. Artificial intelligence coupled with communication technology will make the individual's life more secure and will reduce the costs for society. Many of these new technologies will lead to a debate concerning ethical, relational and political decisions regarding the use of the new technology, and also in relation to the increasing proportion of the elderly in the population.

One can compare the human exploration of the external world to the exploration of the body's inner world. The inner world can be monitored by technological entities, for example a sensor integrated in a pacemaker that sends data to the person's physician alerting the physician to any irregular or dangerous symptoms.

The next step will be control and programming of the fine-tuning of all the technical units we have implanted in the body (Hewitt, 2015: 96–98). The next exploration of the inner world of the body using implants is likely to occur in the brain. Control and help with dependence on alcohol and drugs, anorexia, obesity, blood sugar levels, kidney function, liver function, anxiety and even a person's motivation and endurance, can all be adjusted, using artificial intelligence built into units implanted in the brain (Hewitt, 2015: 100).

With this technology, we have a development towards what one can call personal singularity. Each individual can be controlled and assisted by a technology that can measure and diagnose various physical and mental conditions, as well as implement measures to remedy various problems. This personal singularity will, of course, be aided by technological singularity, and will affect economic singularity, as well as having a major impact on social singularity. In this way, singularity will be given a whole new meaning for the individual. We have shown these relationships in Figure 5.2.

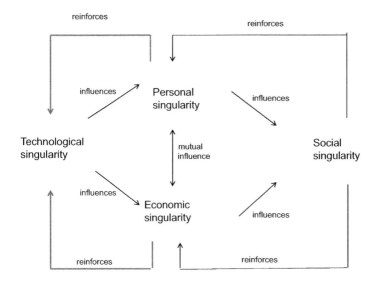

Figure 5.2 Personal singularity.

Personal singularity will occur when technological entities implanted in the body know more about ourselves than we do, and when those entities control our physical, emotional and mental states without our being aware of it.[8] Personal singularity will most probably also arrive with different types of implants:

- Memory implants that can help people with various memory disorders such as Alzheimer's, but also work for people who need to strengthen their memory.
- Sensory implants for the visually impaired and the blind.
- Different types of implants that enhance a particular ability or skill of a person. In this context, Robin Hanson (2016) mentions EMS.[9]

Two scenarios: human and artificial intelligence

In the first scenario, the rate of change is small and people and businesses have time to adapt to the new technology in a balanced and composed way. In Scenario 2, the changes come as cascades of innovations and result in continual chaos with staccato behaviour.

Scenario 1: everyone adapts to the new technology, resulting in harmonious development

The new technology generates new educational programmes that maintain and develop the new technology. This technology and the new educational programmes result in higher economic growth and productivity, leading to increased value creation that benefits both owners and wage earners in a relatively equal way. Work tasks are increasingly taken over by intelligent robots, but at a rate that allows individuals, businesses and the education system to adapt to developments. Value creation increases and each person experiences the benefits of balanced economic growth.

The relationship between people and the tools they produce is perceived as harmonious, although the new technology still amazes most people. People experience a new technology which they have only read about in science-fiction novels, such as tiny robot submarines in the blood vessels that help surgeons diagnose and operate on patients; brain implants that amplify memory and improve specific abilities; and 3D printers that print new organs such as kidneys and livers. Nevertheless, developments are not so rapid that people are unable to adjust, and they accept the new situation as beneficial.

Most people know something about intelligent robots and artificial intelligence via the media or from school or college, and do not think the new situation is all that strange. They know that even the chess world champion is unable to beat a chess robot, so they do not think it at all strange that a super-intelligent robot can perform a surgical procedure that is better, safer and of higher quality than an expert human surgeon can achieve.

Employees experience a fall in their income, because an increasing proportion of the value creation goes to the owners of the new technology (Karabarbounis and Neiman, 2014). However, this fall in income will be partly compensated for by a universal basic income and an increase in part-time work that is available on various short-time projects. People adapt to this new development, for instance, by accepting a lower standard of living in terms of housing, and learning to appreciate their increasing degree of leisure time, alongside other people in a similar situation.

Scenario 2: the rapid change in the development of new technology leads to continual chaos with staccato behaviour

The rapid change in technological developments surprises most people. The new technology is introduced almost overnight, relatively speaking, over a period of 10–20 years. Intelligent robots take over all of the industrial production, so there is no longer any need for industrial workers. During the same period, service robots and other types of intelligent robots take over the work of unskilled workers. In the construction industry, robots take over most of the work. The same is the case in many professional fields, such as the medical profession, education, engineering and so on. This development occurs so rapidly that society is unable to adapt to the changes. The education system is unable to deliver the necessary expertise. The trade unions lose their strength, as fewer workers are now organized in unions. As a result of this development, a very large underclass emerges, living on universal basic income and random jobs. Educational qualifications no longer guarantee work, and people's abilities and intelligence are not so important, compared to what an intelligent robot can handle.

The wage share for the majority of the population will fall dramatically, while the income of the 1 per cent will greatly increase, resulting in an overabundance being consumed by this small section of society. The universal basic income does no more than keep people from starving, while many will experience being socially violated. The social storm that breaks out will result in widespread machine-smashing. The tension between the class of owners and those living on universal basic income and random jobs will increase, breaking out into conflicts and uprisings. In order to keep the peace, the police and army will be used. We will see a development towards a totalitarian structure, where the very rich minority feast from the technological cornucopia, while the many poor live on the meagre crumbs of the universal basic income.

Technology development is further enhanced, th ande human brain is imitated copied, and many new technological innovations emerge. Almost all human work, both physical and mental, is taken over by intelligent robots. Rebellions are kept down by a continuous adjustment and differentiation of universal basic incomes, which means that those who receive a relatively larger universal basic income will help to quell the rebellious elements. Technological soldiers and surveillance machines provide the necessary information about the rebellious elements and they are removed from society. As in ancient Greece, they are banished from society, and sent to distant colonies, where they start primitive farming, supporting themselves at a low technological level.

Implications

In both scenarios, humans will clump together in urban areas. There will be further differentiation of people on the basis of income. The tension between different social groups will increase, and potential conflicts will break out. The extent to which these assumptions will prove to be true will depend on how well governments manage to develop a social safety net and strengthen social cohesion. In other words, this is not a situation where we need a technological solution, but rather a political solution, if we are to create a society where intelligent robots do not lead to unintelligent social developments.

The good working life

The above description concerning the development of intelligent robots and artificial intelligence can also take many other forms, not just the two scenarios we have suggested. One possible development would be towards a more totalitarian and feudal capitalism (Johannessen, 2018b, 2019). Concerning this line of thinking, says Carl Mortished, it is perhaps not populism we should fear, but totalitarian capitalism.[10] Both technological and capitalist developments will affect the working life of the vast majority. As with the two scenarios mentioned above, working life could also take different directions. It is not particularly interesting to predict specifically how working life might evolve, as a result of the two drivers, technology and capitalism, but more interesting to suggest the possibilities that a whole new technology may have for working life. Thus, in this section we will present the optimistic and positive aspects of the new technology. In other words, we will investigate here how intelligent robots can change working life in a positive way, and help people to handle their lives better. Having said this, we are of course aware that the opposite development is also out there knocking on the door. Therefore, the technology pessimists can also benefit from reading further, because they only need to turn our presentation on its head, and they will see that their view is also correct. As we have tried to suggest in other places in this book, the truth is probably somewhere in the middle, between the view of the technology optimists and the view of the technology pessimists. Regarding the development of capitalism, it seems more reasonable to assume that the concentration of capital, whether private or state, will lead to certain value and behavioural changes in those who have access to capital. Capitalism will thus take on a new level, moving from democratic capitalism towards a more feudal-like capitalism (Johannessen, 2019).

The positive aspects of technology development

One can imagine a situation where qualified intelligent robots take over our tasks and functions in the workplace. How will this affect working life? We can imagine a society that replaces human competencies with qualified intelligent robots within specific defined functional areas. One can further imagine a society providing meaningful work for everyone who is made redundant when the robots take over. The working day may also be reduced to a three-hour day plus an extra three hours of competence development.

Of course, nobody knows exactly what will constitute meaningful work for each individual. Therefore, it is the individual's choice that is essential here. Society can help the individual to make a choice, by offering free education at all levels. In practice, this means that a person can train for a special function in working life, and if the robots take over this function, the person can then be re-educated in a new field. This is based on the assumption that the individual will also receive some form of universal basic income. This model thus integrates business and education throughout the life cycle of the individual.

Society has some difficult choices ahead. Should we base ourselves on a model where the individual's free choice forms the basis of his/her future, which is the model that has been dominant in the West, or should we introduce innovative solutions, based on the new intelligent robots that will take over most of the functions in the workplace? If we continue as now, we will most likely end up with a society of winners and losers. This will in turn lead to greater differences in society than we are used to. If we choose innovative solutions that safeguard those who fall by the wayside when intelligent robots take over, then we must develop a different society. The new society can be based on some simple transparent premises:

1 We are given the possibility of free lifelong education.
2 The individual will receive a universal basic income, and be able to manage the transitions between working life, education and new work.
3 No one should be allowed to be left behind in situations where they did not successfully manage the transition from working life, and thus ended up with a meaningless life. This means that giving up is not an option, because help will be available and it will be free.
4 It is not thinking (the Cartesian subject), reason (the Kantian man), or wealth which will be decisive for how society treats the individual, but instead a basic secular, humanistic understanding of each individual.
5 The individual's development should be based on his/her burning desires, where they have abilities and have a desire to be good at something.
6 The individual should develop in areas they feel they are mastering.
7 Three ethical principles are the starting point for this society: Respect, responsibility and dignity. You respect the rights of the other person(s). You always take responsibility for those who need help. You never leave another person or group of people without help if their dignity is threatened.
8 Man is not born free, but creates his own freedom through social activism.
9 Flexibility is the basis of social singularity.
10 The individual, not the collective, is the starting point, according to the logic of singularity.

On the one hand, we know with certainty that intelligent robots will increase the productivity of individuals, businesses, institutions and society as a whole. On the other hand, we also know that such great changes will result in many experiencing anxiety and having fears about the future. This will cause some groups to "smash the machines", that is, become a new kind of Luddite movement.[11] Others will experience moral panic, because the way of life established through a long and evolutionary process will be subjected to dramatic changes. Meanwhile, others will oppose the changes for religious reasons, because humans should not tamper with God's creation.

If we as a society can safeguard the individual and the family, while emphasizing competition and economic dynamics, then we will be able to curb anxiety and tensions. The common denominator for such a social development is that people do not feel socially violated. In other words, society should safeguard the individual's respect, responsibility and dignity, and establish a social norm that views the social violation of others as being unacceptable.

One of the points of developing some basic principles for the new society is to prevent the dissolution of the social contract, strengthen social cohesion and ensure that most people have a meaningful life. However, this will not happen if we continue to use social models that are based on the idea that selfishness and greed are good.

Intelligent robots and artificial intelligence are based on the binary system that uses two symbols, 0 and 1. This has become a multi-million-dollar industry. With intelligent nano-computers connected to the global AI network and implanted in the human body, the "post-human man" will become the new multi-million-dollar industry. This development will take us towards personal singularity. In such a scenario, value creation occurs in the encounter between technology and the individual, but where the technology is hidden from an untrained observer.

There is nothing new in this development; throughout history, there has always been a close link between man and technology. The new situation is that technology has moved from the outside world and into the human body. This may sound like science fiction, but it is only science. It is just a matter of time before it becomes a reality.

Looking ahead to the working life in the near future where technological singularity, personal singularity, economic singularity and social singularity have been established in one form or another, the following question arises: What branch of science will provide us with answers regarding the choices we will need to make in the future? Our answer here is a strategic philosophy that helps guide us towards a more humane society based on the principles mentioned above. A strategic philosophy will enable us to reflect on the positive opportunities that the new technology can have for work and social life. It will also enable us to look into the past in order to identify choices and diversions in technological history, and illuminate technology's relationship to man. Moreover, it will enable us to look ahead to uncover emergent patterns in their infancy. A strategic philosophy will also help us to focus on issues regarding population growth and composition, environmental problems and the opportunities that new technology can offer. Relevant in this context is the issue of retirement age. The current retirement age of roughly 60–67 years was established during the industrial society, because after a lifetime of hard work, people were physically and emotionally worn out by the time they had reached 60. No doubt, there will still be some manual workers in 2040 who have physically exhausting occupations, but these will be in the minority. For these, it is natural that the retirement age remain at around 60–67 years. For those who are not physically exhausted, and at the same time have a life expectancy of 85–95 years in 2040, it is not advantageous for the individual or society that the retirement age is set at 60–67 years.

It is not the age of the individual that should be the starting point for deciding when a person should retire, but the individual's work capacity. If the productivity of a 75-year-old is three times the average within his or her field, then it would seem unreasonable and uneconomical to retire this person, just because he/she has reached a preset age. To apply the same yardstick to everybody in this way represents the logic of an industrial society. An industrial logic also requires employees to be physically present at a workplace, despite their work being done online; most important in this context is instead to look at how much work the employee produces. The transition from an industrial logic to a singularity logic should involve a departure from collective thinking and an adoption of individual thinking, i.e. the individual should take precedence over rule-based common norms. In practice, this means that some people will work and take their vacation at the same time. Others will do what is called "work-surfing", for instance, they may work for five years, and then "surf" for two or three years; then they carry on working for a few more years, and so on. Others will plan to work as long as they can, but at the end of their working life choose to work say 20–70 per cent of a full position, depending on the needs of the individual and the business. Others may choose full working hours, but they do their work while they are in Bali or Hawaii, where they have access to the resources required for efficient work. Others again may choose to partially retire and work part-time, for as long as their productivity remains at its peak. The point of this description is to stress that in the future the rule-based neurosis of the industrial society must give way to full flexibility, which will benefit the individual, businesses and society.

The issue of equal working hours and equal working conditions has its origin in the industrial society. In industrial countries, retirement is usually fixed at around 60–67 years, depending on the occupation and national conditions. The retirement age was set because it was assumed that the period after retirement was one of physical and mental decline, and the individual needed to rest after a long and hard working life. However, in the last few years of the industrial society, new technology emerged that made work easier for the industrial worker, and the future after retirement considerably better and brighter.

According to the logic of singularity, the statistical industrial average is of less interest, because the individual takes centre stage. Flexibility is the norm according to the logic of singularity, not a fixed industrial norm that is applied to everyone.

Singularity and working life can become very people-friendly, if we choose a path where social development puts people before profit, and which is based on some basic premises, for example the ten mentioned above. If society is left to regulate itself according to the logic of capital, it will, with a great degree of probability, develop into a society that is beneficial to the few, but one that will be a challenge and burden for the many.

The global brain: informats

We do not quite fully understand what consciousness is (Smith & Jokie, 2003). On the other hand, we know what it means to be conscious. We know this when we observe someone who is not conscious or aware. For example we know what it means to be environmentally aware or conscious, when we see someone who is not environmentally aware. The point of this little play on words with the same root is to draw attention to the fact that although we may not be fully aware of all the workings of the internet, supernet and AI-net, we can nevertheless imagine how informats will, with time, develop into a "global brain". The "global brain" should be understood figuratively, not literally. The informats and the AI network will improve the logical intelligence of everyone who has access to the informats and AI network.

When we talk about informats and AI networks, we should remember that the internet, as we know it today, is no more than about 25 years old, "born" in CERN in 1993.[12] Today (2019) the internet consists of several layers. The internet that most people know is through web browsers such as Firefox, Safari, Chrome, etc. These browsers only allow us to reach one level of today's internet.

However, there are other layers in the internet, such as "the Deep Web" and "the Dark Web".[13] We can only reach the Deep Web using special software. We are then able to access databases that most people do not have access to, for instance, the databases of private companies, or databases that for personal or security reasons are not available to the general public, such as information about health care recipients, crime registries or information concerning the targets of military drones.

The Dark Web, which was developed by the US Navy (Mosco, 2017: 3), is only available to authorized persons with access to special software. It is now used by various groups, ranging from journalists operating undercover to criminals who need to hide their online activities, such as selling illicit drugs and trafficking.

In other words, there are already several layers in the Internet, to which most of us do not have access. With informats, which are intelligent robots connected to other intelligent robots through a special new layer on the internet, an emergent situation arises. In the future, we will have something that begins to resemble a global "brain", where knowledge that develops in one place can immediately be used by others located somewhere else on the planet, not unlike what happens in the brain.

Informats and the global brain are just a new layer of the existing internet, where both the Deep Web and the Dark Web already exist. If we now reflect a little bit on the relationship between information and knowledge, then the short version is that we can retrieve information online, but we only produce knowledge when we use this information to solve a problem or attain a goal. In our own internal "internet", we have a system of skills, knowledge, perceptions, norms, morals and ethical premises, as well as some ideas which we prefer over others. When new ideas and information enter our consciousness, they are met by "gatekeepers" that interpret and consider these new ideas against the closely linked system of ideas and knowledge we already have in our inner "network". It is not easy for the new ideas and information to get past the gatekeeper, because they have to compete with the well-established and proven internal knowledge base. Van Quine et al., (2013) understood just how conservative language and brain functioning are, long before neuroscience was able to establish this through experiments (Shepherd, 2019). Our inner network, that is, our brain, will always be guarded by a gatekeeper, no matter how effectively the global brain develops. This has implications for education and socialization processes, which we will discuss in the next chapter when we examine singularity in relation to education.

The point in this context is that in order to increase our intelligence by means of informats and the global brain, we must have something to increase. The analogy to information and knowledge is obvious. Although we have access to all the world's information resources, the knowledge we get from this will depend on what we know beforehand. This means that information does not become knowledge by simple technical translations, or by the use of codes. Information becomes knowledge because we structure and systematize this information in relation to some clear goals. The same goes for the global brain. We will not become more logically intelligent even though we have access to informats and the AI network, if we do not have the knowledge base for using these resources. One can explain this by referring to a well-known saying from the Bible, also called the Matthew effect or principle: "Those who have will be given more, and those who have little, will receive even less."[14] The point in our context is that the global brain can trigger this paradoxical Matthew principle, that is, the differences between people's logical intelligence levels will increase sharply with the development of informats and the global brain. This is a paradox, because such a technology should really raise everyone to a higher level. Although the logical intelligence of everyone will be raised to a higher level by means of informats and the global brain, the Matthew principle will come into effect, that is, some will be raised much higher than others. In this way, the differences in intelligence will be much greater, although everyone will be raised to a higher level. However, with the use of informats and the global brain, even those who are not so bright will, with their increased intelligence, become aware of how other people have been raised to a much higher level. Increased intelligence and increased income are thus not necessarily always a good thing. It will make some realize just how far below the others they really are. If, on the other hand, we choose to disregard the psychological aspects of the Matthew principle in this area, it is beyond doubt that informats and the global brain will increase productivity and value creation for businesses and society. However, how this productivity growth will be distributed will depend on the political actions that are implemented.

The global brain is something qualitatively different from the internet of things, cloud computing and big data analytics. It is about informats and intelligent robots that are continuously in contact with each other, in analogy with the neurons in a brain. Understanding development towards the global brain requires more than just having insight into technology. The development towards informats will have implications for all social institutions, the economic system, the political system, the cultural system and, not least, for the relations between people.

Where the global economy has led to global competition, a more multicultural system, local unemployment and political Trumpism,[15] there is much to suggest that the global brain will bring back jobs; not the old industrial jobs, but jobs in the local areas where people want to live. This assumption is based on the knowledge that distribution is the new production (distriduction). In distriduction, people will be able to live where they want to live for various reasons, and at the same time will be able to work and produce at their home office, the local café, the local library, and so on. Informats and the global brain will effectively put a stop to all political, economic and cultural Trumpism. The reason is that when the global brain with informats, intelligent robots and an AI network has been established, the local and national jobs will not be threatened by cheap labour. The mass immigration we have seen to Europe and the US will also lose some of its foothold, because the jobs will emerge where people are already living. One can say that informats and the global brain bring an extra layer to human consciousness, where collective consciousness emerges from the global brain. We need these visions for the simple reason that the transition from what today goes under the name of globalization, to a society that is both closed and at the same time open, will create many social problems. The global brain and the informats will be cognitively open, but will largely remain normatively closed. This means that society becomes open to learning, knowledge development and economic transactions. On the other hand, the culture will be closed around the local and regional norms and values, which are different from place to place. In such a society, Trumpism will have no breeding ground, because "strangers" will no longer be viewed as enemies, but instead as partners, who are located in another place in the world. These partners allow each person to live and work in their local environment, safeguarding their own cultural values and identity. The stranger will not be a threat, but instead a necessary prerequisite for their own existence.

If we define technology as the scientific study of tools (Bunge, 1985: 219–231), then technology also becomes the human interface with nature. When technology becomes more and more invisible to the naked eye via biotechnology, synthetic biology, nano-computers, etc., nature will also be perceived as being more subtle, for increasing numbers of people. This development may easily result in people attributing supernatural powers to nature. The point of this reasoning is to suggest one of the possible consequences of the development towards the global brain, which is that people may be attracted by a new form of the Gaia hypothesis,[16] which also sprang out of technological development.

When artificial intelligence, biotechnology, 3D printers, cloud computing, informats, the AI network, nanotechnology, "gene chips" and genetic data analysis are all integrated into a systemic entity, the global brain will have emerged. This development has been emerging over a long period, but will be manifested with the integration of different areas of knowledge into one single intelligent robot. It is beyond doubt that such a development will transform working life into something qualitatively new. A name has not yet been given to this future new social and technological phenomenon, but it will definitely not be related to communism, and definitely not to Trumpism. The new working life will probably have more in common with the distribution mechanisms in hunter-gatherer society than with the industrial and knowledge society. The reason is that the new production and distribution logic, called distriduction, makes "tribal culture" possible, even though these "tribes" choose to live in urban areas. It is generally believed that human relationships are necessary to human beings; that is, people are social creatures and need human relationships in order to thrive. In this context, the new distriduction logic will be able to re-establish the family, clan and tribal culture of the hunter-gatherer society, but now operating within urban-like communities.

The first step in the development towards such a society will paradoxically be an integration of artificial intelligence into robots of all kinds. The next step will be to connect these robots globally, such as medical robots to other medical robots. This will be a step towards the development of informats. We could say that robots that are connected within specific disciplines, such as medicine, are small-scale informats with a small "i". Large-scale informats with a capital "I" are when all the specific professional robots are interconnected with all other specific robots, regardless of their field of expertise. It is at this level that we can talk about a global brain, where one can metaphorically say that all neurons have access to all the other neurons. This development will represent a process shift from the local towards the global.

The simplest example of this kind of intelligent robot is probably the self-driving car. These will radically transform cities, freeing up large areas that are currently used for parking spaces. When the car has driven its owner to their place of work, it may then be used for other purposes. For instance, it may be rented to people who do not have a car themselves. Yet another purpose will be unmanned trips to a supermarket, where items that have been ordered beforehand are loaded into the car. The car loaded with shopping will park in an adjacent parking lot, and then later drive back to the place of work to pick up its owner at the end of the working day. The car may also park outside the city and wait there until it is needed again. All the cars will be electrically propelled, to reduce pollution. Another scenario is that there are parking spaces outside the cities, and collective transport solutions will be provided from an outer ring road into the city centre – this will result in the city centres being car-free.

Robots will most probably be widely used in the construction industry, which together with the use of large 3D copying machines will enable a reduction in costs, and sharply increase productivity. In turn, this development will probably lead to an increase in the populations of large cities, because of the reduction in house prices brought about by improved productivity in the construction industry. The transport industry and the construction industry will most probably experience radical innovations, with the use of intelligent robots and electrically powered transport drones.

As early as around 2020–2035, the technology in most industries will be interconnected globally, so that it may be understood metaphorically as a global brain. With such a development, in which most work activities will be automated, the labour market will be completely transformed (Nazareth, 2015: 139–142). On the one hand, one can imagine that a sharp increase in productivity will raise the demand for a three-hour day plus an extra three hours of skills development, instead of the 36–40 hour week. Another scenario is mass unemployment and a universal basic income. Both scenarios will be possible with the utilization of future technology, but the outcome will depend on which political decisions are made.

Conclusion

The question we investigated in this chapter was: What impact will social singularity have on working life? The answer to this question is related to four considerations:

- Intelligent robots.
- Artificial intelligence and humans.
- The good working life.
- Informats and "the global brain".

One of the very probable consequences of the developments discussed above is that singularity will revolutionize working life through technology and automation. Intelligent robots will bring despair to the many people who will lose their jobs, while people who are working on intelligent robots will find that their previous experience loses its value.

In parallel with the technological developments, there will be political developments, whereby the market will gain acceptance as a problem-solver. The problem will be simply that the market that emerges will not be a free market, but a form of managed market in which technological development will be driven forward by a small number of key actors, who accordingly will dominate the development of the market. On the one hand, unemployment will grow as a result of intelligent robots and artificial intelligence. On the other hand, economic inequality will increase, both globally and nationally. In addition, problems relating to pollution and global warming will become more severe. Tensions, unrest and military conflicts will follow in the wake of these developments. Informats and other technological systems will be used to obtain the information necessary to control these developments.

In any event, it seems reasonable to assume that the technological developments discussed above will ultimately be beneficial for working life, after some turbulent transitions. It also seems reasonable to assume that these technological innovations will bring about minor and major economic and social crises, both locally, nationally and globally.

Very probably, one cultural consequence of these developments will be demands for and the imposition of greater security and greater stability. Such demands, as we have seen already with the election of the American president, Brexit and so on, represent nostalgia for an analogue culture where stability and predictability were the basic elements of people's lives.

Artificial intelligence and intelligent robots will inevitably bring about changes in working life in the future, both physically and socially. Although we don't know exactly how things will change, we do know that workplaces will change completely. From the automated robots that we see today in the production, service and consumer sectors, we will see a trend towards sophisticated communications robots, along the lines of Google Translate. In the construction industry, robots will take over difficult and dangerous tasks. Nanotechnology will be developed so that various diseases will be monitored continuously and medication will be delivered by minuscule computers targeting the diseases affecting particular individuals.

In addition, we can envisage the increasing economic growth being distributed among the population at large. This means that in the near future, many people will live without having to think about earning a living. In around 2035–2040, when intelligent robots will be as logically and rationally intelligent as intelligent people, then singularity will have occurred.

From the 1960s up until today, we have seen ever more rapid technological development, leading to the automation of many functions and processes in working life. Most recently, digitization has started to automate administrative processes and functions in working life. This means that the question of how few people are needed to complete tasks becomes highly relevant. Against this background, the concept of work will take on a new meaning. We may experience mass unemployment with major social challenges, or we may see the development of completely different ways of working, such as a three-hour day plus an extra three hours of skills development. We may also experience mass unemployment linked to some form of minimum wage. Our intention here is not to highlight what form new things may take, but to show that developments in productivity may make a good life possible for many, or a miserable life possible for most. Technology is there to tackle challenges, and the political system is there to resolve the social challenges posed by technological

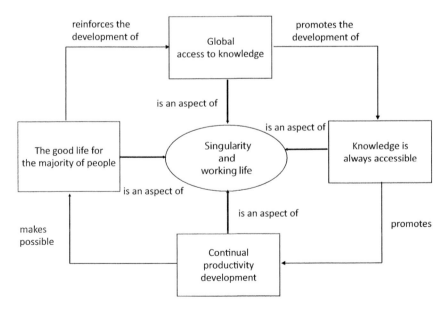

Figure 5.3 Possible consequences of singularity on working life.

development. This technology will lead to enormous economic growth. The question is simply how this economic growth will be distributed.

We have shown how singularity can impact working life in Figure 5.3. This is, of course, only one perspective of a possible development; but this is the perspective we have argued for, described and analysed in this chapter.

Notes

1 An informat is a robot that is linked to other similar robots, with the assistance of artificial intelligence. In this way, a medical robot, for example will be able to obtain in real time all the information it needs within its functional area, as new knowledge is developed.
2 It is uncertain exactly who is the author of this quote, as it has also been attributed to others, such as Niels Bohr and Storm Petersen.
3 The citation from Lincoln can be found in Goertzel and Goertzel, 2015b: 32.
4 We can study trends and cyclical patterns by various methods, such as natural resources analyses, analyses of economic cycles, patent analyses, cultural change analyses, statistical meta-analyses, anthropological meta-analyses, conceptual generalizations, analogue thinking, geopolitical investigations, innovation analyses and so on; there are also many specific methods used in studies of the future, such as the Delphi method, phenomenological modelling, curve fitting, extrapolation, indicator analysis, cyclical analysis, black box prediction and interactive planning methodology, to name a few.
5 Written on the cover of Ross, 2016.
6 "Mirroring" is understood here in relation to the person the intelligent robot helps. For instance, the intelligent robot may be a nano computer that is implanted in someone's ear to help them by making suggestions in certain challenging social interactions.
7 Those who are interested in exact prognoses can refer to Eurostat, amongst other sources, to find figures for the various countries.
8 See Hewitt's (2015: 101) definition of personal singularity.
9 In Hanson, EMS stands for "emulate the human brain".
10 Cited in Mosco (2017: 57).
11 https://en.wikipedia.org/wiki/Luddite.
12 Some date the internet back to 1969, but only those with expert technical knowledge were able to send and receive emails at that time. It was not until 1993 that people had general access to what we now know as the internet (Mosco, 2017: 1).
13 https://en.wikipedia.org/wiki/Darknet.
14 Matthew, 13:12. However, in the Bible the saying refers to faith, not to material wealth.
15 Trumpism here refers to the politics that emerged as a consequence of globalization, which materialized through the election of Donald Trump as president of the United States. This applies to the areas of politics, economics, culture and social relations.
16 https://en.wikipedia.org/wiki/Gaia_hypothesis.

References

Ackoff, R.L. (1981). *Creating the corporate future: Plan or be planned for*, John Wiley & Sons, New York.

Bunge, M. (1985). *Philosophy of Science and Technology. Part II*, Reidel, Dordrecht.

Goertzel, B., & Goertzel, T. (2015a). Introduction, in B. Goertzel & T. Goertzel, (eds.), *The end of the beginning: Life, society and economy on the brink of the singularity*, pp. 6–31, Humanity+ Press, New York.

Goertzel, B., & Goertzel, T. (2015b). Predicting the age of post-human intelligence, in B. Goertzel & T. Goertzel (eds.) *The end of the beginning: Life, society and economy on the brink of the singularity*, pp. 32–57, Humanity+ Press, New York.

Hanson, R. (2016). *The age of EM: Love and Life when robots rule the Earth*, Oxford University Press, Oxford.

Hewitt, J. (2015). Implanting post-human intelligence in human bodies, in B. Goertzel & T. Goertzel (eds.), *The end of the beginning: Life, society and economy on the brink of the singularity*, pp. 96–109, Humanity Press, New York.

Huang, Y., Wu, H., & Liu, H. (eds.) (2017). *Intelligent robotics and applications: 10th international conference*, ICIRA 2017, Wuhan, China, August 16–18, 2017, proceedings, part III, Springer, Cham.

Johannessen, J.-A. (2017). *Innovations lead to economic crises*, Palgrave Macmillan, Cham.

Johannessen, J.-A. (2018a). *Automation, innovation and economic crises: Surviving the Fourth Industrial Revolution*, Routledge, London.

Johannessen, J.-A. (2018b). *The Workplace of the future: The Fourth Industrial Revolution, the precariat and the end of hierarchies?* Routledge, London.

Johannessen, J.-A. (2019). *From democratic capitalism to feudal capitalism in the Fourth Industrial Revolution*, Routledge, London.

Karabarbounis, L., & Neiman, B. (2014). The global decline of the labor share, *Quarterly Journal of Economics*, 129(1): 61–103.

Kurzweil, R. (2006). *The singularity is near*, Penguin, New York.

Miller, J.G. (1978). *Living systems*, McGraw-Hill, New York.

Mosco, V. (2017). *Becoming digital: Towards a post internet society*, Emerald, London.

Nazareth, D. (2015). Robotics and AI: Impact felt on every aspect of our future world, in B. Goertzel & T. Goertzel (eds.), *The end of the beginning: Life, society and economy on the brink of the singularity*, pp. 131–148, Humanity+ Press, New York.

Ross, A. (2016). *The industries of the future*, Simon & Schuster, New York.

Shepherd, S.V. (ed.) (2019). *The Wiley handbook of evolutionary neuroscience*, Wiley-Blackwell, London.

Smith, Q., & Jokie, A. (eds.) (2003). *Consciousness: New philosophical perspectives*, Clarendon Press, Oxford.

Van Quine, W.O., Churchland, P.S., & Føllesdal, D. (2013). *Word and object*, MIT Press, Cambridge, MA.

6 Singularity and education

Introduction

The key ideas in this chapter:

- Today the focus is largely on educating young students to prepare them for a particular profession, or to work in a particular field. In the near future, this will be only a minor aspect of a university's role. Lifelong learning is becoming a practical reality, rather than a slogan.
- Four areas of competence will be particularly in demand in the Fourth Industrial Revolution: coding competence; communicative competence; team-working competence; and problem-solving competence.
- The majority of non-elite national and local universities will take on the role of supervising students, as well as such functions as legitimizing and issuing diplomas for consortia of the world's leading universities.

The possibility that intelligent robots may take over most human functions has been noted by most authors in the field of future research (Goertzel & Goertzel, 2015a, 2015b; Huang et al., 2017; Mosco, 2017). However, despite this, few if any have so far examined how technological singularity and the Fourth Industrial Revolution will transform higher education. That is the topic of this chapter.

The Fourth Industrial Revolution can be understood as being a metamorphosis on a par with the transition from a hunter-gatherer society to an agrarian society, or from an agrarian society to an industrial society. In both of these revolutions, people had to learn something qualitatively new in order to gain maximum benefit from the upheaval. Gradually, parts of the educational system came to evolve around food production, and later around industrial production, information technology and digitization. In the same way, it seems reasonable to assume that the Fourth Industrial Revolution will change the educational system. Since intelligent robots and artificial intelligence will be the driving forces behind the Fourth Industrial Revolution, the same forces will also be significant for the educational system. It seems reasonable to assume that in the same way as we tried to abolish illiteracy, coding will become an important part of the whole educational system.

Just as hunters were despatched to the plains to plough fields, and farm workers were sent from villages to the cities to work in factories, so industrial workers will become knowledge workers (Ross, 2016). Like the first two developments, the latter development will force qualitative changes within the educational system (Doucet & Evers, 2018).

Just as the innovations of the first two revolutions resulted in the value of past experience being eroded, much of our experience from the industrial society will have little or no value. Those aspects of the industrial society which were felt to be safe and stable have already been replaced by change processes and uncertainty. Just as the hunter had to learn how to use the plough in the transition from a hunter-gatherer society to an agrarian society, and the farm worker had to learn to operate a spinning machine in the transition to the industrial society, the industrial worker will have to take on new roles and functions in the innovation society. Relevant in this context is the probable time-lag in the way of thinking from the industrial society to the innovation society. Specifically, thinking from the industrial society will slow down the transition to the innovation economy and so prevent it from flourishing in the initial stages.

There have always been predictions of unemployment when new technology is introduced, ever since the 1800s when the Luddites smashed weaving machines, because they feared the new machines would take away their jobs. In the short perspective, those who ended up unemployed because of the introduction of labour-saving machines were proved to be right. However, from a slightly longer time perspective, we have seen that new technology generates new jobs at a higher salary, because productivity increases. Historically, we have also seen how the trade union movement struggled to establish the introduction of an eight-hour day. A similar development may also take place in the Fourth Industrial Revolution. However, while automation has previously largely affected jobs in production, the new technology will further automate production, but in addition, information and administration processes in businesses and public administration will also be automated. This may lead to two possibilities. The first is mass unemployment; a second possibility is a reduction in working hours from an eight-hour day to a three-hour day, that is, a sharing of work; employees will receive an increase in wages due to a large productivity increase resulting from the utilization of the new technology. In order to adapt to the considerable changes, the three-hour workday may be supplemented by an additional three hours of skills development.

If anything close to this happens, then the education sector will be completely transformed. One of the changes in this sector is likely to be the use of intelligent robots and artificial intelligence (Doucet & Evers, 2018). Regardless of new technology, the teacher will still have an important role to play, especially in the guidance of the student. This also applies to those seeking lifelong learning through shorter or longer courses.

The teacher's function will change with the introduction of the new technology, but the teacher's role will change to a lesser extent. We will examine how the major global changes will have an impact on the individual student. The innovation processes that take place in technology, the economic system, the political system and the workplace are all important for how we design our education system, and for the individual teacher's everyday life.

The Fourth Industrial Revolution and its impact on the educational system directly influence those who design education policy, as well as the individual teacher. Technology is a means of communicating information and developing knowledge. Understood in this way, the new technology, and how it is used in the educational system, however intelligent it may inherently be, is still only a means of achieving something. For instance, this may involve reaching an understanding of what constitutes empathy. It could also involve understanding what it means to help those who have been humiliated and offended. Or, one may wish to examine how we can develop and maintain a healthy and sustainable society. Investigating and teaching both these themes and others, presupposes our having teachers who can act as role models for pupils and students.

On the threshold of the Fourth Industrial Revolution, it is important to understand how we can develop practical strategies, overall models and policies in the field of education. The education system is not significantly different from any other system where major changes are taking place. People are reluctant to change and anxious as to how the changes may affect their jobs. With regard to expectations concerning the approaching new technology, with its intelligent robots and artificial intelligence, the individual teacher is affected by hopes, anxiety, challenges and fears.

New forces are becoming more visible in the education sector. It is not just new technology with intelligent robots that affects us – globalization has an impact on most of us as well. This development has led to very great economic inequalities (Dorling, 2015; McGill, 2016). Policy developers in the education sector should create a policy that takes this development into account. Will they let it continue, will they do something about the uneven allocation of resources, or will they take a neutral position concerning the growing economic inequality?

Employability is a cornerstone of university education, that is, how study programmes are linked to the job market. One positive aspect concerning the development of intelligent robots and artificial intelligence is that millions of people will no longer have to do boring and tedious routine work. Both society and the individual will dramatically change as a result of the new intelligent technology, which will have more logical intelligence than humans. In order to cope with these changes, employees will need to understand the consequences of the technological development. Amongst other things, it will be an important responsibility of the universities to educate these people, so they are able to tackle the new situation.

Another task that universities already have, but which will become more important in the future, is the continual education of employees, that is, ensuring that those who already have work are constantly updated on the latest developments and knowledge within their field. The rapid rate of change and increasing complexity in the outside world will most likely transform the organization, structure and focus of universities. Today the focus is largely on educating young students to prepare them for a particular profession, or to work in a particular field. In the near future, this will be only a minor aspect of a university's role. The most important task will be the continual competence development of those who have work. Lifelong learning is becoming a practical reality, rather than just a slogan. Such a change of focus will also bring about changes in the distribution channels of education and result in the creation of new educational models. In both this and the next chapter, we will draw a roadmap for the new university that will take into consideration technology, the distribution of education, new educational models, management and organization, and how these factors relate to each other.

We will investigate the following question: What impact will singularity have on the educational system?

To answer this question, we have developed three sub-questions:

1   What impact will singularity have on educational technology?
2   What impact will singularity have on the universities' curricula?
3   What impact will singularity have on the development of new educational models?

The introduction is shown in Figure 6.1, which also shows how this chapter is organized.

New educational technology

The question we are investigating here is as follows: What impact will singularity have on educational technology?

Artificial intelligence is just one of the things with which robots and computers will be equipped. Robots will have artificial eyes, artificial emotions, artificial ears, artificial feet and arms, the capacity to conduct artificial relationships and so on (Aoun, 2017: x). Achieving this will be dependent on competence in different fields of technology and in different disciplines, including biology, synthetic biology, nanotechnology, communications technology and so on. It will be essential for the whole educational system, from Year 1 at primary school to PhD level, to reflect this development, in one way or another. Failure to do so would cause the betrayal of an entire generation, whose members will find it difficult to gain access to the labour market (Ainley, 2016).

Industrial robots are already a familiar feature in many industries. In 2015, sales of industrial robots increased by 15 per cent over the previous year, indicating that there is already a strong trend towards the automation of production (Aoun, 2017: x). Demand will increase for people with the skills necessary to develop and apply industrial robots.

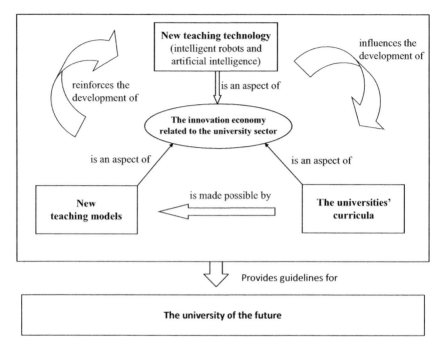

Figure 6.1 Singularity and education.

Robots are already analysing stock market trends, meaning that stockbrokers will find there is less demand for their particular competences. In addition, there are increasing numbers of robots in the banking and financial sectors, meaning that banks need to employ fewer and fewer people. Basically, banks are asking themselves about the minimum number of people they need in order to conduct banking operations.

Drones are already replacing soldiers. Increasing numbers of drones are also being used in the farming and fishing sectors, as well as in the transport sector, among others. Accordingly, there will be strong demand for people who are competent in drone technology.

The health care sector is likely to experience the greatest demand for competence in the areas of artificial intelligence, big data analytics and intelligent robots. In the majority of highly complex situations in medical research, where there is an enormous amount of information available, no doctor – not even a specialist – would be able to access all the necessary information. Intelligent robots and informats will be able to access this information, however. Doctors can ask these robots for advice and receive guidance when diagnosing, and prescribing medication for patients. Accordingly, competence in the use of this technology will be important for medical personnel. There will also be a demand for people with the competence to develop and maintain these intelligent medical robots. In practice, this means that medical technology, and the engineers who have mastered this technology, will be just as important in a hospital environment as doctors and nurses.

In the educational sector, the same types of robots, which will have access to big data in various fields, will initially serve as assistants or "co-pilots" for teaching staff. The robots will scan and analyse different areas of the field in question and will then assist the teacher or lecturer in disseminating the relevant knowledge. In addition, the "co-pilot" will have access to data about each individual pupil's or student's level of progress and will be aware of their particular needs. Accordingly, teaching can be individualized in a way that would be impossible for a single teacher to achieve. In addition, the "co-pilot" will be able to employ emotional scanning and sensors, as well as access to big data, in order to analyse each pupil's or student's emotional state in real time. In this way, teaching can be adjusted in real time to take account of each individual's capacity at that particular time.

It will be possible to use these co-pilots in the various stages of the educational system. In this way, the co-pilot will become an important technology for individualized learning, which will enable teachers to do their job much better than they could without the co-pilot. However, the point here, as with coding competence, is that we should make a distinction between short-term and long-term perspectives. Up until around 2040, the co-pilot will be a helper for the teacher. After 2040, the co-pilot will, to a large extent, be able to perform the teacher function alone; in such a situation, the teacher will be given another function, first as a co-pilot to the robot, and then later, a completely different function in the educational system in relation to the individual student. In other words, in the long term, the intelligent robots will also replace employees with relatively high competence. Whereas earlier in the history of automation, it was first unskilled workers, and then a little later skilled workers, who were replaced in the labour market, singularity will also replace people with very high competence. This does not necessarily mean that we will end up with mass unemployment, but this may happen if nothing is done to address this problem at the political and policy level.

Against this background, it is not difficult to envisage that intelligent robots will transform the entire educational system, as well as the economic and competence structure that is built up around the needs of the industrial society. If this scenario is somewhat in agreement with the developments that emerge, then the entire educational system will need to undergo a metamorphosis, i.e. the larva must be transformed into a butterfly. When the social reality changes, the educational system will need to adjust very quickly; if not, the students will end up with an outdated education by the time they enter the new labour market.

Up until now, computers are programmed, whereas in the very near future they will be able to learn by accessing global data and using sensors that scan the outside world (Aoun, 2017: ix). It is this revolutionary change that scares people – the idea that robots with artificial intelligence will no longer need human input (Ford, 2015: xvi).

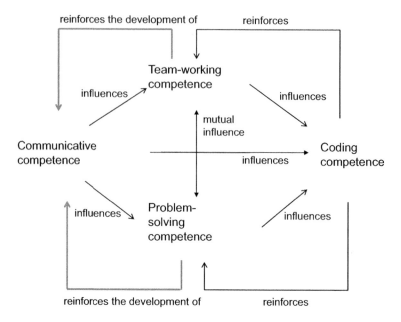

Figure 6.2 Competencies that will be necessary in the future.

On the one hand, it is an accepted truth that coding expertise will be important for everyone in the near future. On the other hand, some assume that coding skills will not be so important further on in the future, because intelligent robots will be able to encode themselves via access to global data through various sensors. This contradictory understanding makes it very diffi-cult to build up a stable educational system that will be of help to individuals, businesses and society (Brynjolfsson & McAfee, 2014: 9). It is reasonable to assume that for this aspect too, one can make a distinction between the near and the distant future. There will be an increasing need for coding expertise up until 2040, while after this date, when it is believed singularity will occur, it is reasonable to believe that artificial intelligence will provide itself with coding, through sensors and access to global data.

However, we do know that four areas of competence (Figure 6.2) will be particularly in demand in the Fourth Industrial Revolution: coding compe-tence; communicative competence; team-working competence; and problem-solving competence (Atkinson, 2010; Murphy, 2016; Ross, 2016). Many jobs will disappear in the near future, some new ones will be created, and others will be transformed as a result of the new technology. However, the educa-tional system is currently designed for the needs of the industrial society. We risk giving students an education that is out of date and for which there is no demand (Ainley, 2014; Aoun, 2017).

The innovation economy is defined and shaped by new technology. Therefore, the educational system should take this into account, and design educational programmes that are suited to future needs.

In the First, Second and Third Industrial Revolutions, newly educated young people were able to find various white-collar jobs. When the Fourth Industrial Revolution approaches singularity in around 2040, many of these jobs will be automated. Consequently, the need for people in such administrative positions will be greatly reduced, and will be much less than the number of students who complete an education in this field today.

As before, young people will be able to use education to climb up the social and economic ladder. However, there will be more people entering higher education, but fewer people who are in demand, in a market where most functions will be automated. This would indicate that those who do get jobs will also receive a higher salary, and those who do not get permanent positions will have to compete for temporary contracts on an hourly basis (Avent, 2017: 5). If the assumptions of Avent and several other researchers are correct (Johannessen, 2018a, 2018b, 2019), then we have a choice between mass unemployment for highly educated people, or a reconstruction of society and the educational system.

This reconstruction may take many forms. One way would be to have a three-hour day working for an employer, and an extra three hours of skills development. In this way, we would avoid mass unemployment and a universal basic income. In Figure 6.3, we have presented four scenarios of a possible future and the challenges for the educational system. As can be seen from the scenarios, the educational system is closely linked to the outside world where the education will be used. This is of course nothing new. The point is that when the rate of change and complexity increase, it is important to continually adapt the educational system, so that it meets the challenges of a changing world.

The emergence of new industries will require new expertise, which will be provided by the educational system. These industries will most likely be related to robotic design, robotic manufacturing, robotic customization, intelligent robotics subcontractors, as well as to various functions and processes of artificial intelligence development, nanotechnology, synthetic biology, new computer technology, molecular technology, new educational technology based on holographic technology, health technology, transport technology, agora robots, pet robots, emotional robots, sex robots, relational robots, care robots, new material technology, new automation technology, etc. In other words, taking into account the above description, it is evident that there will be a need to train millions of young people so they will be equipped to work with the new technology. This is all well and good. However, we need to put this into perspective. Already, by 2024 in the US, it is projected that there will be a need for approximately 4.4 million workers with high expertise in some of these new professions; the total American workforce is projected to be 163.7 million in the same period. The workforce of the traditional major companies such as General

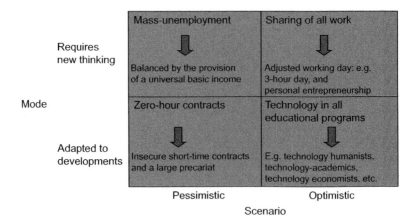

Figure 6.3 Four scenarios showing the possible roles of the educational system in the future.

Motors was 600,000 at its peak. In contrast, at the start of the Fourth Industrial Revolution, Google, a company typical of the new economy, employed around only 60,000 workers in 2015, one tenth that of General Motors' figure. We have also seen a similar development regarding the case of Kodak and Instagram, where Instagram, although they had very few employees, was able to take over much of Kodak's business (Aoun, 2017: xiv).

The above description suggests that in the future we will be facing mass unemployment on a scale never witnessed before. The assumption for this pessimistic view is of course that we do nothing to remedy the situation. Figure 6.3 shows that we can organize society differently, for example by sharing the work, by introducing a three-hour day. However, we may also choose not to implement an overall plan, but instead continually adapt to changes in the outside world. Figure 6.3 shows that if we do not attempt to implement an overall plan, we risk ending up in a situation with zero-hour contracts, uncertain working conditions and the emergence of a large precariat (Johannessen, 2018b).

With regard to the four scenarios above, it should be noted that globalization is likely to enhance technology development and increase automation. The reasoning is simple. Globalization promotes competition, and thus a stronger focus on costs and productivity. In addition to globalization, demographic changes will also affect society. If the political system does not respond to these new developments, then the growing economic inequality that is already evident will only be reinforced (Johannessen, 2018a). The educational system will need to relate to these developments in the outside world.

There is one factor that cannot be emphasized enough, and that is the survival instinct. When people see that mass unemployment and an insecure working life are becoming a reality, we will very likely also see an increase in status for so-called personal entrepreneurship. Personal entrepreneurship will not necessarily create any new businesses, but will be of the one-man-business type, such as cleaning jobs, network taxi driving, hamburger kiosks, freelance travel guides, short-term contracts for transport companies, pizza deliveries, Google coding, proofreading for newspapers and magazines and so on, otherwise known as the "gig economy" (Kessler, 2018). Although personal entrepreneurship does not necessarily create any new businesses, it creates expectations of opportunities and a belief that it pays to be creative.[1] The point in this context is that entrepreneurship in all its forms will increase in status, both personal entrepreneurship, and also entrepreneurship and innovation that lead to new businesses, not least social entrepreneurship. The development of the "gig economy" may also be viewed as an offspring of the precariat and "the working poor" (Johannessen, 2018a, 2018b, 2019).

The emerging personal entrepreneurship is a sign of the "struggle for survival" that is becoming more evident in the current economic climate, something that is also becoming visible in the education sector – for instance, the demands from students to be able to acquire their knowledge "intravenously" in a way that will guarantee them a job and income after graduation. This increases the level of frustration with educational programmes, because there is an expectation that all knowledge that is disseminated should have immediate relevance. This will most likely lead to an increasing intolerance for reflection generally, and for reflection on ethics and cultural and historical knowledge, specifically. The students will want "value for money", and will demand study programmes that address current issues, not study programmes that were designed five to ten years ago. The teachers will be pressured into becoming suppliers of a type of "Wikipedia knowledge". This type of thinking will reinforce the demand for intelligent robots and artificial intelligence as assistants to teachers, because intelligent robots will be superior to teachers in disseminating this type of knowledge, that is, "Wikipedia knowledge".

It is beyond doubt that working life will change dramatically in the not too distant future. Similarly, it is highly probable that the educational system will also change as a result of changes in the outside world. However, no one can say with any certainty exactly how the educational system will change. The four scenarios in Figure 6.3 suggest some aspects of the upcoming changes.

The universities' curricula

The question we are investigating here is as follows: How will technological, economic and social singularity affect university teaching plans and curricula?

Education has at least two purposes:

1   The development of the individual.
2   Equipping people with the competences they need to perform a job.

Over the last hundred years, education has been used as a springboard to get a better job than our parents had. Without a college education, most would find it difficult to rise above their parents' social status and position. However, there is much to suggest that using education to climb up the social class and economic ladder is about to come to an end. It seems that education will now become a necessary condition for having a job at all. A college education in the near future will only function as an economic parachute, so that one does not fall further down the economic ladder. The point here is that it is not education that has changed, but the economic system. At the start of the Fourth Industrial Revolution, and when singularity occurs in the future, this development will only be reinforced (Johannessen, 2018b, 2019). This is the main reason why the educational system will also have to change, not only regarding content, but in how we distribute education and learning.

Those without a master's degree will find that they are slipping down the economic ladder to insecure, poorly paid jobs and hourly paid contracts. To sum up: previously, higher education was a necessary if not sufficient prerequisite to get a well-paid job. In the near future, higher education will be a necessary prerequisite to avoid falling too far down the economic ladder.

As a general rule, university education has always been linked to what society has considered to be respected and valued professions, such as law, medicine, economics, engineering and so on. Previously, it was considered that the clergy, humanists, philosophers and the like contributed important values to society. Education linked to such intellectual and specialist occupations is becoming less important, as society increasingly demands so-called utilitarian and market-related knowledge.

In the near future, it seems reasonable to assume that in the Fourth Industrial Revolution the following fields will be more highly valued by society: technology, neuroscience (brain science), biology and chemistry. Of course, there will also be a need for other types of knowledge and professions, such as lawyers, economists, humanists and so on. The point here is that there will be a difference between what is considered most valuable to society and what is necessary merely to make the wheels of society go round. Consequently, those students who wish to climb up the economic and social ladder should choose an education that society (read: the market) values, demands and is willing to pay for.

Today, education is distributed in many ways, such as on campus, online, at work, as modules together with work, etc. While the universities previously required students to be physically present on campus, today one can complete a degree, up to and including PhD level, without being on campus. In the future, the "campus" will increasingly be a virtual university online. Students at undergraduate level will still attend their studies on campus, but as soon as they begin a master's degree, alternating between studies and work will be offered as a worthwhile alternative. The reason is that working life is constantly changing, and in order to keep up to date with crucial competencies, the student should also have employment that is related to their studies.

Knowledge of "facts", a type of Wikipedia competence, was required in the industrial society. In the knowledge society and the innovation economy, knowledge of facts is uninteresting as a university competence, because this type of "knowledge" is only one key-press away from us, or we can get the answer instantly from an intelligent little robot we carry around with us, that is perhaps integrated into a watch or spectacles, and the like.

We do not need to use our capacity and time to acquire knowledge of the largest rivers and capitals of the various countries, the population of Mali, the population of New York, and so on. Of course, this can be interesting as a party game, but knowledge of "facts" and Wikipedia competence will not be of interest in the innovation economy. Instead, there will be a demand for education that focuses on a type of creative intelligent robot competence. In order to facilitate this type of education, the universities will need to redesign all their curricula (Aoun, 2017: xvii). It is not technology facts that are at the core of such creative intelligent robot competence, but the creative element, which is a necessary prerequisite for developing the innovative new. Technology, creativity and neuroscience will become crucial elements in the primary sought-after competence needed to design and maintain the intelligent robots. What society values is what the universities should deliver, and this will be innovation in the innovation economy. Therefore, creativity, flexibility and complexity will be important elements. The necessary competences needed to promote innovation include idea development, knowledge-sharing, communication skills and co-creation. The overall competence that is needed to bind the other competencies together into a functioning whole is ethics. This refers to ethics relating to innovation development and the application of innovation, for example ethics relating to the design and application of intelligent robots. These robots can be autonomous or interconnected in a network. When intelligent robots work side by side with people, it is important that the skills of the people are complementary to the intelligent robots.

The various competencies are shown in Figure 6.4.

It seems reasonable to assume that the curricula in the various studies will be divided into two. One part will be related to the specific subject. For instance, medical studies will have subject-specific curricula, as will law, economics, management, etc. In addition to the subject-specific part of the curricula, Figure 6.4 shows what type of competence will be important for all subjects to include. There are many ways to organize the five levels of competence that appear in Figure 6.4. One way to organize these five levels would be to think in terms of a five-year master of science study programme. With this in mind, the first year would focus on level 1 and then the further levels successively up to the fifth year, where level 5, ethics and systems thinking, would be given special attention. The inclusion of ethics is self-explanatory. Systems thinking is included so that students will be able to gain an understanding of the relationships between the parts and the whole, as well as the increasing complexity of the outside world.

There is a very simple reason for the competencies shown in Figure 6.4. Even though Joseph Aoun does not specifically mention the five levels of Figure 6.4

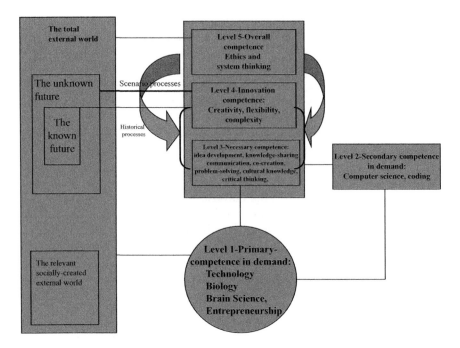

Figure 6.4 Competencies that will be needed in the future innovation economy.

for the innovation economy, he gives a very good reason for why these competencies are important: "people can no longer thrive in a digitized world using merely analogue tools" (Aoun, 2017: xix). I also agree with Aoun that subject-specific competence and technological competence are not sufficient (Aoun, 2017: xix). In a world where the parts are fragmented and where it is difficult to see the connection between the parts, it is important that employees are able to reach an understanding of the relationships between the parts. They can acquire this by adopting a systems-perspective approach to the part and the whole, so that patterns may more easily be discovered (Aoun, 2017: xix). This is the idea behind level 5, where ethics and systems thinking are introduced.

New teaching models

The question we are investigating here is as follows: What impact will singularity have on the development of new educational models?

The more that teaching structures change as a result of changes in the surrounding world, the more that changes will occur in the philosophy of education itself. Teaching models have already changed to become more interactive, compared to the lecture-based model, where a knowledgeable person taught people who lacked that knowledge what they needed to know (Hoidn, 2016).

We have seen a general trend whereby universities have attempted to develop teaching models with a greater resemblance to interactions in working life (Carson, 2018). There is a historical obstacle, however, which relates to students' expectations and lecturers' established practices. Due to these two factors, the lecture-based model continues to dominate, even though pedagogical research tells us that this is not the most effective teaching model (Hoidn, 2016). One reason is that students arrive at university with the idea that they will get topped up with knowledge, as though they are empty tanks that need to be filled. They think of people who are knowledgeable about their subjects as cans of knowledge, which will fill up the students' own "knowledge cans". Throughout history, teachers have prioritized lectures as the means of disseminating knowledge, and they will be reluctant to change their practice. An explanation for this reluctance to change may lie in prospect theory (Tversky & Kahneman, 1974, 1981, 1983, 2000).

If universities fail to change their lecture-based teaching models, then they will become outdated. This would most likely result in private companies taking over the dissemination of knowledge. It is essential that new teaching models are in harmony with changes in the rest of the world (Hoidn, 2016). In practice, this means that the new technology will be linked to the new teaching models (Carson, 2018).

If universities listen to what employers say they are looking for in prospective employees, it will then be easy for them to develop new teaching models that conform to these requirements. In Figure 6.4 above, we have described the competences that will be in demand in the future. If one were to suggest teaching models based on these competences, one could describe them as problem-based learning and process-based learning. In process-based learning, as we understand it here and as it is described in the Appendix, the objective is to educate students to be professional practitioners in a particular field, as well as creative individuals who can develop the field to new heights.

When teaching models are developed in academia in the era of singularity, it will be crucial not to think of bachelor's and master's degrees as representing the conclusion of an educational process. Rather, they will be the basis for a continual process of lifelong learning that will take place through the interaction of workplaces and universities. This will require new approaches to distributing learning. Firstly, the crucial factor will not be a student's age, but instead the knowledge that the student is seeking, regardless of his or her age. Secondly, it will no longer be the case that knowledge is acquired at university and then applied in the workplace. The new model for universities will involve interaction between business and academia. This is the point of intersection where the new innovation economy will present universities with both challenges and opportunities.

One such opportunity which is already available is through free online courses in a variety of subjects, offered by the leading universities in the world. These courses have been named MOOCs (massive open online courses) (Ford, 2015: 136). It is just a matter of time before the leading universities develop a joint overall framework in relation to various subject-specific educational programmes. In the future, such an overall framework will enable students to complete a full bachelor's or master's degree online and have it conferred by a university such as Harvard, Wharton, MIT, Oxford, Cambridge, etc. The idea is that students choose courses from the overall framework of the various collaborating online universities. The final diploma will then be awarded by the partners/consortia, such as Harvard and MIT, or Oxford and Cambridge, etc. Students will be able to acquire knowledge free when they take these online courses, but they will have to pay for the final diploma, for example a master of science degree at MIT/Harvard. In the various countries, the growing competition between universities will most probably result in the less well-known universities losing in the competition with those universities with the best reputations.

One example that illustrates the entrepreneurial opportunities that exist for the type of free online course referred to above, as well as a possible future source of income, is an introductory course in artificial intelligence that was offered by Stanford University; in 2011, they received 160,000 enrolled students from 190 countries for this particular course; 23,000 students completed the entire course and received a certificate from Stanford stating that they had successfully completed it. The students who signed up for the course ranged in age from 10 to 70 years. From Lithuania alone, the number of online students who enrolled in the course exceeded the total number of students enrolled at campus at Stanford (Ford, 2015: 137).

Despite this, it has been shown that these free courses, which are not integrated into a full university degree, do not retain students' interest for long. Student interest declines, and many students drop out after only one to two weeks. Another challenge for the MOOCs is that the students who graduate having taken the online course perform qualitatively more poorly than those who take the course on campus (Ford, 2015: 138). However, the point we are making here is not that MOOCs are the solution, but that they indicate an educational trend. Consequently, the new opportunities that may emerge can result in many universities losing out in the competition between universities.

It seems reasonable to assume that business opportunities lie in offering an integrated degree in collaboration with a consortium of leading universities, which can, for instance, confer a bachelor or master of science degree to students. In addition, one can imagine this consortium collaborating with local universities that can offer guidance on campus, organize examinations and carry out administrative tasks, etc. In this way, the students will receive personal follow-up and an assurance that administrative processes will be carried out efficiently. When such a business model is launched, it will transform the university sector in many countries.

One driver that will promote the development of a situation where the elite universities provide the content and delivery of knowledge is the possibility offered by digitization to increase the numbers enrolled at elite universities such as Stanford, MIT, Harvard and the like. When the numbers enrolling at such universities are high enough, it is probable that the fees will be considerably less than the $40,000 that students on campus currently pay to attend, for example, Stanford (Ford, 2015: 140). One important question is the following: Who would take up a very large loan for an education at a third- or fourth-tier university, when they can get the same education much cheaper at an international elite university? It is assumed that the students will also have the opportunity to attend a campus locally. If such a development takes off, it will completely transform higher education.

When, not if, education is digitized through MOOCs and similar arrangements, the preference will be for education on a large scale, which will affect any university that fails to transform their educational programmes using the new educational model. This may lead either to bankruptcies or else to mergers in the education sector. The latter possibility is the most probable, because the large-scale benefits of large universities can significantly reduce the cost of education.

When digitization and intelligent robots become a reality in most universities, the competition for students will become global. The best students will be attracted by reputation, quality and price. In this transformation, many universities will either go bankrupt or become local departments for the major elite universities. Local universities will probably take on the role of supervising students, as well as functions such as legitimizing and issuing diplomas.

Higher education is big business. In 2014, in the UK alone, the industry employed 750,000 people (Ford, 2015: 144). If digitization leads to major changes in the industry, it will affect many people. No one knows specifically who will be affected, but it is reasonable to believe that the universities that have the best reputation, and are best known for quality, will drive the digital development on a global basis. Furthermore, there is a possibility that the smaller universities will have to refocus and become guidance institutions for the large universities. Moreover, it is also very likely that they will hire PhD students instead of having a large permanent staff of professionals. This is nothing new. We have already seen trends pointing in this direction in the UK and the United States (Ford, 2015: 145).

The universities that are likely to be worst affected are the middling institutions in terms of reputation and quality. These universities will try to compete with the better universities – some will succeed, but most will lose in the global competition, because students wish to receive their education at elite universities. For the individual student, such global competition is likely to be positive, for two reasons. Firstly, the cost of completing a bachelor's or master's degree will drop sharply. Secondly, they will receive a diploma from an elite university, at the same time as they receive guidance and follow-up locally at the universities that choose to collaborate in order to meet the challenges of digitization. For most students globally, a diploma from Oxford, Cambridge, MIT, Harvard, Stanford, etc. will be preferred, rather than a diploma from a third-tier or fourth-tier university, even though this may be a public university offering free education. The scenarios described above will most likely weaken the national public universities that have middling or poor reputations. These may easily become third-tier universities.

An important point in this context is that the students who graduate in the future will face a labour market where automation has taken over many of the jobs they could previously have applied for. This development suggests that in the future students will attempt to secure jobs by applying to the elite universities. They can do this at a lower cost than currently possible, by taking a digitized education offered by an elite university that collaborates with a local university.

When employers discover the opportunities that candidates have to acquire a university degree from an elite university, also locally, they are likely to prefer graduates with elite university diplomas. This will put further pressure on those universities with a lesser reputation, and we may end up with a clear division of three or four levels of universities based on reputation and quality.

Conclusion

The question we have investigated in this chapter is as follows: What impact will singularity have on the educational system?

Singularity is the essence of the Fourth Industrial Revolution. Intelligent robots, artificial intelligence, artificial emotions and artificial relationships are some of the new technologies we are seeing in their early stages, as we stand on the threshold of the Fourth Industrial Revolution. This is the background to the enormous pressure to change which is now being experienced by the educational system, in particular the universities. New technology is affecting both how universities are organized and, in a very fundamental way, their teaching models. University teaching plans and curricula will also change when technology becomes the central component. They will become focused on intelligent robots, artificial intelligence and, to a certain extent, artificial emotions and artificial relationships.

Some people refer to this as the Digital Age, others as the innovation economy, yet others as the Fourth Industrial Revolution, and others again as the knowledge society. Our point is simply that something new is in the process of breaking through, and we do not know exactly what is going to materialize. We also do not know what the consequences will be of whatever does materialize. What we do know, however, is that everyone will be affected, not least educational institutions, in one way or other.

In addition to technology, the political system is also in a state of change. The prevailing political ideology is based on neoclassical, and partly neoliberal, thinking. For universities in the Western world, this has led to an increase in competition, benchmarking, assessments, the development of indicators and a strong focus on leadership and governance.

The short answer to the question posed above is that singularity will promote the development of new or expanded teaching plans, whereby technology and coding skills will become an important part of all education. In addition, most

Level 4 Integration model	(Business world ⟶ Educational world)
Level 3 Learning model	Process and problem-based learning
Level 2 Organisation model	Team-based learning
Level 1 Content model (Curriculum)	Coding, part-whole understanding, understanding of patterns

Figure 6.5 The impact of singularity on the educational system.

professions will be "technologized": a doctor will become a medical engineer, a nurse will become a nursing technician, and so on. This will also cause changes to the teaching models used by universities.

The core of singularity is technology, a technology that resembles human intelligence and, a little further into the future, human emotions and relationships. New teaching models will emerge in the wake of these developments. It is very probable that this type of teaching model will be focused on an integration of universities and businesses, because the prevailing ideology is that universities should deliver the knowledge demanded by private- and public-sector businesses and bureaucracies. This kind of integration will have the potential to provide a seamless transition between universities and businesses. It will also be supported by the idea that learning is a lifelong process. While the logic of the industrial society has been that learning takes place at school, and that people then apply what they have learned at work, the innovation economy promotes the idea that learning, and applying what one has learned, is a circular, rather than a linear, process.

The new teaching models that will engage businesses in the process of learning, and vice versa, will also trigger changes to the more didactic teaching models. What will happen, and what has already started to happen, is a transition from the medieval lecture-based model to a learning model where processes and problems are at the centre of learning, rather than a random lecturer who disseminates material that is available by other means, such as on the internet, YouTube, MOOC and so on. In addition, life in the university sector will reflect working methods in businesses. For example team-based learning models will be preferred to individual learning models.

A figurative response to the question that was asked in the Introduction is shown in Figure 6.5.

Note

1 https://en.wikipedia.org/wiki/Gig_worker.

References

Ainley, P. (2014). Follow your dreams and attend university if possible, Latitude, 21 December.

Aoun, J.E. (2017). *Robot-proof: Higher education in the age of artificial intelligence*, MIT Press, Cambridge, MA.

Atkinson, W. (2010). The myth of the reflexive worker: Class and work histories in neo-liberal times, *Work, Employment & Society*, 24(3): 413–429.

Avent, R. (2017). *The wealth of humans: Work, power, and status in the twenty-first century*, St. Martin Press, New York.

Brynjolfsson, E., & McAfee, A. (2014). *The second machine age*, W.W. Norton, New York.

Carson, C. (ed.) (2018). *Educational processes and learning methods*, Willford Press, New York.

Dorling, D. (2015). *Inequality and the 1%*, Verso, London.

Doucet, A., & Evers, J. (2018). Introduction, in A. Doucet, J. Evers, E. Guerra, N. Lopez, M. Soskil, & K. Timmers, *Teaching in the Fourth Industrial Revolution: Standing at the precipice*, pp. 1–7, Routledge, London.

Ford, M. (2015). *The rise of robots*, Basic, New York.

Goertzel, B., & Goertzel, T. (2015a). Introduction, in B. Goertzel & T. Goertzel (eds.), *The end of the beginning: Life, society and economy on the brink of the Singularity*, pp. 6–31, Humanity+ Press, Los Angeles, CA.

Goertzel, B., & Goertzel, T. (2015b). Predicting the age of post-human intelligence, in B. Goertzel & T. Goertzel (eds.), *The end of the beginning: Life, society and economy on the brink of the Singularity*, pp. 32–57, Humanity+ Press, Los Angeles, CA.

Hoidn, S. (2016). *Student-centered learning environments in higher education classrooms*, Palgrave Macmillan, New York.

Huang, Y., Wu, H., & Liu, H. (eds.) (2017). *Intelligent robotics and applications: 10th international conference*, ICIRA 2017, Wuhan, China, August 16–18, 2017, proceedings, part III, Springer, Cham.

Johannessen, J.-A. (2018a). *Automation, innovation and economic crises: How to survive the Fourth Industrial Revolution*, Routledge, London.

Johannessen, J.-A. (2018b). *The workplace of the future*, Routledge, London.

Johannessen, J.-A. (2019). *From democratic capitalism to feudal capitalism in the Fourth Industrial Revolution*, Routledge, London.

Kessler, S. (2018). *Gigged*, Random House, New York.

McGill, K. (2016). *Global inequality*, University of Toronto Press, Toronto.

Mosco, V. (2017). *Becoming digital: Towards a post internet society*, Emerald, London.

Murphy, A. (2016). *The optimistic workplace*, Amacom, New York.

Ross, A. (2016). *The industries of the future*, Simon & Schuster, New York.

Tversky, A., & Kahneman, D. (1974). Judgment under uncertainty: Heuristics and biases, *Science*, 185: 1124–1131.

Tversky, A., & Kahneman, D. (1981). The framing of decisions and the psychology of choice, *Science*, 211: 453–458.

Tversky, A., & Kahneman, D. (1983). Extensional versus intuitive reasoning: The conjunction fallacy in probability judgment, *Psychological review*, 90: 293–315.

Tversky, A., & Kahneman, D. (2000). Loss aversion in riskless choice, in D. Kahneman & A. Tversky (eds.). *Choices, values and frames*, pp. 143–158, Cambridge University Press, Cambridge.

7 Singularity and the universities of the future

Introduction

The key ideas in this chapter:

- There are five drivers, or megatrends, that will determine the form of the universities of the future. These are: demographics, urbanization, info-structures, turbulence and new organizational logic.
- Four types of university will develop in the Fourth Industrial Revolution: the traditional university, the focus university, the global conglomerate university and the global focus university.
- In the universities of the future, the employees will mainly spend their time supervising and researching, while intelligent robots will take care of disseminating knowledge.
- When teaching productivity explodes as a result of intelligent robots taking over the dissemination of knowledge, we will see a side-effect resulting from global competition. We can describe this side-effect as "the winner takes all". This means that small and medium-sized universities worldwide will become campuses for elite universities, such as Harvard, MIT, Stanford and so on, and for the consortia of these universities.

Singularity and developments within the university sector cannot be disassociated from the context within which university teaching takes place. At a general level, this context is linked to technology, globalization, automation, unemployment and a high degree of uncertainty (Johannessen, 2018a, 2018b). This uncertainty is apparent, both to many people in work, and also to many people currently in education, who will be looking for work in the future. Young people are particularly vulnerable, because we know that the labour market is going to undergo extensive changes, even if we do not know exactly what form these changes will take. We know that there will be a strong increase in productivity, because intelligent robots will enter the labour market (Gordon, 2018). Increasing productivity, in both production and administration, as well as in the service and knowledge sectors, means that there is a real danger of mass unemployment.

Education is also taking place at a time when economic inequalities are increasing rapidly and exponentially (Dorling, 2015; Johannessen, 2018a, 2018b). At the same time, democracy is also under pressure in many places (Doucet & Evers, 2018). Against this background, we are educating young people for a labour market that is insecure, that is in a state of rapid change, and that will be unable to offer secure, well-paid, full-time jobs to everyone in education (Finlayson & Hayward, 2010; Boden, 2016).

Technological singularity and big data will make simulation technologies possible in most areas of higher education (Bartholomew & Hayes, 2017). That is to say, it is the continuous development of artificial intelligence and intelligent robots that will facilitate simulation technologies in educational institutions (Gordon, 2018). While flight simulators are used in the training of pilots today, in the near future there will be simulator programmes in all subject areas, for example in educational fields such as management, medical studies and engineering, and so on (Kozma et al., 2018). As a consequence of this development, the work of university teachers will move away from giving lectures to instead focusing more on coaching and supervising. When intelligent machines, robots and informats penetrate the whole economy, they will be able to reproduce themselves, like the mythological phoenix bird, that hatched from the egg created by itself. The new robots will be able to reproduce themselves in exact copies, just like the phoenix bird. When we reach this situation of singularity, which Kurzweil (2005, 2008) assures us is looming in the future, intelligent machines will have taken over most of the functions that humans perform today. It is in such a situation that higher education institutions will change both their educational technology and also the way they distribute knowledge (Lane, 2014; Skilton & Hovsepian, 2018). Lectures will be viewed as an ineffective and outdated method, and also pedagogically counterproductive. When teaching productivity explodes with the help of new teaching technology, we will have a side-effect due to global competition, which we can call "the winner takes all". By this, we mean that small and medium-sized universities around the world will function as campuses for the elite universities, such as Harvard, MIT, Stanford, etc., as shown in Chapter 6.

Innovations will emerge where productivity and quality are declining (Johannessen, 2017, 2018a, 2018b). This explains why we will witness innovations emerging in teaching technology, because it will become too costly, in relation to the desired quality, to use highly qualified academics to disseminate knowledge in lectures, when intelligent robots can do the job just as well; moreover, this will probably result in improving students' competence, because the robots will be able to focus on the individual student's potential.

Higher education will experience an extremely critical period when singularity occurs. It is not only innovations in teaching technology that will transform educational institutions within higher education. They will also undergo innovations in management, organization and knowledge distribution, and their function in society will change radically. In higher education, practical utility is being given greater focus by owners and administrators, because an economic mindset has already crept into educational arenas that previously largely did not focus on a utility perspective and on economic considerations.

Artificial logical, rational and instrumental intelligence has many advantages over the similar kind of intelligence in humans. In short, intelligent robots have a larger memory function than humans, greater information-processing capacity, superior mathematical and statistics processing capacity, larger multi-tasking capacity, and greater multi-sensory capacity (Brynjolfsson & McAfee, 2014; Susskind & Susskind, 2017;). Intelligent robots are also better equipped to uncover patterns in large volumes of data (big data), and they have a greater ability to analyse big data (Callaghan et al., 2017: v–vii).

When technological singularity occurs in around 2035–2040 (Kurzweil, 2005, 2008; Levesque, 2017), we will see an explosion in student learning capacity, because it will be possible for the student to learn on the basis of their own background and ability to a greater extent than before. While a lecturer and a supervisor have limited capacity, competence and time, intelligent robots will have almost unlimited capacity and time. The intelligent robots will also possess what may be called requisite variety;[1] the Law of Requisite Variety in this context may be understood in terms of the fact that the intelligent robots will constantly be able to adapt their teaching to the level of the students, while bringing them up to a higher level of competence. The individual academic at universities is also able to do this but this is becoming increasingly difficult, because of the explosion in the number of students globally over the last 30 years (Lane, 2014). The intelligent robots will be able to contextualize and exemplify the teaching better than the most capable lecturers. The robots will also be able to provide simulation models using big data. This innovation technology in the universities will lead to a new distribution paradigm for knowledge transfer, that will constitute changes as profound as any since Gutenberg and the printing press. As global competition is considerable and expected to increase, while the development and application of these intelligent robots will require expertise and financial muscle, it seems likely that size will be a dominant factor in the university world when singularity occurs, i.e. "the winner takes all".

It is reasonable to assume that when singularity occurs, and probably before then, our current teaching methodology will receive less emphasis and appear as partially outdated. Consequently, traditional teaching methods, such as giving lectures, will be scaled down and viewed as being less important. If learning activities and processes become the focus of attention, then it is in relation to these elements that the new teaching technology will emerge.

Contextualized teaching and learning relates subject matter to meaningful situations that are relevant to the context where the students will practise and further develop their competence. Using intelligent robots, the contextualization of teaching can be facilitated by simulating situations in analogy with a flight simulator, as suggested above. Without intelligent robots with access to big data, professors and lecturers will not have the sufficient variation (requisite variety) to adapt their teaching to the individual student's abilities and goals.

The question that lies implicit in this description is: What will happen to the universities, if teachers can be mass-produced according to the needs of the market? The mass-production in this case is of course the mass production of intelligent robots with access to big data.

The intelligent robots will be able to develop simulation programmes for use in, for example, cancer research, software production, history teaching, anthropology education, economics education, management education, etc. The assumption here is that if the largest expense item on the budget of universities is wage costs, then it is most probable that innovations will emerge in this area (Johannessen, 2018a). It is in this context that teaching technology using intelligent robots will see the light of day in the near future. The question that arises here is: When this teaching technology becomes a reality, will students need to be physically present on campus? It is most probable that the new teaching technology will result in the adoption of a new distribution paradigm in higher education.

The perception of ourselves as teachers can be completely changed as a result of the introduction of artificial intelligence and intelligent robots in higher education. It will not necessarily be advantageous to imagine that the use of artificial intelligence and intelligent robots in education only concerns a new teaching technology, similar to other technologies we have seen emerge over the last fifty years. The reason is that these new technologies will deprive university teachers of many of the functions they currently have in relation to teaching. The danger of such an attitude is that we will not be prepared for the major upheavals the new technology will bring about in higher education. Instead of hiring staff to teach, it may be the case that in the future universities will mainly hire staff to supervise and conduct research. If such a development occurs as a result of the two technologies, intelligent robots and intelligent informats based on artificial intelligence, then the lecturing role of academics in universities will to a great extent disappear. If the lectures disappear, the function of the academic staff will change significantly. One consequence of this is that many of those who currently work mainly as lecturers will no longer be in demand. It will be those with competence in supervision and research who will be in demand, and this is, as a general rule, those with a PhD, and the ability to research and publish research.

It is not so much the case that human capital will become less important, and artificial intelligence and robots take over, as reflected in the above scenario, but rather that human capital will be utilized in different ways. One of the relevant scenarios concerning intelligent robots, informats and artificial intelligence may be understood as follows: while a human being needs 18+ years to acquire a basic professional education, an artificial robot will require no more than 18 seconds. The point here, however, is not the time the robot uses to acquire learning, but the speed with which it can transmit this knowledge to another intelligent robot. Furthermore, when robots are connected through intelligent networks, all the robots will be continuously upgraded with new knowledge. When these robots can use big data and simulation technology to transfer this

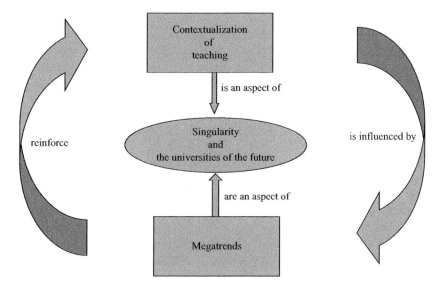

Figure 7.1 Singularity and the universities of the future.

knowledge to students, there will no longer be a need for teachers at universities as mediators of knowledge. An obvious question that also emerges in this context is: Why should students take a university education to get a job, when intelligent robots already do most of the jobs?

In this chapter, we will therefore examine the following question: How will singularity affect the universities of the future?

We have developed two sub-questions to answer the main question.

1   How will the contextualization of teaching affect the universities of the future?
2   How will megatrends affect the universities of the future?

We have illustrated the Introduction in Figure 7.1, which also shows how the chapter is organized.

Contextualization of teaching

If intelligence is the ability to achieve goals in different areas (Armstrong, 2017: 3), then we must anticipate that intelligent robots will rapidly supersede human intelligence. The question that many people are asking is whether intelligent robots can achieve creative, emotional and relationship goals – in other words, the attributes that we associate with being human. We have discussed this in great detail in Chapters 1–5. At a general level, the answer is that "agora robots" will be developed, which will possess artificial intelligence, artificial emotions and the capacity to conduct artificial relationships. If such a development occurs, and there is much to suggest that it will (Johannessen, 2018b; Grandeur and Hughes, 2019), we can then envisage intelligent robots having more logical intelligence than us, in the same way that we are more intelligent than dogs. This comparison is terrifying but can also be a trigger for us to reflect on human values and to develop moral intelligence. If this comes about, or if something comparable to this situation manifests itself, then we need to start reflecting on the following questions right away: What kinds of competence will it be useful for humans to develop? What kinds of competence should the universities develop, if such a scenario, or a comparable one, should become a reality? These are some aspects of what we are exploring in this chapter.

In this context, the contextualization of education means the customization of the teaching process to suit each individual's wishes and interests, as well as the demands of the labour market. To a large extent, good teaching is associated with enthusiasm, passion, the student's own interests and the areas where the student wants to make a difference (Doucet, 2018: 89). In light of this knowledge, student projects should be driven by their own interests, and relate to areas about which they really care and want to gain knowledge, and areas where they will experience a sense of mastery and progress. Over the last 20 years, there has been a complete change in the ways that students gather data and information. They find some information in books and journals, but they find most of their material by searching online. The role of teachers has changed in step with this development. From being walking encyclopaedias, they have become guides and coaches in a learning process (Shirley, 2017).

For the individual teacher, at all levels of the education system, contextualization has so far only been an ideal, but not a practical possibility. However, new teaching technology, together with intelligent robots and artificial intelligence, will make contextualization possible. Contextualization is nothing new in teaching, it goes back at least as far as Socrates, roughly 2,500 years ago. On the other hand, the current teaching model used at universities is based on relics of ideas from the First Industrial Revolution and scientific management; in this context, one often hears the metaphor "topping up" your knowledge – which implies students are half-full tanks that need filling up again. This expression is often heard on continuing education courses, that is, adults attending college to "top up" their knowledge. The use of the metaphor creates expectations regarding the teaching model. When students think that they just need a refill, they expect the lectures to consist of a knowledge tap where they can fill up with knowledge; then once they have tanked up with knowledge, they can carry on going again for many miles with their new full tank. Within the field of education, it is difficult to think of a more inappropriate and unproductive metaphor. Learning has nothing to do with "tanking up" new knowledge, as if students were empty cans that only needed filling up. It is the logic of the industrial society that is largely responsible for this type of thinking and learning practice. The industrial society needed people who could do repetitive tasks, day in and day out, as if they were working on a conveyor belt. The learning methods related to this learning model are of the following types: learning catechisms, memorizing formulas, learning a foreign language parrot-fashion, memorizing the capitals of the world, and so on.

At the overall level, the university learning models also followed an industrial logic. According to this logic, raw materials are transformed through production processes into finished products, which are distributed and then consumed. Then the process is repeated: raw material, finished products, distribution, consumption. In teaching, this became the logic of learning, acquiring competence, application of competence and then a long-awaited otium and retirement from active work, before death helped the worn-out worker over the river of oblivion to paradise on the other side, or via the river Styx down into Hades. Religion was an aid to this industrial logic, in that those who struggled through the hell of working life could receive eternal rest and walk on the gold-plated streets of heaven, if, and only if, they did not violate the norms of church and society.

The industrial logic does not apply to the innovation economy and the knowledge society. However, we should be aware of the fact that the logic of the industrial society is used in models of thought, long after the industrial society's production logic has ceased to exist.

This is what may be referred to as the "anchor" of history, as mentioned in Chapter 5; the anchor of history holds us back and hinders the necessary change processes. History's anchor, or more specifically resistance to change, can be found in the "prospect theory" of the Nobel laureates in economics, Tversky and Kahneman (1974, 1981, 1983, 2000).

The empty tank metaphor for learning and the linear logic of the industrial society are not appropriate for the new logic. The old industrial logic was organized into a linear time sequence: learning, and then application of acquired competence. When one needed to renew one's competence, one attended a university for a "refill". In the new logic, learning is interactive and circular. Firstly, learning is an activity process, where the person who is learning actively works with a problem area and a question related to the problem area. Thus, the person who wishes to learn actively works with both the problem and the related question, searching for knowledge under supervision. Secondly, it is not the case that you first learn something, and then apply it in practice. Learning, practice and application go hand in hand. Nor is it the case that in the knowledge society one first learns, then uses the competence in a job for life, receives a pension and then dies. In the knowledge society and the innovation economy, learning, application of learning and leisure are together a holistic process that takes place every day. As long as one is healthy and can contribute something to an organization and society, one participates in creative work. One develops new competence in relation to the context in which the competence is used, for example using a 3 + 3 model. This means that you work for three hours and build new competence for an additional three hours every day throughout the working year.

Contextualization is a preferred learning model, not because teaching technology or the business world favour the model, but because it is the best learning model for students and employees (Shirley, 2017; Doucet, 2018). Students who receive individual supervision perform qualitatively better than students who receive other types of supervision (Doucet, 2018: 94). It is only through the automation of lectures that this form of educational support is possible, because otherwise the cost would be too prohibitive for most universities.

With the new emerging technology, where intelligent robots and artificial intelligence are continually improving, one does not need to think along the lines of standardization. Standardization belongs to the automation of industrial production. The automation of information and knowledge processes does not need to use standardization, because artificial intelligence and intelligent robots make standardization superfluous (Xie, 2017; Zhao et al., 2017). On the other hand, all categories of teachers at universities will be more or less replaced by intelligent robots, artificial intelligence and intelligent networks. The simple reason for this is that the cost of teachers at universities is the largest expenditure item, and according to innovation theory, innovations emerge where costs are high (Johannessen, 2018a, 2018b); innovations will replace the traditional type of pedagogy, that is, lectures. The contextualization of the teaching does not require teachers of flesh and blood. It is not teachers, but learning, that is essential in educational institutions.

The fear that robots will take over our jobs is great. In an American survey, it appears that people fear this more than they fear death.[2] Future technological solutions will most likely take over most of the work tasks we perform today (Aoun, 2017: 1–23). The fear that robots will take over our jobs is real. On the other hand, this does not necessarily have to lead to mass unemployment. If we share work, for example by doing a three-hour day instead of an eight-hour day, then technology will improve our well-being and not steal our jobs. The intelligent robots will be working for us, rather than against us. It may be envisaged that this development could be possible in all sectors, including in the higher education sector. However, for this to happen, it will require a redistribution of the increased value creation, which will be the result of increased productivity, brought about by robotization. This redistribution is possible, but it is more doubtful that it will occur.

Machines have always replaced workers. This has led to higher productivity, more prosperity and a better life for most people. Throughout history, we have always changed our attitude towards work as a result of machines taking over certain tasks. The new factor regarding intelligent robots is that they will take over information- and knowledge-based jobs, for example at universities. If we want this to benefit most employees, then a strategy of work-sharing needs to be implemented, such as the 3+3 model mentioned above. The new factor around intelligent robots and artificial intelligence is that the robots will take over the jobs of the middle class, such as work relating to information and knowledge, as well as in the service sector, rather than just the jobs of those in industry. Why should it be a cause for more concern that middle-class workers are made redundant, than it is if those working in the factories lose their jobs? Technology has always – ever since the wheel was invented roughly 5,000 years ago, progressing to intelligent robots entering the labour market – changed work functions. Thus, it is nothing new that people have to find themselves new jobs, in this case the university teachers. On the other hand, the universities will flourish with the introduction of artificial intelligence, intelligent robots and artificial intelligence networks. They will flourish because they will be able to more effectively perform the task they are designed to do, that is, teach students new subjects and knowledge, and publish research.

The teaching will become more efficient, because intelligent robots will be able to adapt the teaching to the level of the individual. Research will get better, because academics will be able to devote their time to research, instead of spending time giving lectures. In addition, the researchers will now have a personal assistant in the form of an intelligent robot, which can collect and compile data, and help to find patterns and connections in the data. The abstraction process and the dissemination, on the other hand, will be the sole responsibility of the researcher.

Throughout human history, man has devoted his energy to finding food, shelter and clothing, and fashioning objects and tools to make life easier and more comfortable. The single factor that has helped us most in this process is technology (Sprague, 2015; Srinivasan, 2017). This applies to all areas of work, including the field of higher education. One million years have passed from when we learned to control fire until the time when we have become able to develop human logical intelligence artificially.[3] The history of innovation in brief outlines has gone from controlling fire to steam power to electric power and then to nuclear power, and most recently, to digital technology and artificial intelligence. Throughout this history of innovation, there have always been some who have opposed technological development. In a slightly longer perspective, however, most people's lives have been improved, even though some may have had it worse in a transitional period. This will most likely be the case for the universities, when intelligent robots, artificial intelligence and artificial intelligent networks become established throughout higher education. The basis for the information revolution is the digitization of all information processes, and the development of technologies such as computers, digital communication and artificial intelligence.

The university is a social institution, whose two main objectives are to develop and disseminate knowledge. These two main objectives answer the question: What is a university designed to do? To fulfil the two main objectives, universities need to be in close contact with the society they are designed to serve. Maintaining closeness to the business world, public sector and social institutions is an important function of universities. Consequently, we emphasize the necessity of contextualization of all teaching, because it is important that there is a closeness between the various knowledge domains. The reasoning is simple. It has always been the task of universities to educate and create future employees. Through education at the universities, students acquire the necessary skills to perform a job. The first universities educated priests, philosophers and lawyers. Later, the universities started to educate students for other professions.

Common to all the students who are educated at a university is that they are trained to participate in working life. This is at the heart of contextualization: the closeness between the universities and working life.

Technological development has always led to the development of the universities. The Industrial Revolution resulted in the faculties of theology, law and philosophy having to compete for educational resources with the technological, medical and economics faculties. The digitization of society led to new faculties seeing the light of day, such as data and systems theory, computer science, etc. The growing field of artificial intelligence also seems to be leading to the development of new faculties. However, it seems reasonable to assume that these faculties at the universities will integrate various subject areas, such as technology and information, biology and technology, neuroscience and nanotechnology, etc. The point is that the new faculties at universities are likely to integrate existing disciplines.

The educational system in the Western world and in its universities in particular has been criticized for resembling a factory model (Baird & Henderson, 2001; Barrat, 2015). Metaphorically, students enter through one door of the factory-university as raw materials, are then transformed through various manufacturing processes, and finally go out the other door as finished "products"; the students as finished products are then able to apply their knowledge in social production. This industrial logic of the universities will most probably change at the beginning of the Fourth Industrial Revolution (Johannessen, 2018a, 2018b). Using such a factory model in teaching may have been effective in the industrial economy, but in the innovation economy it is counterproductive (Johannessen, 2018b). It is difficult to educate students to be creative and innovative by treating them as if they were raw materials on an assembly line, that need to be transformed into manufactured products. The conveyor belt metaphor has no place in the innovation economy, because innovation does not involve a process of manufacture, where products can be constructed from parts on an assembly line. Innovation may instead be considered more as creative chaos, a process no one can predict, which certainly cannot be designed and constructed along a factory assembly line (Brynjolfsson & Saunders, 2013). The problem, however, is that ways of thought in relation to models and concepts in institutions, such as the university system, tend to be maintained long after the terrain has changed (Christensen & Raynor, 2003). It is this historic "anchor" that can get stuck in the bottom and overturn many universities, when the storm's violent winds reach the factory walls behind which these institutions hide from the changes in the outside world. The hypothesis is that the longer they remain in hiding, maintaining their concepts and thinking from the industrial age, the more they will be vulnerable to the consequences of the changes. Clearly, this means that if universities do not change in step with the changes in the outside world and relate to the new underlying logic, they will disappear or end up being assimilated in another context.

Some of the changes in the outside world that will affect universities are automation, robotization, digitization, use of intelligent robots and artificial intelligence, and the use of intelligent robots capable of artificial emotions and artificial relationships. It is highly probable that such changes will lead to mass unemployment, if the regulations regarding working hours remain unchanged. One obvious way to prevent mass unemployment would be to implement a process of sharing work, such as a three-hour day plus an extra three hours of competence development, a process that could be introduced in all workplaces. This would give the universities a completely new role in the information economy. So-called "working-life universities" (that cater for working-life needs) will not only become a possibility, but will be a necessity for society's survival in the Fourth Industrial Revolution. If this does not happen, the cohesive forces in society may crumble, and the tensions may be so great that social crises will become a reality. By the simple step of sharing work, while introducing three hours per day of competence development, we can change the universities' role from the classic Humboldtian tradition to becoming working-life universities.

This is not the first time the universities have had to change. After World War II, when US soldiers returned home, the GI Bill was enacted, giving veterans education opportunities; in the immediate post-war period the veterans made up about 50 per cent of US college enrolment.[4] At that time, both the curriculum changed, as well as the content of what was being taught. If the entire workforce were to set aside three hours per day for competence development, this would most likely change the universities' curricula and teaching methods.

When the entire workforce around the world has to go back to school, it seems reasonable to assume that creativity, ideas development, innovations and entrepreneurship will flourish. In order to cope with the increasing amount of people enrolling at the universities, the new university technology will be crucial for coping with the major challenges. On the one hand, the universities must be close to working lives and deliver what they demand. On the other hand, they must also provide knowledge that intelligent robots cannot deliver. One can ask the question: What can humans do that intelligent robots will never be able to do, even if they develop artificial emotions and are capable of artificial relationships? The answer is obvious: being human for the other person(s); ethical reflection; philosophical reflection; the ability to believe, hope and love; the ability to imagine; the ability to create myths; the ability to construct ideologies; the ability to formulate human rights; these are all areas of knowledge that it is difficult to imagine an intelligent robot will ever be able to master. In brief, what separates people from intelligent robots is the ability to imagine a future and then create that future, as well as being creative and living in creative chaos in order to create the innovative new, such as creating the next intelligent robot with artificial emotions and the capability of having artificial relationships.

Students bring different backgrounds and abilities with them into the teaching situation. This is what contextualization attempts to take into account. To illustrate, we can use the analogy of the teacher as a gardener. All the flowers in a garden are different. Some only need a little care and looking after, while others need a lot of attention in order to bloom. After they bloom, they do not require the same level of attention, and can manage on their own. This is also the case with students. If all the students are treated equally, the results will be poor. By turning away from the lecture-based model and going over to more process-related teaching methods, it will be easier for the teacher to guide the individual appropriately. We know that the results of individual supervision are better than from other types of supervision (Doucet, 2018: 94).

By linking new teaching technology to contextualization, the gardening analogy can be further expanded. One can think of the new technology in this context as a tool for improving the soil, so that the plants can thrive and grow better. Using the new technology, such as robot-teachers, artificial intelligence, artificial intelligence networks, artificial emotions, artificial relations, etc., we will not need the same mass of physical buildings as was needed by educational institutions before. Large symbolic buildings will not be needed when the teaching is contextualized and improved by new technology. The large lecture rooms will not be needed if lectures as a method of teaching become passé. With the new technology and a greater focus on contextualization, the teaching can also become more distance-oriented, such as the new MOOC systems have already shown. If such a new teaching paradigm becomes a general trend, then the university campuses will become smaller and more dispersed in the cityscape. Why would we need large symbolic buildings with large lecture halls, when traditional lectures are given less focus? The answer is that we will not need these symbolic buildings. One can also imagine smaller campuses scattered around the region which the university services. On these campuses, students will be provided with group rooms, discussion arenas and supervision rooms, when needed.

If it is learning that is essential to the universities, then it is this that should be emphasized, not architectonic buildings that only drive up costs and inflate the pomposity of principals and directors with elephant-sized egos. It is the activities that make the learning flourish, and the learning which is essential, not the buildings. These activities can be linked to process- or problem-based learning. In both of these teaching models, it is small group rooms and a well-developed infrastructure, as well as an information structure (info-structure), that are the most important prerequisites for learning. The tools we need to facilitate the learning process in both of these pedagogical models are the various forms of learning technology that help to advance learning.

Learning technology is a collective term that we define as the broad range of technological tools whose purpose is to support the learning of the individual. We view the emergence of a new university model as contextualization linked to the emerging new learning technology. The new aspect is the development away from a teaching model based on the metaphor of getting a "refill" of knowledge. The metaphor is based on a knowledgeable person transferring knowledge to people who lack that knowledge. The new model, in which contextualization is central, is activity-based, and is based on the individual student's ability and background, needs, desires, what they are passionate about, what they want to be good at. The new learning model facilitates the student's mastering ability.

In the context-based teaching approach, co-creation is the key to learning. In the transfer of knowledge model, the key to learning is lectures; hence the metaphor, filling up with knowledge. The thinking behind this metaphor is so widespread that when the students are served another pedagogical model, such as project-based learning based on process pedagogy, many respond negatively and want to return to lecture-based teaching, even though they know that learning in such a model is less effective than in the activity-based model.

The activity-based model must be contextualized through real projects, not cases. The reason is that real projects create engagement and closeness to the context the students will use as a basis for learning. With such a model, learning takes place through co-creation, where everyone shares their knowledge to create new knowledge.

Automation is about to reach the universities in two ways. Firstly, the administrative work will be digitized and automated, which we have seen happening in industrial production. Secondly, the actual learning will be automated through various forms of technology-enhanced learning (Branch et al., 2017). The hypothesis is that when robotization establishes itself in the universities, the amount of lectures given by the academic staff will be greatly reduced. Even the introductory lectures for a course can be carried out by robots, and the students will not need to be physically present on campus. They can listen to the "lecturer" and the information from the administration when it suits them best.

Students will be able to study at the time of day when their learning capacity is optimal. This may be at five in the morning or eleven at night. The learning will then be adapted to the student's biological clock, rather than the lecturer's timetable. When, not if, this situation occurs, where robots take over most of the work of the lecturers, then the university's employees will be given new and different functions. This new situation may be described as a tectonic transformation of the universities. This will be the impact that the Fourth Industrial Revolution will have on the universities, where the tectonic plates will shift, and figuratively create new mountain ranges and continents.

The new continent that will be created at the universities is, *firstly*, a completely new learning process. We have seen the beginning of this learning process in the form of the MOOC system. Robotization will turn the MOOC system into an old technology overnight.

Secondly, the actual robotization will be something qualitatively new that will transform the universities into something completely different from today. First and foremost, the emphasis on building stock and symbolic buildings will be a thing of the past.

The "campus" will be located wherever the students feel is their best learning environment. Figuratively, this will be like building more buildings, but without roads and paths between them. Only after a few years will the "roads and paths" be built, once one has seen where students choose to go. If we transfer this metaphor to the campuses of the universities, then the infrastructure and info-structure will be established once we have seen where the students choose to do their learning. This may be in a café, a fitness centre, in the city's library, etc. The university's "campus" will be located where the learning takes place, and the supervisors can then move out to the students and not vice versa. It is possible that it may be appropriate to have an actual building where the employees and the students can meet as needed. This building may be called the "university". Unlike earlier symbolic university buildings, such as those of Oxford University, Cambridge University, MIT, Harvard University, etc., these buildings will figuratively be more like a large tent or marquee. The marquee metaphor is used because marquees, or large canopy-like tents, will be part of a flexible system that one can easily move to a new geographical area when needed.

Thirdly, an old important tectonic plate at the universities will be changed – the requirements concerning the competence of the academic staff. Traditionally, one of the university professor's greatest attributes is his/her ability to give lectures. If this function is taken over by intelligent robots and intelligent networks, this means that the professors will primarily develop knowledge through research and disseminate it via supervision. The research will be disseminated in journals, books and through popularization of the research to a larger audience. The lecturing function of the academic staff will disappear, but not the teaching part, which will mean that much more emphasis will be given to supervision.

Megatrends

The success of the individual universities will be dependent on how they prepare themselves for the times we know are coming. We do not know exactly when these times will arrive, or how robotization will affect universities at a detailed level. It would be a mistake to look in the rear-view mirror when steering towards the future. The past can give us few, if any, indications of what the future may bring. There are some megatrends, however, that will release the metaphorical tectonic plates, including in the world of universities. We can investigate these megatrends to see how they may affect the universities, as part of the education sector. By examining these megatrends, the universities can prepare for the future that lies ahead.

The megatrends we describe here have been adapted from Tse and Esposito (2017). The megatrends that Tse and Esposito highlight are demographics, scarcity of resources, economic inequality, turbulence and the rate of change, and increasing dynamics in the outside world. If we consider these megatrends, how will future universities be affected? While Tse and Esposito focus on how businesses will be affected, we will examine how the universities will be affected. We have selected just some of the aspects of the megatrends that Tse and Esposito investigate, because we wish to focus here on the development of the universities.

The five megatrends we have selected from Tse and Esposito, which will have a direct impact on the development of the universities, are as

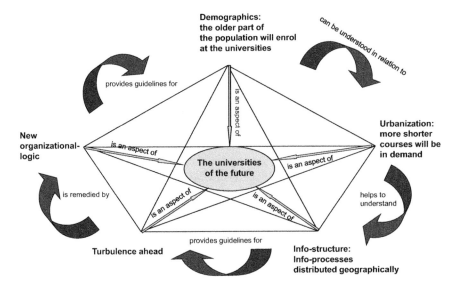

Figure 7.2 Megatrends and the universities.

follows: demographics (an older population); urbanization; info-structure; turbulence; and a new organizational logic. We will describe and analyse these megatrends in what follows. In Figure 7.2, these megatrends are shown in context. Figure 7.2 also shows how the rest of this section is organized.

A growing elderly population

Population demographics are changing. Like Japan, Europe will experience a growing elderly population. In relation to this demographic variable, we can predict with a high degree of certainty what will happen in the future. We also have empirical evidence from Japan that allows us to make very accurate predictions about what will happen in Europe. Firstly, there will be a debate about the burden of taxation, because a smaller number of young people will have to support a larger number of elderly people. Secondly, there will be a debate about pensions, and we will see the emergence of a pensions crisis. At the same time, investment in infrastructure for the elderly will become a central topic. As a consequence of these developments, new ways of living and new housing strategies will become relevant. For example we will see types of housing that will allow elderly people to manage everyday life and avoid having to move into care homes.

Elderly people will not only live longer, they will also stay healthy for longer. In such a situation, it seems reasonable that elderly people will apply to universities, in order to gain knowledge of areas about which they feel they need to know more. Universities that will no longer be able to expand as a result of a larger number of young people flocking to universities, will be able to compensate for this situation in two ways. Firstly, it is very likely that the introduction of new technology will mean that people in work will need to develop their competences on a continual basis. Secondly, universities will make available courses, one-year study programmes and so on, for the growing elderly population. If elderly people get the opportunity to do so, they will be able to continue to work much longer in jobs that are not physically exhausting. As a result, more people will continue to pay tax, and pension pay-outs will be reduced. For universities, this will mean that more elderly people will need to have their competences topped up, so they can continue to perform their roles in the labour market. We can envisage that instead of a mandatory retirement age of 70, for example people whose competences are in demand by employers will be able to continue working for as long as it is in both parties' interests. In this way, a future pension crisis can be avoided, and the burden of taxation on people in work (30–75) can be reduced. If more people choose to continue working after reaching the traditional retirement age, more people will also need to gain new competence from the universities. This will also lead to changes in how knowledge is disseminated and generated at universities, since the learning needs of a 20-year-old are completely different from those of a 70-year-old. Moreover, we should not ignore the fact that people of 70 face different health challenges to people in their twenties. This factor alone will be challenging for universities in respect of their physical architecture.

The population pyramid is in the course of being reversed, and the result will be an upside-down pyramid, i.e. few young people and more elderly people. This will have major consequences for social development in the future and also for competence development. People in the elderly segment of the population are living longer and also staying healthier for longer. This has major implications for the whole of society, including universities.

Universities will have an increasing number of older people on their courses, and they will alter the ranges of courses they offer in response. This is both because older people will demand different types of competences than younger students, and also because there will be a need for more areas of competence targeted at the older part of the population.

If people in the elderly segment of the population fail to keep themselves healthier than older people do today, then society may face catastrophic challenges. Accordingly, larger numbers of older people will apply to universities to keep themselves mentally alert. Many older people will seek out fitness centres to maintain their physical health. Universities will meet this trend by providing more study programmes for older people and more study programmes for fitness-centre instructors who will be working with people in the elderly segment of the population. If we fail to stop age-related diseases such as diabetes, dementia, Alzheimer's, obesity and other age-related "epidemics", then the strain on the socioeconomic system will be unsustainable. Simply for this reason, it is reasonable to believe that attitudes will change about what should be done about older people's competences in order to avoid them becoming a burden on society. When this happens, we will see that 70-year-olds become the new 50-year-olds.

This will have consequences in many areas of society – everywhere from economics to health, politics, social relations and culture. There must be a change in attitude away from the idea that health services are there to fix what goes wrong when we get older, to the idea that we must keep ourselves active to prevent age-related diseases, in so far as possible. The social norm will be that everyone has a responsibility for his or her own health. Values will change, and those who can't take care of their own health will be seen as pariahs, because they will drain societal resources.

Urbanization

This trend is being boosted by the fact that women, for various reasons, are having fewer children. In the United States alone, half of all women are choosing not to have children (Tse and Esposito, 2017:8 4). If this trend continues, this will further amplify the trends we have described above, such as the pensions crisis, the burden on taxpayers, the pressure to work longer and so on. If the trends of lower birth rates and a growing elderly population continue, then the obvious consequence is that more people will want to live in cities, because it is there that they can satisfy their sexual, cultural, economic and social needs, among other things. Quite simply, this demographic trend will boost the increasing urbanization that we are experiencing already.

Cities attract people for many reasons. Possibly the most important reason is the diverse and numerous employment opportunities. Secondly, the cultural opportunities are greater in cities than in rural areas, and, as a rule, universities are located in cities. New technology offers the possibility for more and more people to work remotely via computers and access to networks. However, this does not mean that cities will become less attractive, rather the opposite. It simply provides the opportunity of a respite from the fixed workplace, and the possibility of alternating between work and leisure time in a different way than before.

There are several reasons why the authorities promote urban development:

1   It is cheaper to develop both infrastructure and info-structure in densely populated areas than in rural areas.
2   It is also simpler to develop competence centres, such as universities, in the cities.
3   Costs are reduced on most investments when people live in urban areas.
4   The quality of service increases.
5   There is a greater concentration of expertise in urban areas than in rural areas.
6   Innovations are developed more quickly when people are in close contact with each other, such as in various types of clusters.
7   Innovations spread faster when there is greater population density (West, 2018).

8   There is a positive link between economic growth (GDP) and densely populated urban areas (Kresl, 2015).
9   It is easier to change employment in urban areas.
10 It is easier to take additional education at a university.

These ten factors suggest that urbanization will only increase in the future. Based on this, a hypothesis is that the greater the urbanization, the greater the probability that universities' services will be more in demand. On the other hand, the universities will need to offer more study programmes of one year's duration or less, because many of those who want to acquire new skills already have a bachelor's or master's degree and in some case even a PhD. If the universities are to keep up with the new dynamics, then they should have a greater focus on continuing and further education, which often comprises one-month courses or one-year study programmes, as well as the traditional bachelor's, master's and PhD study programmes.

Info-structure

The infrastructure comprises the physical structures and facilities of a society, such as the roads, bridges, airports, railroads, networks of various types, etc. The information structure (info-structure), on the other hand, is something quite different. While industrialization requires an infrastructure, the Fourth Industrial Revolution requires an info-structure. Just as infrastructure can be viewed from different levels, such as the city, district, nation, region and globe, the info-structure can also be viewed from different perspectives. Moreover, there is a close connection between the development of the infrastructure and the info-structure. The hypothesis is that the better developed the infrastructure, the greater the probability that the info-structure will also be developed to an acceptable level.

The info-structure can be described in an abstract manner as being nine information processes. These nine processes exist at all system levels, for example in an organization, in a country, etc. The nine processes are shown in Figure 7.3.

The purpose of a university is to produce and distribute knowledge. To achieve this, it is necessary that the university follow the central rule: that all nine information processes, shown above, function efficiently and effectively. Given the nine info-structure processes in a university, is it necessary to organize all of them under one roof? The question implies that large architectonic buildings, or several campuses, such as at Oxford and Cambridge, will not be needed in the future development of universities. It is not the buildings that make a university a university, but the knowledge they develop and distribute. Given this assumption, the nine information processes of which a university consists can be distributed over a larger geographical area. This is especially important in the big cities, because of the lack of space; for instance, the space occupied by the universities could be used for housing. When singularity becomes a

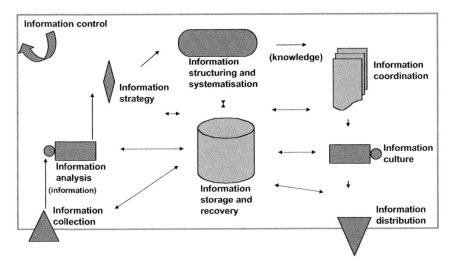

Figure 7.3 Info-structure processes.

reality, scope not scale will be the most important factor for the development of universities.

The resource that will always be scarce, at whatever technological level, is relevant competence. It is this relevant competence that the universities should deliver, and they should deliver it where the customers work and live, not necessarily on campus.

Turbulence and complexity ahead

As a result of the Fourth Industrial Revolution, technological singularity will cause changes to happen more rapidly than we are used to, and also to take different directions from those we expect. To sum up the situation in a single sentence, this means that there will be an increase in turbulence and complexity, for universities as well.

One of the results of an increase in turbulence will be that established courses and disciplines will undergo rapid change, and new courses and disciplines will be established. In addition, the increasing complexity will lead to the emergence of new disciplines, as the result of contacts between disciplines that were never previously in contact with each other. We have already seen how information and technology have spawned the new disciplines of information technology and informatics. We have also seen the emergence of biotechnology from biology and technology, along with other examples.

The new aspect is that what we do not expect to happen will happen; for example it may well be that philosophy and technology, ethics and technology, religion and technology, anthropology and technology, economics and technology, medicine and technology, biology and material technology, will all become new disciplines, which will also change the established disciplines from which they emerge.

One of the consequences of the increasing turbulence and complexity of the universities is that size matters. Let us elaborate on this, because we have argued elsewhere in this book that universities do not need to be large in order to have the right competence when singularity is established. We are still of the opinion that size will be less relevant to maintaining competence. We also believe that the universities' architectonic structures will change to smaller distributed campuses in areas close to the students. On the other hand, it seems reasonable to assume, given the increasing turbulence and complexity, that the universities should be organized in large conglomerates, in order to facilitate new study programmes and discontinue old ones, without this compromising the dissemination and development of knowledge. For this reason, it seems reasonable to suggest that the organization of universities should be two-sided. On the one hand, they will be organized for scope, and on the other hand, for scale. This apparent paradox can be solved by organizing the universities so that both scale and scope are ensured. Taking into consideration the increasing turbulence and complexity, Figure 7.4 shows a two-sided organization of the universities, with the aim of ensuring scale and scope.

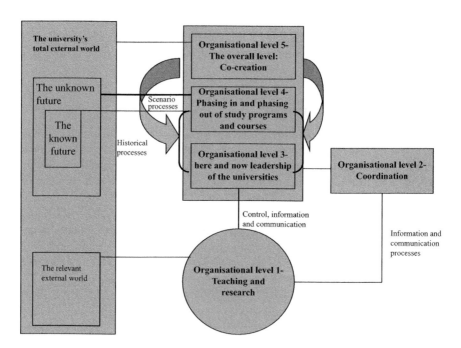

Figure 7.4 The two-sided organization of the universities.

New organizational logic

In light of the four megatrends discussed above, it seems reasonable to assume that the universities of the future will not resemble traditional universities, as we have known them for several hundred years.

Firstly, we will see the establishment of some universities that are focused on just one or two subject areas, for example economics and management, or medicine. A mere scrap of paper can abolish the current restrictions that require an institution to cover several subject areas, and to have several faculties, in order to qualify as a university. The criteria used to determine whether an institution qualifies as a university should be based on its levels of competence, not on its breadth of competence or bureaucratic limitations.

Secondly, in the future, we will still have universities, as we know them today, with many faculties and many fields of study under the same administration. This is what is called the traditional Humboldtian university.[5] They are driven by a logic based on scale, cost, quality, competence and innovation. The Humboldtian tradition emphasizes humanist educational ideals and research-based teaching. The model emerged during the first wave of industrialization and originated from Prussia around the time of the Napoleonic wars. These traditional universities will not be integrated into any fixed organizational associations, even though they may cooperate with other universities, locally and globally. The Humboldtian tradition represents the industrial society's organization of higher education.

Thirdly, we will see the emergence of global conglomerates. Here one can imagine, for example, that Harvard will be a leading force in one such conglomerate. The global conglomerates will have two types of basic organizational logic: information flow and communication. In other words, it will not be important where the student is located, as long as the conglomerate can operate according to these two logics. In practice, this will mean that students who are enrolled at a Harvard conglomerate will receive a Harvard education and a Harvard diploma, although the actual education takes place on a campus located in other regions, such as the Pyrenees in Spain, the Atlas Mountains in Morocco, or in European capital cities such Oslo, Copenhagen or Berlin, to mention a few examples.

Fourthly, it seems probable that when the bureaucratic limitations are abolished regarding how many academic disciplines an institution of higher education must offer in order to be called a university, then local focus universities will emerge that will enter into association with similar focus universities globally. These associations may be organized in relation to strong and weak ties. In practice, this will mean that they can be independent but still collaborate closely with other focus universities, or enter into tightly-knit organizational constellations. Regardless of the form of organization, these focus universities will benefit from each other's research within specific fields, such as technology, medicine, biology, etc.

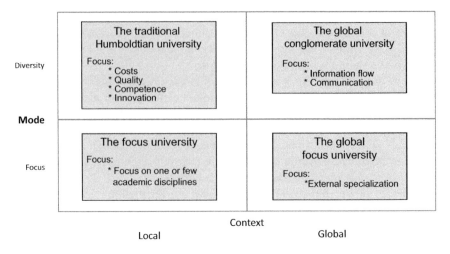

Figure 7.5 The organization of the universities in the future.

In Figure 7.5 we have shown a typology of what the universities of the future may look like, given the conditions discussed above.

Conclusion

The question we have discussed in this chapter is as follows: How will singularity affect the universities of the future?

In the innovation economy, the universities should be drivers for entrepreneurship and innovation. In this context, we should not understand entrepreneurship as referring to business start-ups, or even to small- or medium-sized businesses. When we refer to entrepreneurship here, we mean innovative entrepreneurship, i.e. new companies starting up against the background of innovation. The reason is that in the innovation economy, innovation itself will be the main competitive parameter, and each individual society must ensure that economic growth results from innovation. Universities must also change in order to encourage innovation. Some universities will continue to be organized as they are now, i.e. in accordance with the classical Humboldtian tradition. We will also see the emergence of other types of university. These are similar to what one might call a focus university, because they are focused on one, or a very few, fields. A third type that will develop will be the result of a number of focus universities merging with other focus universities to form a global focus university. A fourth type of university that will emerge is what we refer to here as the global conglomerate university. This will happen when a leading traditional university, Harvard or Oxford for example, establishes new campuses

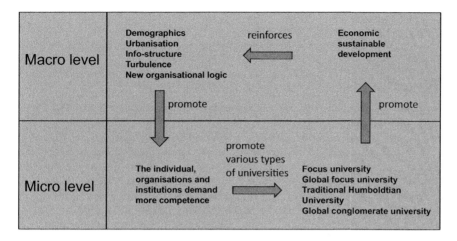

Figure 7.6 The Boudon–Coleman model for the university of the future.

or buys up local universities and uses the Harvard model to educate students globally under the Harvard umbrella.

In the Fourth Industrial Revolution, universities will change in response to the social mechanisms that are driving the economy. The fundamental drivers in the innovation economy are robotization, digitization, intelligent robots and intelligent algorithms. Many factors suggest that the rate of economic change will affect the rate of change in the university sector. This suggests that those universities that fail to keep up with the rate of change in the surrounding world will be merged with universities that do succeed in doing so.

Nor is it the case that the university structures that emerged during the First Industrial Revolution – the so-called Humboldtian universities – will be the drivers for the universities of the future. Quite the contrary. These universities are weighed down by bureaucratic red-tape and resistance to change, and will have little willingness to change beyond their own scholarly level. The drivers of the innovation economy will be the completely new university structures that will emerge in response to the Fourth Industrial Revolution and the innovation economy. Here we refer to these universities as focus universities, global focus universities and global conglomerate universities.

The answer to the question asked at the beginning of this conclusion is shown in the following Boudon–Coleman model (Figure 7.6).

Notes

1 https://en.wikipedia.org/wiki/Variety_(cybernetics).
2 https://blogs.chapman.edu/wilkinson/2016/10/11/americas-top-fears-2016.

3 http://discovermagazine.com/2013/may/09-archaeologists-find-earliest-evidence-of-humans-cooking-with-fire.
4 http://fliphtml5.com/xpbg/iqtn/basic.
5 https://en.wikipedia.org/wiki/Humboldtian_model_of_higher_education.

References

Aoun, J.E. (2017). *Robot-Proof: Higher education in the age of artificial intelligence*, MIT Press, Cambridge, MA.

Armstrong, S. (2017). Introduction to the technological singularity, in V. Callaghan, J. Miller, R. Yampolskiy, & S. Armstrong (eds.), *The technological singularity*, pp. 1–8, Springer, Berlin.

Baird, L., & Henderson, J.C. (2001). *The knowledge engine*, Berrett-Koehler, San Francisco, CA.

Barrat, J. (2015). *Our final invention*, St. Martin's Griffin, London.

Bartholomew, P., & Hayes, S. (2017). An introduction to technology enhanced learning policy, in J. Branch, P. Bartholomew & C. Nygaard (eds.), *Technology-enhanced learning in higher education*, pp. 17–29, Libri, New York.

Boden, M.A. (2016). *AI: Its nature and future*, Oxford University Press, Oxford.

Branch, J. Bartholomew, P., & Nygaard, C. (2017). Introducing technology enhanced learning, in J. Branch, P. Bartholomew and C. Nygaard (eds.), *Technology-enhanced learning in higher education*, pp. 1–17, Libri, New York.

Brynjolfsson, E., & McAfee, A. (2014). *The second machine age: Work, progress and prosperity in a time of brilliant technologies*, W.W.Norton, New York.

Brynjolfsson, E., & Saunders, A. (2013). *Wired for innovation: How information technology is reshaping the economy*, MIT Press, Cambridge, MA.

Callaghan, V., Miller, J., Yampolskiy, R., & Armstrong, S. (eds.) (2017). *The technological singularity*, Springer, Berlin.

Christensen, C.M., & Raynor, M.E. (2003). *Innovator's solution: Creating and sustaining successful growth*, Harvard Business School Press, Boston, MA.

Dorling, D. (2015). *Inequality and the 1%*, Verso, London.

Doucet, A. (2018). Contextualizing personalization in education, in A. Doucet, J. Evers, E. Guerra, N. Lopez, M. Soskil, & K. Timmers (eds.), *Teaching in the fourth industrial revolution: Standing at the precipice*, pp. 89–105, Routledge, London.

Doucet, A. & Evers, J. (2018). Introduction, in A. Doucet, J. Evers, E. Guerra, N. Lopez, M. Soskil, & K. Timmers (eds.), *Teaching in the fourth industrial revolution: Standing at the precipice*, pp. 1–7, Routledge, London.

Finlayson, G., & Hayward, D. (2010). *Education towards heteronomy: A critical analysis of the reform of UK universities since 1978*, online resource: https://libcom.org/history/education-towards-heteronomy-critical-analysis-reform-uk-universities-1978.

Gordon, E. (2018). *Future jobs: Solving the employment and skills crisis*, Praeger, New York.

Grandeur, K., & Hughes, J.J. (2019). *Surviving the machine age: Intelligent technology and the transformation of human work*, Palgrave Macmillan, Cham.

Johannessen, J.-A. (2017). *Innovation leads to economic crises*, Palgrave Macmillan, Cham.

Johannessen, J.-A. (2018a). *Automation, innovation and economic crises: Surviving the Fourth Industrial Revolution*, Routledge, London.

Johannessen, J.-A. (2018b). *The future of work*, Routledge, London.

Kozma, R., Alippi, C., Choe, Y., & Morabito, F.C. (2018). *Artificial intelligence in the age of neural networks and brain computing*, Academic Press, London

Kresl, P. (ed.). (2015). *Cities and partnerships for sustainable urban development*, Edward Elgar, London.

Kurzweil, R. (2005). *The singularity is near*, Penguin, London.

Kurzweil, R. (2008). *The age of spiritual machines: When computers exceed human intelligence*, Penguin, London.

Lane, J.E. (2014). *Building a smarter university*, State University of New York Press, New York.

Levesque, H.J. (2017). *Common sense, the Turing test, and the quest for real AI*, MIT Press, Cambridge, MA.

Shirley, D. (2017). *The new imperatives of educational change*, Routledge, London.

Skilton, M., & Hovsepian, F. (2018). *The 4th Industrial Revolution: Responding to the impact of artificial intelligence on business*, Palgrave Macmillan, Cham.

Sprague, S. (2015). What can labor productivity tell us about the US economy, *US Bureau of Labor Statistics: Beyond the Numbers*, 3(12): 1–9.

Srinivasan, R. (2017)., *Whose global village? Rethinking how technology shapes the world* New York University Press, New York.

Susskind, R., & Susskind, D. (2017). *The future of professions: How technology will transform the work of human experts*, Oxford University Press, Oxford.

Tse, T.C.M., & Esposito, M. (2017). *Understanding how the future unfolds*, Lioncrest, New York.

Tversky, A., & Kahneman, D. (1974). Judgment under uncertainty: Heuristics and biases, *Science*, 185: 1124–1131.

Tversky, A., & Kahneman, D. (1981). The framing of decisions and the psychology of choice, *Science*, 211: 453–458.

Tversky, A., & Kahneman, D. (1983). Extensional versus intuitive reasoning: The conjunction fallacy in probability judgment, *Psychological review*, 90: 293–315.

Tversky, A., & Kahneman, D. (2000). Loss aversion in riskless choice, in D. Kahneman & A. Tversky (eds.), *Choices, values and frames*, pp. 143–158, Cambridge University Press, Cambridge.

West, G. (2018). *Scale: The universal laws of growth, innovation, sustainability, and the pace of life in organisms, cities, economies, and companies*, Penguin, New York.

Xie, S. (2017). *Advanced robotics for medical rehabilitation*, Springer, Cham.

Zhao, J., Feng, Z., Chu, F., & Ma, N. (2017). *Advanced theory of constraint and motion analysis for robot mechanisms*, Academic Press, London.

Appendix: Process pedagogy

Process learning aims to develop the students' action competence, and their ability to reflect upon their own learning.

The purpose of process learning is to develop the students' ability to act, reflect and communicate, as well as their social awareness.

Ability to act: The students are able to prioritize their work tasks, take initiatives, and make decisions – even when they have limited time. Students will acquire the ability to know when they need information, and how to find, evaluate and use information.

Reflective: Students will gain knowledge, be able to use and find knowledge, reflect upon and discuss knowledge, gain self-insight and reflect upon it.

Communicative: Students can present their views, cases and ideas; and can lead and participate in debates.

Socially aware: Students can take responsibility for others, both in close relationships with colleagues, but also for others in a global perspective. They can understand the usefulness of networking relationships, and they are able to work actively with ethics.

The teaching method aims to provide students with the opportunity to work with real cross-disciplinary issues and challenges. On the basis of relevant theory, they will collaborate in teams, with close follow-up by the teaching staff, in order to solve various problems.

Process learning will also provide students with a working method that will give them the opportunity of learning skills so they can become attractive workers in tomorrow's business world, in the public sector and in the area of research. The teaching method emphasizes active participation and knowledge-sharing, rather than passive learning through lectures. This will involve students working with cases, case letters[1] and also projects that use real situations corresponding to what they will experience in future workplaces.

Students will:

- Train to lead and be led by others.
- Present and be able to gain recognition for their ideas and views.

- Give and accept criticism in public forums.
- Maintain responsibility for results.
- Establish and utilize networks.
- Learn to adapt to new situations and rapid change.
- Practise reflection upon their own learning and development.

Process learning is an educational method that will activate and engage the student through various methods, such as interdisciplinary project assignments, problem-based learning and "key lectures". The teaching method involves students working in fixed groups (teams); they will be guided individually and in teams throughout the whole of the study period. The students should reflect on their own learning, team-working competence and ability to act. The teaching method will enable students to acquire theoretical knowledge, as well as knowledge of working life. This will provide students with the skills and abilities to become proactive and engaged employees in the future.

An overview of the categories of process learning is given below (see Figure A1); the content will be described below.

Projects and cases

As part of the process learning, students will also work on various projects and cases.

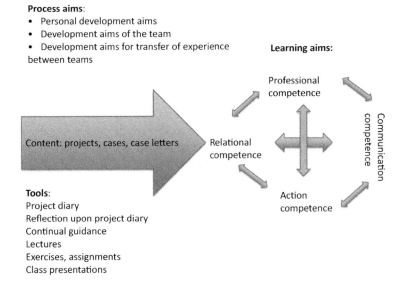

Figure A1 Process learning

1   The cases presented by the teaching staff (not the business-related cases). The cases may be problem-based learning cases or smaller cases, which will give students practice in working with case-solving and project methods.
2   Projects where students work with real businesses and organizations. The students will independently attempt to find problems, solve them using theory and possibly find better solutions for the "client".

Tools

Project diary

For each assignment, students will keep a continuous journal of the work process in their project diaries. This should include reflections on their own learning, team collaboration, collaboration between teams, and also reflections on their own learning in relation to lectures, the syllabus and projects. The project diary should include questions and a summary of the discussion with their supervisor. The student must submit their project diary together with the mandatory project assignments. The project diary constitutes an important element in the guidance process.

Guidance

Students and teams will be given guidance, which will take different forms. It may take the form of direct guidance of a student in relation to a problem or assignment. Groups (teams) will also be given guidance. It may also involve taking responsibility for panel discussions in the class and giving feedback on panel discussions.

Lectures

Every subject will include key lectures. These will mainly be given in "blocks" and will be related to ongoing projects. The purpose of the lectures is to provide students with an introduction to topics, focus interest on a subject area, provide a summary of a subject area, and illuminate or present current research in a particular area. However, the main emphasis of the teaching is guidance-based. Please refer to the overview of ECTS and lectures.

Exercises, presentations

All the major projects should have a written presentation. However, the students will also present the projects in other ways. For instance, this could be an oral formal presentation, such as a report to a board. Other types of presentations could be creative presentations such as giving a performance, making a video film, a dramatic presentation, creating a visual experience, etc. The objectives of the projects may be to get media coverage, a non-profit project to help others, and so on.

Process learning views the student as a whole human being, where the intellect is stimulated by artistic experiences, physical pursuits, altruistic experiences, etc. All the students' projects should include aspects of these elements.

The students will be given clear assessment criteria for those assignments that will be assessed (which will be handed out together with the assignments).

The working methods of the teams

The students will mainly work in teams consisting of five to nive students. A plan for the team's work must be prepared. The plan will specify who is the team leader, the expectations of the individual participants, the project "milestones", the team's working methods, the team's development goals, and development goals for the transfer of experiences between teams.

- The teams will work together for a single semester.
- The leaders of the teams will meet and exchange experiences concerning professional development and regarding the challenges related to the teams' work and composition. The team leader will be chosen for each new project.
- The team leaders will have regular meetings with the semester teams of the respective study programmes.
- A quality manager should also be selected for each team, who should focus on the professional aspects. They will have regular meetings with study programme coordinators, where they will provide feedback in relation to the quality of the learning process and learning outcomes of the subjects.
- When submitting compulsory projects, the teams will be divided into three (the teams can alternate regarding division within the team). One submission during the semester will be individual, although the students work in teams.

Note

1 Case letters are brief statements about a theoretical or practical phenomenon.

Index

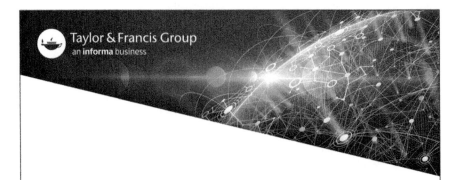